Gravely Concerned
Southern Writers' Graves

LECTOR, SI MONUMENTUM REQUIRIS, CIRCUMSPICE

— Christopher Wren

Gravely Concerned
Southern Writers' Graves

by John Soward Bayne

Copyright 2010, 2012 by Clemson University
ISBN 978-0-9842598-4-7
First edition published 2010. Second edition 2012

Published by Clemson University Press in Clemson, South Carolina

Editorial Assistants: Ashley Dannelly, Christina Cook, and Jared Jameson

Cover design by Ellen Marley Yates

To order copies, please visit the Clemson University Press website: www.clemson.edu/press

Contents

Foreword... viii
Preface xi
Acknowledgments... xiv

David Crockett (1786–1836)........................2
Richard Henry Wilde (1789–1847) 4
Alexander Gallatin McNutt (1802–1848) 6
Edgar Allan Poe (1809–1849) 8
Caroline Lee Hentz (1800–1856)..................10
Thomas Holley Chivers (1809–1858) 12
James Mathewes Legaré (1823–1859)...............14
William Elliott (1788–1863).....................16
Henry Timrod (1829–1867) 18
George Washington Harris (1814–1869)............20
William Gilmore Simms (1806–1870)...............22
Augustus Baldwin Longstreet (1790–1870).........24
John Pendleton Kennedy (1795–1870) 26
Penina Moïse (1797–1880) 28
Sidney Lanier (1842–1881).......................30
Mary Ann Bryan Mason (1802–1881)................32
William Tappan Thompson (1812–1882).............34
Sherwood Bonner (1849–1883) 36
James Gettys McGready Ramsey (1797–1884)........38
Abram Joseph Ryan (1838–1886)...................40
Paul Hamilton Hayne (1830–1886).................42
William Clark Falkner (1825–1889)...............44
Henry Grady (1850–1889) 46
Charles Colcock Jones, Jr. (1831–1893)..........48
Frederick Douglass (1818–1895) 50
Harriett Ann Jacobs (1813–1897) 52
William Malone Baskervill (1850–1899)...........54
Albery Allson Whitman (1851–1901)...............56
Sam Watkins (1839–1901) 58
John Brown Gordon Coogler (1865–1901) 60
Charles Henry Smith (1826–1903).................62
Kate Chopin (1850–1904).........................64
John Charles McNeill (1874–1907) 66
James Ryder Randall (1839–1908).................68
Joel Chandler Harris (1848–1908)................70
Augusta Jane Evans Wilson (1835–1909) 72
Frances Boyd Calhoun (1867–1909)................74
Mark Twain (1835–1910)..........................76
O. Henry (1862–1910) 78
Thomas Cooper DeLeon (1839–1914) 80
Booker Taliaferro Washington (1856–1915) 82

Christian Reid (1846–1920) 84
Mary Noailles Murfree (1850–1922) 86
Frances Hodgson Burnett (1849–1924)..............88
George Washington Cable (1844–1925) 90
Ambrose Elliott Gonzales (1857–1926)..............92
Sarah Bull Barnwell Elliott (1848–1928)............94
Frances Newman (1883–1928) 96
John Trotwood Moore (1856–1929) 98
Grace Elizabeth King (1851–1932) 100
Charles Waddell Chesnutt (1858–1932) 102
Corra Mae White Harris (1869–1935)...............104
Mary Johnston (1870–1936) 106
Robert Ervin Howard (1906–1936) 108
James Weldon Johnson (1871–1938).................110
Thomas Wolfe (1900–1938) 112
Abbie Mandana Holmes Christensen (1852–1938) 114
Harry Stillwell Edwards (1855–1938) 116
Virginia Frazer Boyle (1863–1938) 118
DuBose Heyward (1885–1940) 120
Wilbur Joseph Cash (1900–1941)...................122
William Alexander Percy (1885–1942)...............124
Ben Robertson (1885–1942).......................126
John Peale Bishop (1892–1944) 128
Henry Bellamann (1882–1945).....................130
Ellen Glasgow (1873–1945).......................132
Thomas Dixon, Jr. (1864–1946) 134
Lyle Saxon (1891–1946) 136
George Madden Martin (1866–1946) 138
Margaret Mitchell (1900–1949)....................140
Hervey Allen (1889–1949)........................142
John Gould Fletcher (1886–1950) 144
Douglas Southall Freeman (1866–1953).............146
Emily Clark (1891–1953).........................148
Marjorie Kinnan Rawlings (1896–1953) 150
James Street (1903–1954) 152
James Agee (1909–1955) 154
Beatrice Witte Ravenel (1870–1956) 156
John Bennett (1865–1956) 158
Josephine Pinckney (1895–1957)...................160
James Branch Cabell (1879–1958)..................162
Byron Herbert Reece (1917–1958) 164
Zora Neale Hurston (1891–1960) 166
Julia Peterkin (1880–1961) 168
William Faulkner (1897–1962).....................170
Stark Young (1891–1963) 172
John Faulkner (1901–1963).......................174
Hamilton Basso (1904–1964) 176
Flannery O'Connor (1925–1964)...................178

T. S. Stribling (1881–1965)....................180
Randall Jarrell (1914–1965) 182
Hubert Creekmore (1907–1966) 184
Lillian Smith (1897–1966) 186
Carson McCullers (1917–1967)................188
Donald Davidson (1893–1968)................190
Katherine Drayton Mayrant Simons (1890–1969) 192
John Kennedy Toole (1937–1969).................194
James McBride Dabbs (1896–1970)...............196
Hodding Carter (1907–1972) 198
Arna Wendell Bontemps (1902–1973) 200
Conrad Aiken (1889–1973)....................202
Archibald Rutledge (1883–1973) 204
John Crowe Ransom (1888–1974) 206
Allen Tate (1899–1979)......................208
John Jacob Niles (1892–1980) 210
Katherine Anne Porter (1890–1980) 212
Paul Green (1894–1981)......................214
Harry Golden (1902–1981)....................216
Tennessee Williams (1911–1983) 218
Lillian Hellman (1905–1984) 220
Walter Tevis (1928–1984) 222
Truman Capote (1924–1984) 224
William Bradford Huie (1910–1986)..............226
Robert Penn Warren (1905–1989) 228
Walker Percy (1916–1990).....................230
Alex Haley (1921–1992) 232
Caroline Miller (1903–1992)...................234
Lewis Grizzard (1946–1994)...................236
Andrew Lytle (1902–1995) 238
Eugenia Price (1916–1996) 240
James Dickey (1923–1997) 242
Eugene Walter (1921–1998)....................244
Margaret Walker Alexander (1915–1998)...........246
Willie Morris (1934–1999) 248
Richard Marius (1933–1999) 250
Eudora Welty (1909–2001) 252
Larry Brown (1951–2004).....................254
Shelby Foote (1916–2005) 256
Burke Davis (1913–2006).....................258
William Styron (1925–2006)...................260
Wilma Dykeman (1920–2006) 262

"Scattered, Smothered, and Covered" 264
Bibliography................................269
Index......................................275

FOREWORD

Mister John Bayne and those to whom he gives generous acknowledgment have created here a beautiful and comprehensive work that every person interested in literature should clamor to own. In fact, had I known how splendid the presentation would be, I may well have hastened my own demise so that I might be nominated for inclusion. But alas, I live yet, and so am accorded the honor of a few introductory remarks.

Mister Bayne has limited his work to the graves of Southern writers. This is as it should be, for many of these good people, especially in the antebellum years, received little attention from the Northern literary establishment and even less from an apathetic, largely illiterate, Southern public. Death, reinforced by the hindsight of scholarship, grants them now the attention they deserved in life, a happy circumstance Mister Bayne champions in these pages.

A visitor to any of these literary sites will naturally find himself in the larger context of graveyards where all kinds and conditions of men await Judgment Day. Edgar Lee Masters asks,

> *Where are Elmer, Herman, Bert, Tom and Charley,*
> *The weak of will, the strong of arm, the clown, the boozer,*
>   *the fighter?*

The answer, you will remember, is that *All, all, are sleeping on the hill*, and so shall you and I one day. This fact, like most facts, is uncomfortable for some. We have all known a person who enters cemeteries only because a friend or kinsman has had the poor taste to die and thus remind him of his mortality. On such occasions, the reluctant visitor ventures no further than the funeral home canopy, where he stands with hands clasped and head bowed. He never lingers to hear the clods of earth strike the coffin, and God forbid he should wander with curiosity among the old, established residents of the place. He considers himself an intruder, evidently, for he practices a strict, annoying, and thoroughly modern etiquette: speak in whispers, don't walk on graves or sit on gravestones, do not dare chuckle at the Woodmen of the World tree stumps nor mock the grotesque postmortem vanities of the rich. For the recalcitrant one, certainty can be found only in the busy world outside the fence, and thence he returns with dispatch and relief, the gates of his mind and heart latched tightly so that he might continue to deny the mystery he, too, must meet one day.

I have always taken a different view, one closer to that of the nineteenth century. I believe that a walk through a cemetery is no intrusion but, first, a sojourn into the past and, second, a glimpse into the future of our ephemeral selves. I see no possible harm in walking over a grave, and I think it proper that a man should sit on a tombstone, smoke his pipe, and contemplate his own mortality while the mockingbirds sing in the oaks. I believe the dead, so far as they may be aware, find such occasions enjoyable: footsteps of a visitor from the world they left behind come to acknowledge them as fellow travelers, no different from us, but only gone ahead. I see only virtue in the company of the dead, in the names once spoken but now graven in silent stone, in the lives once lived to good or ill but now vanished from the earth.

This, I have found, is the artist's view as well. Those writers and artists I have been privileged to know are strollers in graveyards; they are students of funeral architecture and symbology; they speculate on those vanished lives beneath the stones. Life, after all, is the artist's subject, and life is a one-way street to Thanatos, a dark neighborhood which no artist worthy of the name can ignore.

The writers, the artists, in this volume lie comfortable, we pray, in their narrow beds, and we trust they are content to be among the people they wrote about in life. Southern writers, with a few exceptions, seem to end up among their kinfolk and fellow townsmen. Miss Eudora Welty, for example, lies in sight of the house where she was born, and Mr. William Faulkner sleeps in close company with those whose stories and culture were the matter of his greatest work.

Many years ago, when some of us boys worked at the Faulkner House in Oxford, one of our unofficial duties--mandated by the late curator Dr. James Webb (who lies just over the ridge from Mr. Faulkner)--was the care of Mr. Faulkner's family plot. It was a hopeless charge, for the grave site, overshadowed by oaks, lies at the foot of a steep clay hill. Rowan Oak groundskeeper Isaiah McQuirt and I, together with assistant curators Danny Toma, Terrell Lewis, and Keith Fudge--each in his appointed time--did our best. We dug drainage trenches to no avail: too much runoff. We planted periwinkle, Mr. and Mrs. Faulkner's favorite groundcover, without success: too much shade from the oaks, too much clay in the ground. Finally, the staff had to be satisfied with periodic sweeping and raking. We policed the cigarette butts and picked up the Jack Daniel's bottles left by devotees who thought it clever to visit Mr. Faulkner in the dark of night and waste good whiskey by pouring it over his grave (another reason, perhaps, why the periwinkle never grew). Visitors left roses, too, and clutches of wildflowers. These we left undisturbed for the nonce, removing them only when their beauty had faded.

As a young artist, Mr. Faulkner, infatuated with the romantic notion of a poet's death, composed a *memento mori* for himself. These lines may be familiar:

> But I shall sleep, for where is any death
> While in these blue hills slumberous overhead
> I'm rooted like a tree? Though I be dead
> This soil that holds me fast will find me breath.

No doubt Mr. Faulkner would have laughed to see us at our labors, digging and trenching and sweeping and raking, trying to keep the earth from reclaiming its own, while all around the blue hills lay slumberous, indifferent to time, prepared to outlast us all. Sometimes we would lean on our tools and look out at the summer green, or the barren gray of winter, and we would see the world we had read about, our own beloved land that Mr. Faulkner had shown us in all its lights and shadows. At such times, that youthful poem would come back to us, and the epitaph of Mr. T. S. Stribling, who rests among his own hills in Tennessee. Land and community, these two, and life and death: once spoken through the dust at our feet. Astonishing! It was not an experience that would appeal to the reluctant, but it never failed to remind us how damned lucky we were.

So, pilgrim, pass by. Be not reluctant at your author's grave. Look at the name indited in stone: what lies beneath the name is only dust, of course, but what lies *behind* it is the record of the artist's suffering and the true monument that is his or her work. Remember that this person once walked the earth, felt the compulsion to create, suffered rejection and frustration, just as you will do, have done, if you have chosen the writer's craft. Ask your questions; you may be astonished at the reply. Study the graves 'round about, and see--*really* see--the landscape. Drink a little whiskey if appropriate, but take your bottles with you. Leave a rose, a clutch of wildflowers. And remember the epitaph Miss Estelle chose for Mr. Faulkner, the words that in autumn are covered by fallen leaves, the words beautiful in their simplicity that speak for all those represented in this book: *Beloved, go with God.*

Howard Bahr
Jackson, Mississippi
May 2010

Preface

This book presents the graves of writers from the American South. The selection is based on the authors' popular or critical reputations and the appeal and accessibility of their gravesites. Some may dispute whether these subjects were sufficiently Southern, and whether they were truly writers, but this is certain: they're all dead. The pictures of their graves, presented chronologically, illustrate Southern literary history, and this book memorializes the artists, some famous and some obscure.

Most of the gravesites are in the Southeastern United States, but some, nearly 20 percent, are removed from their native soil, the land Gerald O'Hara tells Scarlett "is the only thing in the world worth workin' for, worth fightin' for, worth dyin' for, because it's the only thing that lasts." A few who would have been desirable to include are buried outside the country, and so aren't. Others were cremated and left no monument.

Literary pilgrims are not rare. Poets' Corner in Westminster Abbey and Shakespeare's tomb in Stratford-upon-Avon are on most tourist itineraries in England. Although not as popular as the grave of Jim Morrison, Gertrude Stein's and Oscar Wilde's graves draw people to Père Lachaise in Paris. In the United States, probably the most visited writers' graves are at Authors' Ridge in Sleepy Hollow Cemetery, Concord, Massachusetts, where Henry David Thoreau, Louisa May Alcott, Ralph Waldo Emerson, and Nathaniel Hawthorne are buried.

The nearest there is to a "Southern Authors' Ridge" may be Hollywood Cemetery in Richmond, Virginia. Ellen Glasgow, James Branch Cabell, and Douglas Southall Freeman are all buried there, along with other less famous writers, though not as close together as in Sleepy Hollow. Hollywood has other attractions, not literary—J. E. B. Stuart, Fitzhugh Lee, and three Presidents, James Monroe, John Tyler, and Jefferson Davis. Another candidate Authors' Ridge, but it's certainly no ridge, is Magnolia Cemetery in Charleston: William Elliott, William Gilmore Simms, Josephine Pinckney, Beatrice Ravenel, and more.

Many outstanding cemeteries are represented, particularly Oakland in Atlanta, Magnolia in Charleston, Bonaventure in Savannah, and Elmwood in Memphis. These are all representative of the "rural cemetery movement," begun at Mount Auburn in Cambridge, Massachusetts, in 1835, inspired by Père Lachaise. Built away from city centers, they feature curving pathways and roads, and were intended to encourage visitors to view the monuments, contemplate the trees and flowers, and otherwise enjoy themselves—picnics, dates—the first city parks.

Another fine cemetery is Metairie in New Orleans. It was a racetrack before it became a cemetery in 1872, and the oval lanes still reflect its past. Outside the South, some of the more interesting cemeteries are Green-Wood in Brooklyn, New York, Lake View in Cleveland, Ohio, and Westwood in Los Angeles, where Truman Capote, who in life enjoyed mingling with other celebrities, keeps company with Dean Martin, Natalie Wood, Mel Torme, Burt Lancaster, Eva Gabor, and Marilyn Monroe.

The earliest of the writers is the Tennessean Davy Crockett, whose authorial hand in his best-selling autobiography and other volumes is challenged by some experts. Still, the use of humor and tale-spinning is characteristic of early Southern writing, especially of the "Southwest humorists" such as Augustus Baldwin Longstreet and George Washington Harris. Other antebellum writers included are poets, Richard Henry Wilde, Edgar Allan Poe, and his biographer and rival, Thomas Holley Chivers. The planter class is represented by William Elliott, the author of *Carolina Sports*.

From the Civil War era, poets include Henry Timrod, Paul Hamilton Hayne, Father Abram Joseph Ryan, and Sidney Lanier. William Gilmore Simms was a prolific novelist and poet. Augusta Jane Evans Wilson's novels were banned and burned in Union camps, and were so popular that parents named their daughters Edna Earl after the heroine of her novel *St. Elmo*. Harriett Ann Jacobs survived slavery and wrote about it in her *Diary of a Slave Girl*. Another former slave is the poet Albery Allson Whitman, buried at South-View in Atlanta. Sadly, Mary Boykin Miller Chesnut, the Civil War diarist, is buried on private property and her grave couldn't be photographed.

The Reconstruction period produced some writers looking backwards and others looking ahead. Among the former were Thomas Cooper DeLeon, "the Blind Laureate of the Lost Cause," buried in Mobile. Two editors of the Atlanta *Constitution* represented the Old South and the New South, Joel Chandler Harris and Henry Grady. Their graves are near one another in Westview Cemetery, Harris's grave marked with a rough-hewn granite stone, with his portrait in his characteristic floppy hat and bow tie, and Grady's, an elegant marble mausoleum.

Two authors of classic children's books are Frances Boyd Calhoun and Frances Hodgson Burnett. Calhoun died before her *Miss Minerva and William Green Hill* achieved its success (the sequels were written by Emma Speed Sampson, whose grave in Hollywood Cemetery in Richmond is unmarked). The author of *The Secret Garden* and *Little Lord Fauntleroy*, Burnett was an Englishwoman who lived many years in Knoxville, Tennessee. She has a striking monument in Long Island, New York.

The early Twentieth Century marked the Southern Literary Renaissance, or renascence. It was provoked in part by an essay by H. L. Mencken, "The Sahara of the Bozart," in which he scolded the South for its lack of artistic achievement. Literary circles and societies, notably in Charleston, Richmond, and Nashville, brought forth a flowering of Southern letters. By the 1920s, some of the best and most popular American literature was being produced by such writers as DuBose Heyward, Ellen Glasgow, John Crowe Ransom, and William Faulkner. Between 1929 and 1939, half the Pulitzer Prizes for the novel were won by Southerners.

Faulkner is the only Southern writer so far to have won the Nobel Prize for Literature. The themes put forth in his novels, love of the land, genealogy, racial guilt, and distrust of industrialization, are prominent in Southern literature throughout its history. In the second half of the Twentieth Century, notable Southern writers include Katherine Anne Porter, Walker Percy, Flannery O'Connor, Tennessee Williams, Robert Penn Warren, and Eudora Welty. Welty had a particularly close attachment to cemeteries, having grown up in a house overlooking Greenwood Cemetery in Jackson, Mississippi. In the 1930s she took cemetery photographs throughout Mississippi; many of them are published in her last book, *Country Churchyards*, and her novels and stories abound with cemetery scenes.

The most recent grave is that of Wilma Dykeman, historian and folklorist of the Southern Appalachians. She died in December 2006 and was buried in a hillside church yard in Asheville, North Carolina.

There are a few unusual monuments. James Agee's unlettered boulder stands alone on a farm in New York State. Lillian Smith's grave is marked by a stone fireplace. The older tombstones naturally appeal more to cemetery visitors, but some of the newer stones are beautifully designed and executed, even within the confines of a 1' x 2' horizontal slab in the case of Lillian Hellman. There are ledger stones, obelisks, wedge stones, and sarcophaguses, as well as upright markers. Conrad Aiken's monument is a stone bench; he is said to have wanted visitors to sit and have a martini.

The writers' epitaphs are predictably "above average." No one used "Remember friend as you pass by / As you are now so once was I. . . ." or "I told you I was sick!" Among the best are T. S. Stribling's "Through this dust these hills once spoke" and Ben Robertson's "I rest in thy bosom, Carolina, thy skies over me, thine earth and air above and around me. Among my own, in my own country, I sleep."

On 20 April 2008 a new obelisk was unveiled over the presumed grave of George Washington Harris, with an epitaph written by the author in a fragmentary "Parson Bullen's Oration Over the Corpse of Sut Lovingood": "Let us try an' ricollect his virtues—ef he had any—an' forgit his vices—ef we can. *For of sich air the kingdom of heaven!*"

Finding these graves has taken considerable energy. The websites Findagrave.com and PoliticalGraveyard.com have been very helpful, as have been various biographical dictionaries, author biographies, and other references. Google has been indispensable. Sometimes the biographies accompanying authors' collected papers at university libraries provided burial information when it couldn't be found elsewhere. Another source has been genealogical message boards. In a few cases, an author's relative has helped. Particularly, Larry Brown's son Billy Ray, straight from church with his children, showed the way to his father's grave.

For each writer there is a list of works and a short biography. The bibliography in the back of the book lists reference materials, author biographies, and critical analyses. Christopher Wren's famous epitaph in St. Paul's Cathedral in London reminds monument-seekers to look at the artist's work. Likewise, the true monuments for these men and women are the books and poems and plays they wrote. Anyone wanting to know more about them should take Welty's advice: "Read that."

Acknowledgments

This book depended on the knowledge, effort, generosity, hospitality, and cooperation of many people, whose help is gratefully acknowledged. Everyone in my family has endured cemetery visits and detours, including two of my grand-nephews. My colleague Shan Nichols braved rain and cold to take photographs when he was on out-of-town work assignments. Two other people helped in ways "above and beyond." The first is Tige Marston, cemetery specialist in Mobile, who not only led me to the graves of Augusta Evans and Thomas Cooper DeLeon in Magnolia Cemetery on his day off on a Saturday in November 2006, but also drove me to the Old Catholic Cemetery and to City Cemetery, and finished up with a restaurant recommendation. That was true Southern hospitality, shown to a stranger fresh off an overnight Greyhound bus, discouraged by a lack of success. The other is Dr. Randy Cross of Calhoun Community College, who took up the challenge of George Washington Harris with marvelous energy and ability. The unveiling of Harris's obelisk by three generations of his direct descendants, plus Thomas Inge, who had studied Harris for 50 years, was in every way a remarkable occasion. With apologies for omissions and possible misspellings, I convey thanks to:

Jeanne Allen, Valentine Richmond History Center, Richmond VA; Virginia Historical Society, Richmond VA; Michael Berens, Atlanta GA; Richard Saunders, University of Tennessee, Martin TN; Ed Frank, University of Memphis TN; Nick Wyman, University of Tennessee Special Collections Library, Knoxville TN; Deb Haines, Hillcrest Cemetery, Holly Springs MS; the Mel Jones family, Chapel Hill NC; Dave Farmer, Greenville SC; Marty Butler, Austin TX; Tim Seldes, Russell and Volkening, New York NY; Jesseca Salky, Russell and Volkening, New York NY; Joy Azmitia, Russell and Volkening, New York NY; Kimberly Sabo, Lake View Cemetery, Cleveland OH; Gayle Edwards, Anderson SC; Faulkner House Books, New Orleans LA; Pearl McHaney, Georgia State University, Atlanta GA; Tom McHaney, Georgia State University, Atlanta GA; June Haddon Hobbs, Gardner-Webb University, Boiling Springs NC; David Gradwohl, Iowa State University, Ames IA; the late Gary Collison, Pennsylvania State University, York PA; Metairie Cemetery, New Orleans LA; Greenwood Cemetery, New Orleans LA; Valentine Richmond History Center, Richmond VA; Wini Hemphill, South-View Cemetery, Atlanta GA; Judy Long, Byhalia Books, Athens GA; Kevin Kuharic, Oakland Cemetery, Atlanta GA; John Carmichael, Director of Tourism, Camden SC; Maureen Rodgers, The Book Barn, Hillsdale NY; John Agee, Hillsdale NY; Mabel Toney, Hollywood Cemetery, Richmond VA; Maple View Cemetery, Smyrna TN; Carly Colombero, Brewton-Parker College, Mount Vernon GA; Lee Cheek, Athens State University, Athens AL; Ben Fisher, University of Mississippi, Oxford MS; Jack Crouch, Calvary Cemetery, Nashville TN; Paul Engsberg, University Cemetery, Sewanee TN; Shan Nichols, AT&T Consulting,

Atlanta GA; Debbie May, Nashville Public Library TN; Joe Edgette, Widener University, PA; the late Helen Sclair, Bohemian National Cemetery, Chicago IL; Westview Cemetery, Atlanta GA; Michael Segers (email, C. Miller); Mike Ethridge (email, WS Ethridge); Charles Blackburn, Chapel Hill NC; Deborah Cox, Metro Archives of Nashville and Davidson County TN; John Allison, Historian, Decatur AL; Millen Ellis, Due West SC; Bill Butler, email (Roark Bradford); Bill Starr, Georgia Center for the Book, Decatur GA; Betty Brewer, Evergreen Cemetery, Murfreesboro TN; Annette Levy Ratkin, Jewish Federation of Nashville TN; Mt. Olivet Cemetery, Nashville TN; McClung Library, Knoxville TN; Barry Cain, Edgewood Cemetery, Knoxville TN; Robbin Kelley, Town of Harwich MA; Daryl Hannah, Greenhill Cemetery, Waynesville NC; Nancy Smith Fichter, Lillian E. Smith Center for Creative Arts, Clayton GA; Daryl Ballew, West Hills Cemetery, Dalton GA; Jerry Murphy, Magnolia Cemetery, Augusta GA; Jodie Hill, Marietta GA; Jeff Nixon, Austin TX; Wyatt Prunty, Sewanee TN; Bob McNeil, Green Hills Cemetery, Asheville NC; Billy Ray Brown, Tula MS; Randy K. Cross, Decatur AL; Phil Wirey, Decatur AL; David Gwinn, Covington TN; Linda Fogle, University of South Carolina Press, Columbia SC; Sheila Byrd, Decatur AL; Jill Chadwick, Decatur AL; Dr. Bill Pullen, Trenton GA; Michael and Lyndll Yawn, Topsail Island NC; Ruth Ellen Porter, Brewton-Parker College, Mount Vernon GA; Barbara Ladd, Decatur GA; Jimmie Covington, Memphis TN; M. Thomas Inge, Randolph-Macon College, Ashland, VA; Jack Neely, Knoxville TN; Mark Zalesky, Knoxville TN; Michael Toomey, East Tennessee Historical Society, Knoxville TN; Steve Cotham, McClung Historical Collection, Knoxville TN; Mike Lord, Atlanta GA; Dick Lord, Trenton GA; Dawn Gray, Trenton GA; David Cooper, *Chattanooga Times-Free Press*; Lois Swaney, Holly Springs MS; The Very Rev. Bruce McMillan, Holly Springs MS; Beverly McDonald, Magnolia Cemetery, Charleston SC; Melee Laney, Hartselle AL; Stephanie Turner, Michelle Belden, and Carolyn Shankle, University of North Carolina at Greensboro; Carolee Fox, Charleston SC; Janice Kahn, Charleston SC; Brian Jordan, Austin TX; Tom Jordan, Brownwood, TX; Julie Langley, Austin TX; Susan Shaw, Austin TX; Scott Baird, Trinity University, San Antonio TX; P. K. Magruder, Northampton MA; Bill Sullivan, Northampton MA; Thomas L. Johnson, Spartanburg SC; Lain Shakespeare, Atlanta GA; Billy Arant, Chattanooga TN; Brad Russell, Clemson SC; Wayne Chapman, Clemson SC; Ashley Dannelly, Clemson SC; Michael LeSage, Atlanta GA; Ron Rash, Clemson SC; Robert Ward, Los Angeles CA; Christina Cook, Clemson SC; Charis Chapman, Clemson SC; the staff of Budget Car Rentals, Courtland St., Atlanta; Greyhound Bus Lines; Kay Powell, Atlanta, GA.

Howard Bahr, of Jackson, MS, kindly contributed the Foreword. He is the author of *The Black Flower*, *The Year of Jubilo*, *The Judas Field*, and *Pelican Road*. For over a decade he was curator of Rowan Oak, the home of William Faulkner, in Oxford, MS.

The following contributors are credited with respect to the location where their work is to be found in this volume:

Photo Credits

Bill Bayne, 225
Bob Bayne, cover, ii, 25, 49, 53, 65, 77, 91, 119, 129, 145, 171, 219, 221, 229, 251, 257, 261
William C. Bayne, 71
Michael Berens, 141
Dave Farmer, 127
Brian Jordan, 109, 203
Shan Nichols, 211, 223
Jeff Nixon, 3

Writing Credits

Bill Bayne, 2, 38, 58, 82, 146, 180, 224, 232, 234, 254
Harry Bayne, 14, 16, 18, 22, 26, 28, 30, 34, 36, 40, 42, 48, 54, 60, 64, 92, 98, 100, 102, 106, 114, 116, 120, 126, 130, 142, 156, 158, 160, 168, 170, 174, 176, 178, 188, 192, 196, 200, 202, 204, 210, 214, 216, 218, 226, 242
Lauren Bayne, 187, 241
William C. Bayne, 10, 46, 50, 62, 68, 76, 80, 86, 88, 90, 94, 96, 118, 122, 124, 134, 136, 138, 140, 144, 148, 150, 152, 162, 164, 172, 184, 190, 208, 220, 228, 236, 238, 250, 256, 260
Brian Jordan, 12, 66, 78, 108, 110, 128, 132, 194, 206, 212, 222, 230, 244, 246, 248, 258, 262

Gravely Concerned
Southern Writers' Graves

David Crockett
(1786–1836)

Born 17 August 1786, Hawkins Co. TN
Died 6 March 1836, San Antonio TX
Buried San Fernando Cathedral, San Antonio TX

Works: *A Narrative of the Life of David Crockett of the State of Tennessee, An Account of Col. Crockett's Tour to the North and Down East, In the Year of Our Lord One Thousand Eight Hundred and Thirty-Four, The Life of Martin Van Buren: Hair-Apparent to the "Government," and the Appointed Successor of General Jackson*

Colonel David (Davy) Crockett was one of the most famous citizens in the history of the state of Tennessee: a celebrity while living who became a legend after his death. Crockett was a frontiersman, statesman, soldier, adventurer, and politician who was born 17 August 1786 on the banks of the Nolichucky River, in what is now Greene County, Tennessee. He fought in the Creek War in a volunteer militia under the leadership of General Andrew Jackson and rose to the rank of colonel. Crockett was a member of the Tennessee House of Representatives and later served Tennessee in the U.S. Congress from 1827 to 1833.

Crockett wrote *Davy Crockett: His Own Story*, in 1834, and while it was his autobiography, it was also filled with numerous tall tales that helped his acclaim and stature grow. After being narrowly defeated for another term to the Congress, he yearned for other opportunities, and moved to Texas in 1835. Crockett and others from Tennessee served under Colonel William Barrett Travis at the Alamo in San Antonio. Crockett and the other defenders of the Alamo fought bravely for 13 days against General Antonio López de Santa Anna's Mexican Army. On 6 March 1836, Davy Crockett died in battle along with the other 189 men fighting for Texas independence.

With other victims of the massacre, his ashes are at San Fernando Cathedral in San Antonio. San Antonio also has a cenotaph for those who died at the Alamo, at the site where the funeral pyres burned.

Richard Henry Wilde
(1789–1847)

Born 24 September 1789, Dublin, Ireland
Died 10 September 1847, Augusta GA
Buried Magnolia, Augusta GA

Works: *Hesperia, The Lament of the Captive, Conjectures and Researches Concerning the Love, Madness, and Imprisonment of Torquato Tasso*

Wilde came with his parents from Ireland to Baltimore, Maryland when he was a child. After his father died, he and his mother moved to Augusta, Georgia. He studied law and was admitted to the Georgia bar in 1809. After serving as Attorney General of Georgia, he was elected to Congress three times. Afterwards he went to Italy for several years. There he researched Italian literature, including Dante and Torquato Tasso. He returned to Georgia and then moved to New Orleans, where he was a law professor at the University of Louisiana (now Tulane University).

A poem from his unfinished epic about Florida, called "The Lament of the Captive," was very popular, often recited and reprinted, beginning "My Life is like the Summer Rose." It was alleged to be a translation of an ancient Greek poem, but the Greek version instead turned out to have been written by an admirer. Wilde intended to publish books on Dante and other Italian poets, but he died from yellow fever in 1847.

He was buried temporarily in a New Orleans vault, and then moved to a grave beside his infant son's in a family cemetery near Augusta. In 1885 Augustan Charles Colcock Jones, Jr., wrote that Wilde's grave was unmarked and neglected. His essay told the story of Wilde's life, and of his famous poem, and noted, "It frequently comes to pass that ancestral graves lie neglected, and private burial grounds fall a prey to disuse and oblivion. Under such circumstances it seems a folly to commit our dead to the guardianship of aught other than a public cemetery, where sepulture within its walls is practicable." The following year Wilde was reburied in City Cemetery (now Magnolia).

Alexander Gallatin McNutt
(1802–1848)

Born 3 January 1802, Rockbridge Co. VA
Died 22 October 1848, DeSoto Co. MS
Buried Greenwood, Jackson MS

Works: "Chunkey's Fight with the Panthers," "A Swim for a Deer," "Another Story of Jem and Chunkey

Alexander Gallatin McNutt was born in Virginia and studied at Washington College in Lexington, Virginia (now Washington and Lee), where he studied law. He was admitted to the Virginia bar in 1823. He moved to Vicksburg, Mississippi, in the 1830s. He practiced law in Vicksburg, and was married to the widow of his former law partner, who had been murdered by his slaves in 1833. One of the four slaves sentenced to hang for his death implicated McNutt, but McNutt's supporters said this was a smear by his political opponent, Henry S. Foote. Mrs. McNutt married a third time after McNutt's death.

After a celebrated series of debates, McNutt was elected Governor of Mississippi, and served from 1838 to 1842. During his time in office, the Union Bank of Mississippi collapsed, and by the end of his term the state had a debt of over $5 million. The McNutts entertained former President Andrew Jackson when he visited the city named for him in 1841. After his time as governor, McNutt ran unsuccessfully for the U.S. Senate, defeated by the same political rival, Henry Foote.

Stories McNutt wrote for *The Spirit of the Times* were signed "The Turkey Runner," often with comic characters Jem and Chunkey, employed by a cotton planter called the Captain. "The Governor" appears as a character in some of the tales, and Chunkey and Jem are said to be modeled on two workers on McNutt's plantation. Jem and Chunkey hunt panthers and bears, gamble, and drink a lot of whiskey.

The editor of *The Spirit of the Times*, William Trotter Porter, admired McNutt's tales to the extent that several were included in both Porter anthologies, *The Big Bear of Arkansas* (1846) and *A Quarter Race in Kentucky* (1847).

McNutt died while on a campaign trip at Cockrum's Cross Roads, DeSoto County, Mississippi, and is buried at Greenwood Cemetery in Jackson. McNutt's house in Vicksburg, built c. 1826, is now a guest house.

Edgar Allan Poe
(1809–1849)

Born 19 January 1809, Boston MA
Died 9 October 1849, Baltimore MD
Buried Old Westminster, Baltimore MD

Works: *Tamerlane and Other Poems, Al Araaf, Tamerlane and Minor Poems, Poems, The Narrative of Arthur Gordon Pym, of Nantucket, The Conchologist's First Book, Tales of the Grotesque and Arabesque, The Prose Romances of Edgar A. Poe: Uniform Serial Edition, Tales, The Raven and Other Poems, Eureka: A Prose Poem*

Edgar Allan Poe was born in Boston on 19 January 1809, a son of itinerant stage actors. Orphaned young, Poe was taken in by a well-to-do Richmond cotton merchant, John Allan. After schooling in England, he entered the University of Virginia in 1826, where he excelled as a scholar and athlete, but from which Allan forced his withdrawal because of gambling debts and drinking. A stint in the U.S. Army saw Poe stationed at Fort Moultrie near Charleston, South Carolina, later the setting of his stories "The Balloon Hoax" and "The Gold-Bug." Poe subsequently secured an appointment to the U.S. Military Academy at West Point, but his erratic behavior led to his being court-martialed and removed.

In 1835, he married his first cousin, 13-year-old Virginia Clemm, who suffered from chronic ill health and died in 1847.

Over the course of his literary career, Poe lived in Richmond, Baltimore, New York, and Philadelphia, holding editorial positions with several journals, most notably *The Southern Literary Messenger*, all the while producing a wealth of memorable fiction, poetry, and criticism. Regrettably, his volatile temper and intemperate drinking habits cost him important jobs and wounded his reputation.

En route to New York from Virginia in October 1849, Poe inexplicably appeared in Baltimore, disheveled and only intermittently conscious. He died in a local hospital on 9 October 1849. (Recent medical speculations concerning the cause of his death have ranged from diabetes to rabies.) Buried at Old Westminster churchyard, Poe's remains were later moved from an obscure plot to a more prominent location.

The author's grave was visited annually, on Poe's birthday, by an anonymous caped figure who left gifts of cognac and three roses. This tradition continued for more than 60 years, until this Poe toaster failed to appear 19 January 2010, the year after Poe's bicentennial.

Caroline Lee Hentz
(1800–1856)

Born 1 June 1800, Lancaster MA
Died 11 February 1856, Marianna FL
Buried St. Luke's Episcopal Cemetery, Marianna FL

Works: *Lovell's Folly, a Novel, De Lara; or, The Moorish Bride, Aunt Patty's Scrap-Bag, Linda; or, The Young Pilot of the Belle Creole, The Mob Cap and other Tales, Ugly Effie; or, The Neglected One and the Pet Beaty, and Other Tales, Rena; or, The Snowbird, The Banished Son and Other Stories of the Heart, Eoline; or, Magnolia Vale, Marcus Warland; or, The Long Moss Spring: A Tale of the South, Helen and Arthur; or, Miss Thusa's Spinning Wheel, The Victim of Excitement, The Bosom Serpent, etc., etc., etc., Wild Jack; or, The Stolen Child, and Other Stories, The Planter's Northern Bride, The Flowers of Elocution: A Class Book, Robert Graham, a Novel, Courtship and Marriage; or, The Joys and Sorrows of American Life, Ernest Linwood, a Novel, The Lost Daughter and Other Stories of the Heart, Love after Marriage and Other Stories of the Heart, The Planter's Daughter: A Tale of Louisiana*

Caroline Lee Whiting Hentz was a seventh-generation native of Massachusetts who earned fame and considerable fortune as a Southern writer, known for her defense of slavery and her feminist views of marriage and motherhood.

She married Nicholas Marcellus Hentz, a schoolmaster at Round Hill Academy in Northampton, Massachusetts, in 1824. Two years later they moved to Chapel Hill, North Carolina, where he became a professor of languages for the state university. At Chapel Hill, she gave guidance to George Moses Horton, a slave who became the first professional American-born black poet, known as the Sable Bard of North Carolina. Horton became her protégé and she helped him in getting published in the North as well as in North Carolina.

She wrote and entered her first play, *De Lara, or The Moorish Bride*, in a literary contest in 1831. She won, but the contest host could not pay the posted $500 prize, so he returned her copyright to her. The win, however, gave her some fame and paved the way for subsequent efforts.

In 1832 she and her husband moved to Cincinnati, where she became a personal friend of Harriet Beecher Stowe, a fellow native of Massachusetts.

In 1834, the Hentz family moved to Florence, Alabama, and her literary career soared. She became one of the Deep South's most prolific writers, publishing three plays, eight novels, and nine collections of stories. She was an avid anti-abolitionist, and her themes upheld the South's widely held fear of a slave uprising.

She lived in Tuscaloosa and Tuskegee in Alabama, then in Columbus, Georgia, and finally in Marianna, Florida, where she died 11 February 1856.

Thomas Holley Chivers
(1809–1858)

Born 18 October 1809, Washington GA
Died 18 December 1858, Decatur GA
Buried Decatur Cemetery, Decatur GA

Works: *The Path of Sorrow, Conrad and Eudora, Nacoochee, The Lost Pleiad, Search After Truth, Enochs of Ruby, Virginalia, Memoralia, Atlanta, Heroes of Freedom, The Sons of Usna, Selected Poems of Thomas Holley Chivers, Chivers' Life of Poe, The Correspondence of Thomas Holley Chivers*

Thomas Holley Chivers was born into a wealthy Georgian plantation-owning family on 18 October 1807. He became interested in poetry at a young age after reading William Cowper's "The Rose." He married, but even though the couple produced a daughter, the marriage was short lived. Chivers then studied medicine in Kentucky at Transylvania University, but his medical career was brief; poetry and publishing were his true passions. He wrote and travelled throughout the United States, writing and publishing at various stops along the way. In 1834 he married Harriet Hunt in Georgia, where he had returned two years prior. As a poet, Chivers wrote poems with religious overtones, emphasizing death and the afterlife, drawing heavily upon Native American imagery. He published several volumes of poetry including *The Lost Pleiad* (1845) and *The Path of Sorrow* (1832), as well as several plays.

Chivers is perhaps best known for his sometimes friendly, sometimes competitive relationship with Edgar Allan Poe. Poe and Chivers met in 1845 and quickly became friends. Chivers admired Poe's work. In fact, he offered to support Poe financially throughout the rest of his life, if Poe would move to the South and leave the job he had with *Graham's Magazine*, which Chivers viewed as a vastly underpaid position. Poe was a fan of Chivers as well, writing, "His figures of speech are metaphor run mad, and his grammar is often none at all. Yet there are as fine individual passages to be found in the poems of Dr. Chivers, as in those of any poet whatsoever." Chivers's medical knowledge led him to lecture Poe endlessly on the dangers of alcohol, and the two argued about what made a poet truly a poet. After Poe's death in 1845, Chivers defended the validity of Poe's works while at the same time claiming that Poe had all but plagiarized "The Raven" and "Ulalume" from him. He even suggested that Poe learned to write poetry from reading his works. Literary scholar Randy Nelson wrote, "Anybody who's read both Poe and Thomas Holley Chivers can see that one of them 'influenced' the other, but just who took what from whom isn't clear."

Chivers died in Decatur and is buried in Decatur Cemetery. A monument to him stands in front of the DeKalb County Public Library.

James Mathewes Legaré
(1823–1859)

Born 26 November 1823, Charleston SC
Died 30 May 1859, Aiken SC
Buried St Thaddeus, Aiken SC

Works: *Orta-Undis, and Other Poems*

James Mathewes Legaré might well have been considered a Renaissance man had he been born a century later. He was a writer, poet, inventor, and painter who also served as a postmaster during the administration of President Millard Fillmore.

He was born in Charleston in 1823 to French Huguenot parents. His father, John D. Legaré, was an agricultural editor, and his mother, Mary D. M. Legaré, was socially prominent. Hugh Swinton Legaré, Legaré's third cousin, served as attorney general of the United States, appointed by President John Tyler.

Legaré was graduated from the College of Charleston in 1842 and attended St. Mary's College in Baltimore, Maryland, for a year following his graduation.

While at St. Mary's, he created a fictional genealogy of his family that he buried in an iron casket in a Charleston garden. When it was discovered, the hoax was reported in the *Charleston Courier*, and the story spread nationally. The notoriety from the story of the elaborate hoax may have served to provide Harriet Beecher Stowe with a villainous name for her novel, *Uncle Tom's Cabin*. Simon Legree is a phonetic rendering of the Legaré surname.

He returned to Charleston and studied law under James L. Petigru. Legaré also published verse and fiction, and his landscapes were hung in Apprentices' Hall. He drew the sponsorship of James J. Audubon and William G. Simms, but he had contracted tuberculosis, and a family financial reversal forced his father to move to Aiken, South Carolina.

Legaré conducted experiments with lignin cotton furniture and with a creation he called the "dual air-engine." He was awarded two United States patents.

He died of tuberculosis in Aiken in 1859 and was buried there in the St. Thaddeus's Episcopal Church Cemetery. Many years after his death local high school students raised funds to erect an appropriate monument over his grave, which previously had been unmarked.

William Elliott
(1788–1863)

Born 27 April 1788, Beaufort SC
Died 3 February 1863, Charleston SC
Buried Magnolia, Charleston SC

Works: *Carolina Sports by Land and Water, Fiesco: A Tragedy, Letters from Agricola*

The Elliotts were a well-known family of planters, politicians, and churchmen. Originally from Cornwall, England, they arrived in Charleston around 1685 by way of Barbados. William Elliott's grandfather married Mary Barnwell, of distinguished roots, and settled in Beaufort. His father was a delegate to the state convention which ratified the Constitution, and introduced sea-island cotton to South Carolina.

William Elliott—born in Beaufort, South Carolina, in 1788, and educated at Harvard College—became a Lowcountry planter, with wealthy and honored connections including Episcopal bishops. His wife was of equally prominent ancestry. After a brief involvement in politics, he channeled his energies into his agribusiness enterprises. He gained a wider recognition, however, as a lecturer and essayist. A series of pieces on the great outdoors he wrote for Charleston newspapers became in book form *Carolina Sports by Land and Water* (1846).

The Elliott family owned more than a dozen plantations and more than 300 slaves. Elliott advocated agricultural innovations, including crop diversification, and wrote articles for *The Southern Agriculturist*. He opposed secession until after the Civil War began, but then became a loyal Confederate, and all three of his sons volunteered. During the war, his plantations were seized; some were sold at auction and others were held by the government.

Elliott died in Charleston in 1863, and was buried at Magnolia Cemetery. A grandson, Ambrose Elliott Gonzales, rose to prominence a generation later as founder of *The State* newspaper in Columbia, and as the author of four "Black Border" novels, all rendered in the Gullah dialect, spoken by African-Americans in the Lowcountry of Georgia and South Carolina.

Oak Lawn plantation, mentioned on Elliott's tombstone, and his principal residence, was burned to the ground during the Civil War.

Henry Timrod
(1829–1867)

Born 8 December 1829, Charleston SC
Died 7 October 1867, Columbia SC
Buried Trinity Cathedral, Columbia SC

Works: *Poems, Katie, Verses from the Cotton Boll, Uncollected Poems, Essays*

Henry Timrod (1828-1867), born in Charleston, South Carolina, of German descent, attended the University of Georgia, but because of illness withdrew and returned to his native city, where he undertook the study of law as an apprentice in a law firm. But the writing of verse held more appeal for him, and between 1848 and 1853 he submitted poems to *The Southern Literary Messenger*, one of the South's most prominent journals. In 1856 he took a teaching position at a plantation near Florence, South Carolina. Katie Godwin, one of his pupils, later became his wife. The single collection of his poetry to appear during his lifetime was published in 1860. The book enhanced his public profile, but did not sell well.

Upon the outbreak of the Civil War in 1861, Timrod returned to Charleston. Poetry from this period championed the secessionist cause, leading to his being identified as the Poet Laureate of the Confederacy. "Ethnogenesis," "Charleston," "The Cotton Boll," and a memorial ode to the Confederate dead, sung at Charleston's Magnolia Cemetery in 1867, became his best-known works. Briefly he served in the Confederate army, but his fragile constitution was not equal to the demands of war, and he returned to South Carolina, settling in Columbia to work as associate editor of *The South Carolinian*. In February 1864 he married, and his wife gave birth to their only child, Willie, on 24 December 1864. General Sherman's Union troops destroyed the newspaper's offices when they occupied Columbia in mid-February 1865. Emotionally broken and suffering from tuberculosis, Timrod spent his last two years in poverty. He went unpaid for services as correspondent for a Charleston newspaper, which subsequently went out of business.

His son, Willie, died, presaging the poet's own death on 7 October 1867. Timrod was buried at Trinity Episcopal Cathedral in Columbia. After Timrod's death his reputation steadily grew. His fellow author and friend Paul Hamilton Hayne edited and published in 1873 *The Poems of Henry Timrod* to widespread and appreciative notice. In 1911 the South Carolina General Assembly selected the words of Timrod's poem "Carolina" for the state song, with music by Lily Strickland of Anderson, South Carolina. In 2006 a *New York Times* reporter made mention of contemporary musician Bob Dylan's apparent borrowings—however unacknowledged—from Timrod's verse in Dylan's album *Modern Times*.

George Washington Harris
(1814–1869)

Born 20 March 1814, Allegheny City PA
Died 11 December 1869, Knoxville TN
Buried Brock Cemetery, Trenton GA

Works: *Sut Lovingood. Yarns Spun by a "Nat'ral Born Durn'd Fool"*

Harris moved to Knoxville when he was young and lived with his half-brother Samuel Bell, a silversmith and eventual mayor. At 19, Harris became captain of the steamship *Knoxville*. In this role he participated in the removal of the Cherokees from East Tennessee, the "Trail of Tears." He worked in Knoxville as a jeweler, glassmaker, surveyor, inventor, postmaster, and not-very-successful gentleman farmer. He owned three slaves for a time, and was an elder at First Presbyterian Church in Knoxville. He started writing humorous sketches in the 1840s, using the pseudonyms Mr. Free and later Sugartail. The sketches were printed in *The Spirit of the Times*, a New York sporting journal, and in Tennessee newspapers. His character Sut Lovingood, a free-spirited hillbilly, appeared in 1854. Just before and during the Civil War, pro-Union East Tennessee was inhospitable to someone with Harris's political sensibilities—two of his sons fought for the Confederacy. He lived in Nashville, Chattanooga, Trenton, Georgia, and Decatur, Alabama, often holding railroad jobs. His only book, *Sut Lovingood. Yarns Spun by a "Nat'ral Born Durn'd Fool,"* was published in 1867, and remained in print until the 1920s. It was reviewed by Mark Twain and praised by Faulkner. In 1867 his wife died in Trenton, and in 1869 Harris married a Decatur widow with children.

Two months later, in December 1869, Harris, then working for the railroad in Decatur, went to Virginia, carrying the manuscript for his second book, to be called *High Times and Hard Times*, to arrange for its publication. On the return trip Harris got ill on the train. He was put off at Knoxville, where doctors attended him. He said "Poisoned!" then died, 10 December 1869. The assembled physicians concluded he died from "an unknown cause": some speculated apoplexy or morphia. The original doctors' determination still holds—an unknown cause. According to a newspaper report, his wife collected his body in Knoxville and took it to Chattanooga. The manuscript for *High Times and Hard Times* was lost. The grave was also, until 2007, when Phil Wirey, a cemeterian and genealogist in Decatur, Alabama, located it beside his first wife's grave, in the Brock family cemetery in Trenton. It was marked only with an unlettered fieldstone until the national honor society Sigma Kappa Delta erected a granite obelisk. Three generations of Harris's descendants, plus noted Harris scholar M. Thomas Inge, unveiled the marker 20 April 2008.

William Gilmore Simms
(1806–1870)

Born 17 April 1806, Charleston SC
Died 11 May 1870, Charleston SC
Buried Magnolia, Charleston SC

Works: *Monody, On the Death of Gen. Charles Cotesworth Pinckney, Early Lays, Lyrical and Other Poems, The Vision of Cortes, Cain, and Other Poems, The Tri-Color; or, The Three Days of Blood, in Paris, Atlantis: A Story of the Sea, The Remains of Maynard Davis Richardson, With a Memoir of His Life, Martin Faber: The Story of a Criminal, The Book of My Lady: A Melange, Guy Rivers: A Tale of Georgia, The Yemassee: A Romance of Carolina, The Partisan: A Tale of the Revolution, Mellichampe: A Legend of the Santee, Carl Warner: An Imaginative Story, Richard Hurdis; or, The Avenger of Blood, Pelayo: A Story of the Goth, Southern Passages and Pictures, The Damsel of Darien, Border Beagles: A Tale of Mississippi, The History of South Carolina, The Kinsmen; or, The Black Riders of Congaree, Confession; or, The Blind Heart, Beauchampe; or, The Kentucky Tragedy, Donna Florida: A Tale, The Geography of South Carolina, The Social Principle, The Life of Francis Marion, Castle Dismal; or, The Bachelor's Christmas, Songs of the South, The Life of Captain John Smith, the Founder of Virginia, The Life of Chevalier Bayard: "The Good Knight," Charleston and Her Satirists: A Scribblement, Lays of the Palmetto: A Tribute to the South Carolina Regiment, in the War with Mexico, The Cassique of Accabee, A Supplement to the Plays of William Shakespeare Comprising the Seven Dramas, Which Have Been Ascribed to His Pen but Which are not Included in His Writings in Modern Editions, Father Abbott; or, The Home Tourist, Sabbath Lyrics; or, Songs from Scripture, The Rebel of Winchester, Norman Maurice; or, The Man of the People: An American Drama, Michael Bonham; or, The Fall of Bexar, The Sword and the Distaff; or, Fair, Fat, and Forty: A Story of the South, at the Close of the Revolution, The Golden Christmas: A Chronicle of St. John's, Berkeley, As Good as a Comedy; or, The Tennessean's Story, Vasconselos: A Romance of the New World, Egeria; or, Voices of Thought and Counsel, For the Woods and Wayside, Marie de Berniere: A Tale of the Crescent City, Poems Descriptive, Dramatic, Legendary and Contemplative, South Carolina in the Revolutionary War, Southward Ho! A Tale of Sunshine, The Forayers; or, The Raid of the Dog-Days, Eutaw: A Sequel to the Forayers, The Cassique of Kiawah: A Colonial Romance, Areytos; or, Songs and Ballads of the South, Sack and Destruction of the City of Columbia, S.C., War Poets of the South, The Army Correspondence of Colonel John Laurens in the Years 1777-8, With a Memoir, The Sense of the Beautiful: An Address, The Letters of William Gilmore Simms (6 vols.), Voltmeier; or, The Mountain Men, Paddy McGann; or, The Demon of the Stump, Joscelyn: A Tale of the Revolution, The Cub of the Panther: A Hunter Legend of the "Old North State"*

The name William Gilmore Simms was well known to nineteenth-century readers of fiction and Southern history, although his literary star has been eclipsed by those of his contemporaries Nathaniel Hawthorne, Herman Melville, and James Fenimore Cooper. A planter, politician, journalist, poet, and novelist, Simms was the pre-eminent man of letters in the South prior to the Civil War. His Revolutionary War romances, such as *The Yemassee* (1835) and *A Cassique of Kiawah* (1859), were especially popular and critically well received. But the Civil War exacted its toll on him, and he spent the last five years of his life in genteel poverty. He died in May, 1870. After funeral services at Charleston's St. Paul's Episcopal Church (now the Cathedral of St. Paul and St. Luke), he was buried at Magnolia Cemetery.

Augustus Baldwin Longstreet
(1790–1870)

Born 22 September 1790, Augusta GA
Died 10 July 1870, Oxford MS
Buried St. Peter's, Oxford MS

Works: *Georgia Scenes, Master William Mitten, Stories with a Moral, Letters on the Epistle of Paul to Philemon, A Voice from the South*

Longstreet was one of the first "Southwestern humorists," who lived and wrote when Augusta, Georgia, was considered the Southwest. His father, an inventor and land speculator, had moved from New Jersey to Augusta to make his fortune in about 1785. His most famous work, *Georgia Scenes* (1835), was reviewed favorably by Poe, and was a national best-seller. Poe's review in *The Southern Literary Messenger* called Longstreet "clever...with an exquisitely discriminative and penetrating understanding of character in general, and of Southern character in particular. ...Seldom—perhaps never in our lives—have we laughed as immoderately over any book. ..." *Georgia Scenes* was the first work by a Southwestern humorist to reach a national audience.

Longstreet studied law at Yale, following the example of John C. Calhoun, a family friend. He was admitted to the Georgia bar in 1815 and then had a distinguished career as lawyer, state assemblyman, judge, Methodist minister, and college president at Emory College, Centenary College, the University of Mississippi, and South Carolina College. His experiences as a lawyer in Richmond County, Georgia, inspired the stories in *Georgia Scenes*.

He left Columbia in late 1861, after most of the students had left school to join the Confederates. During the war he supported the South with his writings, and served as a chaplain in the Georgia Militia. His nephew was Lt. Gen. James Longstreet, Lee's "Old War Horse," and his son-in-law was L. Q. C. Lamar II. He returned to Oxford, Mississippi, where his house was burned by Federal troops in December 1862, using his papers as kindling. He moved back to Georgia for the remainder of the war. After the war, he retired back to Oxford, where he died. He was buried in St. Peter's Cemetery.

John Pendleton Kennedy
(1795–1870)

Born 25 October 1795, Baltimore MD
Died 18 August 1870, Newport RI
Buried Green Mount, Baltimore MD

Works: *Swallow Barn: or a Sojourn in the Old Dominion, Horse-Shoe Robinson: A Tale of the Tory Ascendency, Rob of the Bowl: A Legend of St. Inigoe's, Quodlibet, Memoirs of the Work of William Wirt, Collected Works*

John Pendleton Kennedy is best known for his novels *Swallow Barn* (1832) and *Horse-Shoe Robinson* (1835). He was born in Baltimore, was graduated from Baltimore College (now the University of Maryland), and saw military service in the War of 1812. He was admitted to the bar in 1816. Kennedy served in the Maryland House of Delegates and was later a member of the U.S. House of Representatives. He was elected in 1841, and served two terms. He entertained Charles Dickens on his first trip to the United States in 1842, in support of international copyright laws. He rose to prominence and considerable wealth as a writer, while his near-contemporary Edgar Allan Poe struggled against destitution.

Once, when Kennedy invited Poe to his home for dinner, Poe replied pitifully that he would have to decline the invitation because he lacked acceptable clothing to wear to such a grand home. A Whig, Kennedy was appointed Secretary of the Navy by President Millard Fillmore (1852-1853). When the Civil War broke out eight years later, Kennedy staunchly defended the Union's cause. Kennedy died in Newport, Rhode Island, in 1870 and was buried in Green Mount Cemetery in his home city. He had been a featured speaker when Green Mount was dedicated 13 July 1839.

In his speech he identified Green Mount as belonging to the rural cemetery movement begun at Mount Auburn in Cambridge, Massachusetts, in 1831: "Though scarce a half hour's walk from yon living mart, where one hundred thousand human beings toil in their noisy crafts, here the deep quiet of the country reigns, broken by no ruder voice than such as marks the tranquility of rural life,--the voice of 'birds on branches warbling,'—the lowing of distant cattle, and the whetting of the mower's scythe."

Penina Moïse
(1797–1880)

Born 23 April 1797, Charleston SC
Died 13 September 1880, Charleston SC
Buried Kahal Kadosh Beth Elohim (Coming Street)

Work: *Fancy's Sketch Book*

Penina Moïse, a member of Charleston's Sephardic Jewish community, was born in 1797. She holds the distinction of being the first Jewish American female to issue a volume of poetry, *Fancy's Sketch Book*, in 1833. A teacher, linguist, and poet, she suffered the loss of her sight in middle age, but the affliction did not impede her literary output.

Her chief thematic concerns were religious devotion and the Confederate cause. During the Civil War she fled her native city, moving to the town of Sumter, 100 miles inland, because her sometimes-controversial poetry had angered members of the Union army.

After the end of hostilities she returned to Charleston, where she died in 1880. She was buried in historic Kahal Kadosh Beth Elohim Cemetery, the oldest Jewish burial ground in the South, on Coming Street. Today she is best remembered as the author of several works that appear in the hymnal of Reform Judaism.

Beth Elohim was the fourth oldest Jewish congregation in the United States, organized in 1749, and the cemetery was established in 1764. When some members of Beth Elohim voted to install an organ in their synagogue in 1840, rebuilt after a fire, a schism resulted and traditionalists formed a separate Orthodox congregation, Shearit Israel.

Beth Elohim thus became the first Reform Jewish congregation, and Penina Moïse's poetic and teaching contributions were important. She wrote 190 hymns for use at Beth Elohim, and was superintendant of the Sunday school.

Sidney Lanier
(1842–1881)

Born 3 February 1842, Macon GA
Died 8 September 1881, Lynn NC
Buried Green Mount, Baltimore MD

Works: *Tiger-Lilies, Florida: Its Scenery, Climate, and History, Poems, The Science of English Verse, The English Novel and the Principle of its Development, Poems of Sidney Lanier, Music and Poetry, Retrospects and Prospects: Descriptive and Historical Essays, Bob: The Story of Our Mocking-Bird, Letters of Sidney Lanier, Shakespeare and His Forerunners, Poem Outlines, The Centennial Edition of the Works of Sidney Lanier*

Sidney Lanier was born in Macon, Georgia, and graduated with honors from Oglethorpe University (then located near Milledgeville) shortly before entering service in the Confederate signal corps. He was a pilot for English blockade runners, and was captured. As a prisoner of war in Maryland he contracted tuberculosis.

Released at the war's end in 1865, Lanier returned to his native Georgia, where he studied and briefly practiced law. For a time he taught school and served as a church organist in Alabama. In 1867 he wed Mary Day; to them were born three sons. Unable to secure steady work as a musician in New York, Boston, or Philadelphia, he instead settled in Baltimore, where he was employed as a flutist by the Peabody Conservatory's orchestra, and later received a teaching appointment in literature at the new Johns Hopkins University.

Lanier authored a single novel, *Tiger-Lilies* (1867), based upon his war experiences; a technical text on poetry, *The Science of English Verse* (1880); and numerous essays and poems. After years of suffering, Lanier succumbed at age 39 to tuberculosis during a stay in Lynn, North Carolina, in 1881. He was buried in Green Mount Cemetery in Baltimore.

Lanier has been dismissed by some recent scholars and critics as a second-tier poet, but Southern readers have long revered his work. Among his most broadly cherished poems are "The Song of the Chattahoochee," "The Symphony," "Corn," and "The Marshes of Glynn." He was commemorated after his death as towns, counties, lakes, parks, and schools throughout the South were named or re-named in his memory.

Mary Ann Bryan Mason
(1802–1881)

Born 6 September 1802, New Bern NC
Died 31 August 1881, Raleigh NC
Buried Oakwood, Raleigh NC

Works: *The Young Housewife's Counsellor and Friend: Containing Directions in Every Department of Housekeeping, Including the Duties of Wife and Mother, A Wreath from the Woods of Carolina, Her Church and Her Mother: A Story of Filial Piety, Spring-Time for Sowing*

Mary Ann Bryan was born into an old and prominent North Carolina family. Just before her 21st birthday she married the rector of Christ Episcopal Church in New Bern. He later moved to other parishes, and also taught at colleges in New York and Delaware, but from 1840 until 1874, he was rector of Christ Church in Raleigh. They had six children.

Mary Ann Bryan Mason was an artist and musician as well as a writer. She wrote the first book by a North Carolinian exclusively for children, *A Wreath from the Woods of Carolina* (1859), a collection of religious stories, which she illustrated with her own engravings of Tar Heel wildflowers. Her popular guide to housekeeping, *The Young Housewife's Counsellor and Friend, Containing Directions in Every Department of Housekeeping, Including the Duties of Wife and Mother* (1871), was reprinted in 1875 with the title *Mrs. Mason's New Cookery*.

In addition to recipes, *The Young Housewife's Counsellor* gives advice on housecleaning, entertaining, caring for children, and dealing with servants. Mrs. Bryan offers cures for various ailments, including a remedy for cancer: "Pound up a handful of sorrel leaves, stew them together with lard, and apply the poultice to the cancer, taking care to protect the well flesh by means of a large piece of adhesive plaster with a round hole cut in the center just sufficiently large to expose the cancer. This poultice should remain twenty-four hours. Strong potash, applied in the same way, it is said, will destroy a cancer so that it can be pulled out as you would pull up a parsnip from the ground."

Mrs. Mason died in Raleigh and was buried at Oakwood Cemetery there.

William Tappan Thompson
(1812–1882)

Born 31 August 1812, Ravenna OH
Died 24 March 1882, Savannah GA
Buried Laurel Grove, Savannah GA

Works: *Major Jones's Courtship, Major Jones's Chronicles of Pineville, John's Alive: or the Bride of the Ghost, Major Jones's Sketches of Travel, Polly Peablossom's Wedding, Rancy Cotton's Courtship*

William Tappan Thompson was born in 1812 in Ravenna, Portage County, Ohio. As a teenager, Thompson secured a position at a Philadelphia newspaper, and later was employed by the territorial government of Florida. He has become identified as one of the Old Southwest humorists chiefly because of one of his fictional characters, Major Joseph Jones.

He moved to Augusta, Georgia, in 1834, to serve as an apprentice in the law office of another Southwest humorist, Augustus Baldwin Longstreet. He also worked for Longstreet's newspaper, the *State Rights Sentinel*. Thompson fought in the Second Seminole War (1836), returning the following year to Augusta to wed Caroline Amour Carrie.

Thompson was associated with several periodicals, including the *Augusta Mirror*, which he inaugurated in 1838; *The Family Companion and Ladies' Mirror* (Macon, Georgia); *The Southern Miscellany* (Madison, Georgia); and the *Western Continent* (Baltimore). His first volume of humorous dialect tales, *Major Jones's Courtship*, debuted in 1843. Later collections included *Chronicles of Pineville* (1845), *John's Alive; or, The Bride of a Ghost* (1846), and *Major Jones's Sketches of Travel* (1848). In 1850 Thompson became the founding editor of the *Savannah Morning News*, a post he vacated when Union forces captured that city in 1864. For a time the paper was under northern ownership, and Thompson continued his work there.

After a European tour in 1867, Thompson resumed editorial control of the paper. He was an ardent and outspoken Democrat, and his journalism reflected his political leanings. In his capacity as editor he mentored Joel Chandler Harris, who served as the *Morning News*'s associate editor, 1870-1876. Thompson died in Savannah in 1882, and was buried at that city's Laurel Grove Cemetery.

Sherwood Bonner
(1849–1883)

Born 26 February 1849, Holly Springs MS
Died 22 July 1883, Holly Springs MS
Buried Hill Crest, Holly Springs MS

Works: *Dialect Tales, Suwanee River Tales, Like Unto Like, Last Will and Testament, The Valcours*

Born the daughter of a medical doctor, Katherine Sherwood Bonner in her early teens experienced the trauma of the Union Army's occupation of her home town. None other than Gen. U.S. Grant seized the Bonner home, Cedarhurst, and other local homes to accommodate his military entourage before the Vicksburg campaign. In 1871 Sherwood Bonner wed Edward McDowell, but the marriage floundered after the couple moved to Texas.

Bonner and her only child, Lilian, returned to Holly Springs in 1873. She then moved to Boston, leaving her daughter with relatives. In that most literary of northern cities she became Henry Wadsworth Longfellow's amanuensis, and published poems, dialect pieces, and local-color stories in such venues as *Harper's Weekly*, *St. Nicholas*, and *Youth's Companion*. Her popular "Grandmammy" sketches (1875-80) were rendered in African-American dialect.

Other works captured the speech of Tennessee mountaineers and Southern Illinoisans. *Like unto Like*, a novel set during Reconstruction, was published by Harper Brothers in 1878. Granted a divorce in 1881, Bonner returned to her native South, and died from breast cancer in Holly Springs when she was only thirty-four.

Bonner's grave in Hill Crest Cemetery was originally unmarked at her request, according to scholar Anne Gowdy, but a modern marker, placed ca. 1997 by the Very Rev. Mr. Bruce D. McMillan, rector of Christ Episcopal Church in Holly Springs, is inscribed "She Was Much Loved." This epitaph was of Bonner's own choosing, according to biographer Hubert Horton McAlexander. The ashes of Bonner's daughter, Lilian Kirk Hammond, were placed in the same grave, also marked by Fr. McMillan.

James Gettys McGready Ramsey
(1797–1884)

Born 25 March 1797, Swan Pond TN
Died 11 April 1884, Knoxville TN
Buried Lebanon in the Forks, Knoxville TN

Works: *Annals of Tennessee, Dr. J.G.M. Ramsey: Autobiography and Letters*

James Gettys McGready Ramsey was born in East Tennessee in 1796. He was a masterful jack of all trades, who at different stages of his life worked as a physician, a banker, a public servant, a religious leader, and a great historian of Tennessee.

Ramsey's father, Colonel Francis Alexander Ramsey, was a leading figure in the founding of Tennessee's statehood, having served in an official capacity in the failed state of Franklin, a precursor to the state of Tennessee.

J. G. M. Ramsey began his education at Ebenezer Academy in Knox County, Tennessee, and continued his studies at Washington College. Ramsey completed his education at the University of Pennsylvania Medical School.

In 1821, Ramsey married Margaret Crozier, and the couple had 11 children. Ramsey became the president of the Knoxville branch of the Bank of Tennessee, following the death of his father, who had previously held the position. By the 1830's, Ramsey had become interested in the growth of railroads and tried to establish a line between Knoxville and Charleston, with the first train entering Knoxville in 1855.

In 1834, Ramsey founded the East Tennessee Historical and Antiquarian Society, known today as the East Tennessee Historical Society. He served in the role of recording secretary and helped protect and document the relics dating from the early days of Tennessee.

At the outbreak of the War Between the States, Ramsey was a staunch secessionist and served as a treasury agent and field surgeon to the Confederacy. The war inflicted hardships on his family; their home was destroyed, a son was killed, and they had to live in exile in Charlotte, North Carolina. After the war, Ramsey continued to live in North Carolina, where he practiced medicine and began working on his autobiography, published posthumously in 1954 as *Dr. J.G.M. Ramsey: Autobiography and Letters*.

He returned to Knoxville in the early 1870's, and resided there until his death in 1884.

Abram Joseph Ryan
(1838–1886)

Born 5 February 1838, Hagerstown, MD
Died 22 April 1886, Louisville KY
Buried Old Catholic Cemetery, Mobile AL

Works: *Father Ryan's Poems, Poems, Patriotic, Religious, and Miscellaneous, A Crown for Our Queen*

Abram Joseph Ryan was born in Hagerstown, Maryland, to Irish immigrants. Educated by the Christian Brothers (also known as Vincentians) in St. Louis, Missouri, and at Niagara University in New York, he was ordained to the Roman Catholic priesthood in 1856. Father Ryan served as a volunteer chaplain to the Confederate soldiers throughout the Civil War, but never joined the army. Subsequently he was a priest at parishes in Mississippi, Tennessee, Alabama, and Georgia.

During the war and afterward, he produced a large quantity of poetry, much of it lamenting the fallen Confederacy, in whose service Ryan's brother had lost his life. His best-known poems—reminiscent in rhyme and meter of Edgar Allan Poe's—include "The Sword of Robert Lee," "The Conquered Banner," "C.S.A.," and such devotional verse as "Their Story Runneth Thus." Much of his work appeared first in the *Banner of the South*, a newspaper devoted to the Lost Cause that he oversaw while living in Augusta, Georgia.

Today he is remembered as the "Poet-Priest of the Confederacy." Father Ryan died at a Franciscan monastery in Louisville, Kentucky, in the spring of 1886. He was buried in the Old Catholic Cemetery in Mobile. A monument to his memory was erected in that city in 1913, and a Catholic high school in Nashville, Tennessee, was named for him.

His most celebrated poem is "The Conquered Banner." The concluding lines are carved on a footstone at his grave, where formerly a slanting flagpole flew, to support a drooping Confederate battle flag:

> Furl that Banner, softly, slowly!
> Treat it gently—it is holy—
> For it droops above the dead.
> Touch it not, unfold it never,
> Let it droop there, furled forever,
> For its people's hopes are dead.

Paul Hamilton Hayne
(1830–1886)

Born 1 January 1830, Charleston SC
Died 6 July 1886, Grovetown GA
Buried Magnolia, Augusta GA

Works: *Poems, Sonnets and Other Poems, Avolio: A Legend of the Island of Cos. With Poems, Lyrical, Miscellaneous, and Dramatic, Legends and Lyrics,* ed. *The Poems of Henry Timrod, The Mountain of the Lovers With Poems of Nature and Tradition, Poems*

Hayne was graduated from the College of Charleston. An attorney by training, he abandoned the practice of law to devote his energies to writing (especially sonnets), and established close friendships with the Charleston literati, including Henry Timrod and William Gilmore Simms.

In 1857 Hayne helped found the influential *Russell's Magazine.* Physically unsuited for the rigors of military service, he served on the South Carolina governor's staff during the Civil War.

His contemporary biographer wrote, "During the bombardment of his native city, his beautiful home was burned to the ground, and his large, handsome library utterly lost. Even the few valuables, such as the old family silver, which he succeeded in securing and removing to a bank in Columbia for safe-keeping, were swept away in the famous 'march to the sea'; and there was nothing left for the homeless and ruined man but exile among the 'Pine Barrens' of Georgia."

Impoverished by the war, he fled his native city and settled in a cabin near Grovetown, Georgia, a short distance from Augusta.

Hayne wrote prolifically, seeing his poems and prose works published in the *Atlantic Monthly* and *Harper's*. He became known as the "Poet of the Pines" and the "last Southern cavalier," and won the esteem of such writers as Alfred, Lord Tennyson, Henry Wadsworth Longfellow, Sidney Lanier, and William Cullen Bryant.

He died at age fifty-six in Grovetown and was buried in Augusta's Magnolia Cemetery. Today he is respected more for his letters than for his poetry.

WILLIAM CLARK FALKNER (1825–1889)

Born 8 July 1825, Knoxville TN
Died 5 November 1889, Ripley MS
Buried Ripley Cemetery, Ripley MS

Works: *The Life and Confession of A. J. MacCannon, Murderer of the Adcock Family, The White Rose of Memphis, The Siege of Monterey, The Spanish Heroine, The Lost Diamond, Rapid Ramblings in Europe, The Little Brick Church, Lady Olivia, Rapid Ramblings in Europe*

The child William Faulkner said, "I want to be a writer like my great-granddaddy." Faulkner's third novel and first "Yoknapatawpha" novel was *Sartoris* (1929, also known as *Flags in the Dust*, 1975). Many of the life events of Colonel John Sartoris in the novel are taken from the life of Faulkner's great-grandfather William Clark Falkner, known as the "Old Colonel," and himself a novelist.

In particular, Faulkner describes Sartoris's grave monument, the statue with its "carven eyes" gazing out at the railroad he built, and his leg leaning against a stone pylon.

Falkner (born Faulkner, but he dropped the "u") was born in Knox County, Tennessee, and moved with his family to Missouri and Pontotoc, Mississippi, before settling in Ripley, Mississippi. He served in the Mexican War and then practiced law. In 1849 in a business dispute he killed two men, Robert Hindman and Erasmus Moore. His Mexican War experiences inspired an autobiographical poem, *The Siege of Monterrey* (1851), and a novel, *The Spanish Heroine* (1851).

When the Civil War broke out, he was elected Colonel of the Second Mississippi Infantry of the Confederate Army. He led the regiment at the First Battle of Manassas, but was afterwards defeated for re-election. He raised a new regiment, the Mississippi Partisan Rangers, but never regained his former stature. Nevertheless he was known as "Colonel Falkner" or "The Old Colonel" ever after.

After the war he started The Ship Island, Ripley, and Kentucky Railroad, and wrote a play, *The Lost Diamond* (1867), and his best-known novel, *The White Rose of Memphis* (1881). This book, in which various characters tell stories on the maiden cruise of a Mississippi riverboat, against a central murder-mystery plot, was originally serialized in the *Ripley Advertiser*. It was a popular success, reprinted into the 20th century. He tried the same formula in *The Little Brick Church* (1882) with less success. His last book, *Rapid Ramblings in Europe* (1884) is a travel book in the mode of Twain's *Innocents Abroad* (1869).

Falkner was elected to the Mississippi legislature in 1889, and was immediately afterwards shot and killed on the Ripley square by a former business partner, Richard Simon Thurmond.

The "Old Colonel" was buried in the Ripley Cemetery, beneath a statue looking out over the railroad he built, supported by a "pylon" of a stack of books.

Henry Grady
(1850–1889)

Born 24 May 1850, Athens GA
Died 23 December 1889, Atlanta GA
Buried Westview, Atlanta GA

Works: *The New South and Other Addresses, Life and Labors of Henry W. Grady: His Speeches, Writings, etc., The Speeches of Henry W. Grady, The Complete Orations and Speeches of Henry W. Grady, The New South: Writings and Speeches of Henry W. Grady.*

Henry Woodfin Grady wrote no poems, novels, histories, or plays. He was a newspaperman and a distinguished orator.

His father died from a gunshot wound he received during the Civil War in the siege of Petersburg, Virginia, and Henry was reared by his mother. He was graduated from the University of Georgia and went to the University of Virginia with the idea of studying law. Instead, he developed an interest in Greek and Anglo-Saxon languages, history, and literature, and embarked on a career in journalism. He first wrote for the Rome *Courier*, but that newspaper went bankrupt in 1871. After marrying Julia King of Atlanta, he shared ownership in the Atlanta *Daily Herald* with Robert Alston and Alexander St. Clair Adams. On 14 March 1874 Grady published an editorial in the *Daily Herald*, "The New South," advocating industrial development as the tonic to boost the South out of its economic woes.

His aggressive writing style and his promotion of railroad development in the Atlanta area caught the attention of Evan P. Howell and W. A. Hemphill—majority owners of the Atlanta *Constitution*. They offered Grady the position of managing editor and allowed him to purchase a quarter-share interest in the newspaper for $20,000. The *Constitution* gave Grady a wider audience for his pro-industrialization views. He also campaigned for anti-liquor laws, a mix of agricultural crops besides cotton, a new library, and for adequate care for the Confederate veterans. The *Constitution* became the voice for what came to be termed the Atlanta Ring, a loose-knit group of pro-industry Democrats that included Howell and Grady.

Grady was also developing a reputation as a raconteur and orator. In 1886 he was invited to address the prestigious New England Society meeting in New York. He called for greater trust between the North and South and extolled the virtues of investment in the New South, where, he told all who would listen, there was a "willing" labor force. His campaign brought investment capital to Atlanta and helped secure the city with its largely diversified industrial base.

Grady died 23 December 1889 after becoming ill returning from a speech at Faneuil Hall in Boston 11 days earlier.

Charles Colcock Jones, Jr.
(1831–1893)

Born 28 October 1831, Savannah GA
Died 19 July 1893, Augusta GA
Buried Summerville Cemetery, Augusta GA

Works: *Indian Remains in Southern Georgia, The Monumental Remains of Georgia, Historical Sketch of the Chatham Artillery, Historical Sketch of Tom-chi-chi, Mico of Yamacraws, Antiquities of the Southern Indians, The Siege of Savannah in December 1864, The Dead Towns of Georgia, The Life and Services of Commodore Josiah Tattnall, Hernando de Soto, The History of Georgia, Negro Myths from the Georgia Coast*

Jones was born in Savannah in 1831, a son of a nationally prominent Presbyterian clergyman. (The family's absorbing correspondence is collected in the 1973 National Book Award-winning *The Children of Pride*, edited by Robert Manson Myers.) Growing up on Georgia's coastal plain, he became acquainted with the state's early history and with the Gullah dialect spoken by slaves from western Africa. These early exposures formed the foundation of his later literary pursuits. Educated at Princeton University and Harvard Law School, Jones was elected mayor of Savannah in 1860.

Of Sherman's march to the sea, ending with Sherman's presentation to Lincoln of Savannah as a Christmas gift, Jones wrote,

> This sad chapter in the history of Georgia has been written only by those who made light of her afflictions, laughed at her calamities, gloated over her losses, and lauded her spoilers. A predatory expedition, inaugurated with full knowledge of her weakness, conceived in a spirit of wanton destruction, conducted in violation of the rules of civilized warfare, and compassed in the face of feeble resistance, has been magnified into a grand military achievement worthy of all admiration. The easy march of a well-appointed army of seventy thousand men through the heart of a state abounding in every supply save men and materials of war, and at the most delightful season of the year, has been so talked of and written about by those who either participated in the enterprise or sympathized with its leaders, that multitudes have come to regard this holiday excursion as a triumph of consummate military skill and valor—as one of the most wonderful exploits in the history of modern warfare. *Audi alteram partem.*

He was financially ruined by the Civil War, and moved to New York in the hope of rebuilding his life. Jones returned to his native state in 1877 after Reconstruction, settling in Augusta. He died in 1893, a victim of Bright's disease, and was buried at Summerville Cemetery.

Frederick Douglass
(1818–1895)

Born 14 February 1818, Talbot County MD
Died 20 February 1895, Washington DC
Buried Mount Hope, Rochester NY

Works: *Narrative of the Life of Frederick Douglass, an American Slave, Written by Himself, Life and Times of Frederick Douglass, My Bondage and My Freedom, The Life and Writings of Frederick Douglass, The Frederick Douglass Papers, Frederick Douglass: The Narrative and Selected Writings*

Frederick Augustus Washington Bailey (later Douglass) was born into slavery in Talbot County on Maryland's Eastern Shore in 1818. He became a newspaper editor, orator, writer, statesman, suffragist, minister, and the greatest African-American abolitionist. Separated from his mother, Harriet Bailey, when he was an infant, he was reared by his grandmother, Betty Bailey. His mother died when he was about seven years old; nothing is known about his father. Douglass was sent to serve a family in Baltimore when he was about 12.

The wife of his owner began teaching him the letters of the alphabet. Douglass later said he learned to read from white children in the Baltimore neighborhood and from the writing of the men working in the area. He began reading avidly, particularly newspapers, political materials, and books. Douglass soon was teaching other slaves to read. That activity alarmed his owners.

Sold to a harsh owner, known regionally as a "slave breaker," in 1833, Douglass was beaten repeatedly, but once he fought back, the owner stopped the beatings. He attempted to escape in 1836 but failed. Another escape scheme the following year also proved unsuccessful.

On 3 September 1838, he boarded a train at Havre de Grace, Maryland, dressed as a seaman. He made his way to Philadelphia and then on to New York, arriving the following day. He continued on to New Bedford, Massachusetts, where he met William Lloyd Garrison, the fiery abolitionist editor of *The Liberator*. Douglass was asked to speak at one of the abolitionist meetings he attended, and Garrison wrote his story. He delivered his first planned speech at the Massachusetts Anti-Slavery convention in Nantucket, at age 23.

He published *Narrative of the Life of Frederick Douglass, an American Slave* (1845), which became a best-seller among the abolitionists in the North and in England. Douglass toured England and Ireland, speaking to anti-slavery groups. He founded his own abolitionist newspaper, *The North Star*, in 1846. Five years later he merged the newspaper with another publication to form the *Frederick Douglass Paper*. He advised President Abraham Lincoln on the treatment of African-American soldiers and remained an activist for civil rights, suffrage, and equal pay throughout his life. Douglass died in Washington, D. C., in 1895.

Harriet Ann Jacobs
(1813–1897)

Born 1813, Edenton NC
Died 7 March 1897, Washington DC
Buried Mount Auburn, Cambridge MA

Works: *Incidents in the Life of a Slave Girl*

Born into slavery in Edenton, North Carolina, Harriet Jacobs as a young girl was sexually harassed by her owner. She entered a consensual sexual relationship with a white neighbor by whom she had two children, but eventually she had to hide from her owner to avoid his sexual attentions. Jacobs lived in an attic crawl space of her grandmother's house for seven years until she fled north in 1842, first to Philadelphia and then to New York three years later.

She became involved in the abolitionist movement, often relating her experiences as a slave, and telling of her efforts to purchase the freedom of her children, who eventually managed to join her in New York.

Jacobs began writing her autobiography, *Incidents in the Life of a Slave Girl*, as a series of stories for the *New York Tribune*, but when the subject of her sexual abuse at the hands of her owner surfaced, the series was canceled as being too explicit for the New York readers. The *New York Tribune* was edited by Horace Greeley, a leader in the abolitionist movement.

Frustrated by the cancellation of her newspaper series, Jacobs began attempts to have her stories compiled in a book. One publisher agreed to print the book, but went out of business before the project was completed. A second publisher went bankrupt before the book could be printed.

Meanwhile, John S. Jacobs, the author's younger brother, published a condensed version of her book as *A True Tale of Slavery* (1861) in London. The response to the book was sensational, although John Jacobs had expurgated all references to the sexual harassment. Later the same year a Boston firm published Harriet Jacobs's autobiography as originally conceived.

Both versions were far more popular in England than in the United States, but abolitionists used the revelations in the books as justifications for the Civil War as a war to end slavery.

She died in Washington, D.C., and was buried in Mount Auburn Cemetery in Cambridge, Massachusetts.

William Malone Baskervill
(1850–1899)

Born 1 April 1850, Fayette Co. TN
Died 6 September 1899, Nashville TN
Buried Mt. Olivet, Nashville TN

Works: *Andreas: A Legend of St. Andrews, Students' Anglo-Saxon Dictionary, An Outline of Anglo-Saxon Grammar, Shall the Negro Be Educated or Suppressed?, English Grammar for High School and College Use, Southern Writers: Biographical and Critical Studies, School Grammar of the English Language*

William Malone Baskervill was the son of a Methodist minister, medical doctor, and planter.

Born in rural Southwest Tennessee (Fayette County), his mother died when he was four years old. Baskervill moved with his father several times as a youth. He was injured severely when a gun discharged accidentally during a hunting trip, wounding him in the left arm.

Baskervill attended Indiana Asbury University (now DePauw) and Randolph-Macon College in Virginia, then studied in Leipzig, Germany, where he earned his doctorate in 1880. After teaching Latin at Wofford College in South Carolina, he joined the faculty at Vanderbilt University in Nashville and subsequently became chairman of the English department there.

He wrote several books on grammar and proper English usage.

In addition to his scholarly endeavors, Baskervill joined with Louisiana-based George Washington Cable, a local color writer, to promote the civil rights and educational opportunities for African-Americans in the South. The principal vehicle for their efforts was the Open Letter Club, which flourished from 1887 until 1890. Critics charged that the club was churning out purely liberal propaganda and was without merit.

He was an unabashed fan of Joel Chandler Harris and praised Harris's Uncle Remus stories for what he regarded as authentic portrayals of Southern life.

Baskervill had intended to write twelve articles about selected post-Civil War writers in the South, but the project (*Southern Writers: Biographical and Critical Studies*, 1897) ballooned to two volumes, the second of which was completed by his students after his death in 1899.

He died in Nashville at the age of 49 and was buried in Mt. Olivet Cemetery there.

Albery Allson Whitman
(1851–1901)

Born 30 May 1851, Hart Co. KY
Died 29 June 1901, Louisville KY
Buried South-View, Atlanta GA

Works: *Essays on the Ten Plagues, Leelah Misled, Not a Man and Yet a Man, The Rape of Florida, Twasinta's Seminoles, Drifted Leaves, World's Fair Poem, An Idyl of the South*

Born a slave, Whitman attended Wilberforce University after limited formal schooling, and came under the influence of Bishop Daniel Alexander Payne of the African Methodist Episcopal Church. He was ordained an AME minister, and served and founded churches in Kansas, Ohio, Texas, and Georgia. His first book of poetry, *Essays on the Ten Plagues and Other Miscellaneous Poems*, was published in 1873, but no copies survive. His poem "Not a Man Yet a Man," over 5000 lines long, was published in 1877.

His last pastorate was at Allen Temple in Atlanta. His poetic narratives earned him the title "The Poet Laureate of the Negro Race." Along with his wife, Caddie (or Katie, as the grave marker reads), he declaimed his poems at the Chicago World's Fair. These two poems, "The Freedman's Triumphant Song" and "The Veteran," were published together in a pamphlet called *The World's Fair Poem* (1893).

Three of his daughters, Mabel, Alberta, and Effie, together with a fourth "adopted" daughter Alice, formed a famous vaudeville group, the Whitman Sisters, a song-and-dance ensemble that toured the US and Europe, the "Royalty of Negro Vaudeville."

Whitman died from pneumonia, complicated by overuse of alcohol, in Atlanta, and is buried in South-View Cemetery. South-View was created in 1886 by a group of African-American businessmen who resented the poor treatment they had received at Oakland. It is the burial place of many luminaries from the African-American community, including A. C. Herndon, Mr. and Mrs. Martin Luther King, Sr., John Wesley Dobbs, Ralph David Abernathy, and others. Martin Luther King, Jr., was buried there temporarily until his crypt on Auburn Avenue in the MLK Center was completed.

Sam Watkins
(1839–1901)

Born 26 June 1839, Columbia TN
Died 20 July 1901, Ashwood TN
Buried Zion Presbyterian Church Cemetery, Columbia TN

Works: *Company Aytch*

Sam Watkins was born 26 June 1839 in Maury County, Tennessee, near Columbia. He attended Jackson College and worked briefly as a store clerk before enlisting in the Confederate Army. Watkins originally joined the "Bigsby Grays" of the 3rd Tennessee in Mount Pleasant, but soon thereafter he moved on to the First Tennessee Infantry, Company H, also known as the "Maury Grays," in early 1861.

In the "Maury Grays," he participated in some of the most gruesome and famous battles of the War Between the States. Watkins fought in the battles at Shiloh, Chattanooga, Chickamauga, and Atlanta. He was promoted to Fourth Corporal for picking up a Union flag during the Battle of Atlanta.

Watkins was one of only seven out of the original 120 men who enlisted in Company H, when the Army of Tennessee surrendered to General William Tecumseh Sherman in North Carolina in April 1865. After the war, Watkins returned to Maury County, where he married and raised a family.

In 1881, Watkins began working on his memoirs, titled *Co. Aytch: A Side Show of the Big Show*. It was originally published in 1882. The book gave a candid first-hand glimpse of the real-life horrors that the "Maury Grays" suffered. Ken Burns, who produced the much-heralded series *The Civil War* for PBS, used Watkins's writings to help represent the viewpoints of Confederate soldiers.

Sam Watkins died on 20 July 1901 and was buried with honors by the United Confederate Veterans in the cemetery of Zion Presbyterian Church in Maury County.

John Brown Gordon Coogler
(1865–1901)

Born 3 December 1865, Doko (Blythewood) SC
Died 9 September 1901, Columbia SC
Buried Elmwood, Columbia SC

Works: *Purely Original Verse*

John Brown Gordon Coogler chose his name to capitalize on the fame of Confederate General John Brown Gordon. He styled himself as a poet and acquired fans throughout the South as well as in England. At his small print shop in Columbia, South Carolina, he offered "poems while you wait." But the poems were often couplets or quatrains with little substance and even less nuance.

In a more modern setting he might have been termed a wit, but from his humble beginnings, he drew the titles of "The Bard of the Congaree," "Palmetto Poet," "Songbird of the Saluda," and the "Dulcet-Voice Singer of Dixie."

He was born in Doko (now Blythewood) South Carolina in 1865, but his father abandoned his family, leaving three sons and three daughters behind. Coogler's older brothers disappeared, and he was left to help provide for his mother and his sisters from age 15.

He earned a modest living from the print shop operation but added income from his occasional poems sold to customers.

Literary scholars and lay readers have branded Coogler one of the worst versifiers America has produced, but he was warmly praised by his fans.

Munsey's Magazine nominated him for poet laureate, and Henry W. Grady, editor of the *Atlanta Constitution* and president of Atlanta's Coogler Fan Club, wrote, "There must be something in the writings of a man who can attract attention and win applause when corn is thirty cents a bushel and potato bugs have become a burden."

H. L. Mencken may have put Coogler in sharper perspective by quoting two of his lines in "Sahara of the Bozart," in which he described the South as a cultural wasteland: "Alas for the South! Her books have grown fewer -- /She never was much given to literature."

Coogler, who suffered poor health for several years, died in 1901 in Columbia. He is buried in Elmwood Cemetery there.

Charles Henry Smith
(1826–1903)

Born 15 June 1826, Lawrenceville GA
Died 24 August 1903, Cartersville GA
Buried Oak Hill, Cartersville GA

Works: *Bill Arp, So Called, Bill Arp's Peace Papers, Bill Arp's Scrap Book: Humor and Philosophy, The Farm and the Fireside: Sketches of Domestic Life in War and in Peace, A School History of Georgia, Bill Arp: From the Uncivil War to Date*

Charles Henry Smith first came to notice as a writer when he penned a letter to the *Atlanta Constitution* in 1861 responding to President Lincoln's order for the rebels at Fort Sumter to "disperse and retire peaceably." Smith's response: "I tried my darnd'st yesterday to disperse and retire, but it was no go." He signed the letter Bill Arp, supposedly the name of a local Cracker. The letter was widely reprinted in newspapers throughout the South.

Smith, who had been trained as a lawyer, joined the Confederate army and fought in a number of battles. He wrote about 30 letters during the war that were reprinted in Southern newspapers. His family home in Rome, Georgia, was used by several Union generals, including William Tecumseh Sherman. When the Smiths returned after the war, they found the home sacked and gutted.

Returning to civilian life, Smith began writing letters again to the *Constitution*, using backwoods dialect to satirize Reconstruction, politics, hardships, and social trends. He became a weekly columnist at the *Constitution* with his letters from Bill Arp, The Country Philosopher. The columns—keyed strongly to the pleasures of rural living and the need for independence—were syndicated across the South, but also appeared in newspapers in New York, Chicago, San Francisco, and Detroit.

Altogether, his columns appeared in 700 newspapers, making him the South's premier humorist. In the 1890s he wrote a series of columns in support of lynching. In addition to his columns, he was also successful in politics.

He was elected to the Georgia state senate in 1865, afterwards serving as mayor and alderman in Rome, and as a member of a local school board. His final piece of writing appeared in the *Constitution* in 1903—the last of 1,250 columns. He died 24 August 1903 in Cartersville, Georgia.

Kate Chopin (1850–1904)

Born 8 February 1850, St. Louis MO
Died 20 August 1904, St. Louis MO
Buried Calvary, St. Louis MO

Works: *At Fault, Bayou Folk, A Night in Acadie, The Awakening, The Complete Works of Kate Chopin, The Storm, The Story of an Hour, Désirée's Baby, At the Cadian Ball*

As a young woman Kate O'Flaherty was shocking to her neighbors. She openly smoked Cuban cigarettes. She rode horses—alone. She played cards with men. She showed a little too much ankle when she raised her skirts to step off a curb.

Although she had been born in St. Louis, she is almost always identified with Louisiana, the setting for most of her literary works. Her husband, Oscar Chopin, lost his business in New Orleans, forcing a move of the family to Cloutierville, Louisiana. His death in 1882 propelled her into a writing career as a means of supporting her six children. The family home in Cloutierville served as the Bayou Folk Museum until it burned in 2008.

On her honeymoon she had met the suffragist Victoria Claflin Woodhull (1838-1927), who advocated women's rights, birth control, and free love, and who advised Chopin to eschew the useless and degrading life of most married women.

Chopin's talents as a local colorist were well demonstrated in her many short stories, but she began a more significant literary contribution with stories dealing with interracial marriage, venereal disease, adultery, and prostitution – topics regarded as taboo for Southern women.

Her best-known contribution to southern literature was *The Awakening* (1899). The novel traces the life of Edna Pontellier, who undergoes a psychosexual epiphany before walking on the beach at Grand Isle, Louisiana, ripping off her clothing and walking into the choppy surf of the Gulf of Mexico to drown.

The Awakening was initially condemned as being immoral and indecent. The overwhelming negative response to her novel made it difficult for Chopin to publish afterwards.

But after having been out of print for many years, *The Awakening* drew waves of followers when the book was reissued in the late 1960s. Chopin's new readers hailed her as an early feminist and applauded her writing detailing women's efforts to escape from traditional and social restraints. In this and other works she advocated "women's liberation" several generations ahead of its time.

Chopin suffered a brain hemorrhage in St. Louis, where she died in 1904. She is buried in that city's Calvary Cemetery.

John Charles McNeill
(1874–1907)

Born 26 July 1874, Wagram NC
Died 17 October 1907, Wagram NC
Buried Spring Hill Cemetery, Wagram NC

Works: *Songs Merry and Sad, Lyrics from Cotton Land, Possums and Persimmons: Newly Collected Poems, Home in the Sandhills*

John Charles McNeill was born 26 July 1874 in Scotland County, North Carolina, near Wagram. The youngest of Duncan and Euphemia McNeill's five children, he spent a great deal of time outdoors as a child fishing, hunting, swimming, and working alongside laborers in the fields. He studied law at Whiteville Academy and Wake Forest College, where he was an exemplary student. During this time he submitted poems to the Wake Forest literary journal, which he also edited in part.

McNeill continued to write poems and stories for the local newspaper in Lumberton, where he moved at 26. Several years later, after settling in Laurinburg to practice law, he was elected to the state legislature. His poems were published in *Youth's Companion, Century Magazine,* and the Charlotte *Observer*. He accepted a position as a staff writer for the *Observer*, which led to the publication of 467 of his poems. Additionally, two collections of his poems were published in book form. Wildly popular in North Carolina, he was unofficially named poet laureate of the state in 1906, 25 years before such an honor existed.

McNeill died 17 October 1907 at the age of 34. His home was moved in 1960 to the Richmond Temperance and Literary Society's Temperance Hall in Wagram. One of his most beloved poems is "Sunburnt Boys," which concludes

> You will not – will you? – soon forget
> When I was one of you,
> Nor love me less that time has borne
> My craft to currents new;
> Nor shall I ever cease to share
> Your hardships and your joys,
> Robust, rough-spoken, gentle-hearted
> Sunburnt boys!

James Ryder Randall
(1839–1908)

Born 1 January 1839, Baltimore MD
Died 15 January 1908, Augusta GA
Buried Magnolia, Augusta GA

Works: "Maryland, My Maryland"

James Ryder Randall was outraged to learn that Union troops had marched through his hometown of Baltimore, Maryland, and that a friend and classmate of his had been wounded in April 1861. Randall had attended Georgetown University in Washington, but did not graduate. He left school and traveled in South America and the West Indies before accepting a position teaching English at Poydras College in Pointe Coupee, Louisiana.

Prompted by news of the invasion of Baltimore by Federal troops, he wrote the nine-stanza poem, "Maryland, My Maryland." It was first published 26 April 1861 in the New Orleans *Delta* newspaper. It remains the most martial poem in American literature.

A friend of Randall's, Jennie Cary, set the poem to the music of a popular college drinking song of the day, "Lauriger Horatius," better known in later years as "O, Tannenbaum." The song became the favorite war song of the Confederacy, and Randall was tabbed the Poet Laureate of the Lost Cause.

Despite Randall's Confederate sympathies, the state of Maryland, which had remained in the Union, adopted "Maryland, My Maryland" as the state song in 1939.

After the war, Randall accepted a number of newspaper jobs, including serving as Washington correspondent and later editor for the Augusta *Chronicle* in Georgia. He also wrote other poems, many with a religious tone, but none reached the popularity of "Maryland, My Maryland."

He died in Augusta 15 January 1908.

Joel Chandler Harris
(1848–1908)

Born 9 December 1848, Eatonton GA
Died 3 July 1908, Atlanta GA
Buried Westview, Atlanta GA

Works: *Uncle Remus: His Songs and His Sayings, Nights with Uncle Remus, Mingo and Other Sketches in Black and White, Free Joe and other Georgian Sketches, Daddy Jake the Runaway, Balaam and His Master, A Plantation Printer, Uncle Remus and His Friends, Little Mr. Thimblefinger and His Queer Country, Mr. Rabbit at Home, The Story of Aaron, Stories of Georgia*

Joel Chandler Harris learned the printing trade when he worked at Turnbull plantation during the Civil War, and he wrote for newspapers in Macon, New Orleans, Forsyth, Georgia, and Savannah before joining the *Atlanta Constitution* in 1876. There he was co-editor with Henry Grady. While Grady looked forward to the prosperity of the New South, Harris extolled the pleasures of the old, and maintained countrified manners and clothing.

Both Harris and Grady are buried in Westview Cemetery, Grady in an impressive mausoleum and Harris's grave marked with a rustic boulder, with his portrait on it showing him in his characteristic floppy hat. His Uncle Remus character debuted in the *Constitution* in 1878, and his first book of sketches was printed in 1880. He continued to publish volumes of Uncle Remus tales until his death in 1908. The tales were surpassed only by Mark Twain's writing in terms of popularity.

His house in Atlanta, the Wren's Nest, is a lively museum, directed by his great-great-great grandson Lain Shakespeare. Around the base of the house is a peculiar "Authors Walk of Fame," whereon civic and literary groups sponsored cenotaphs of writers to be installed, from the 1940s until the mid-1980s. Besides writers from Georgia and other Southern states, Longfellow and Robert Burns are memorialized, and some people best known for extra-literary effors, such as Confederate President Jefferson Davis and Vice President Alexander Stephens, the physician Crawford Long, and the general, senator, and governor John Brown Gordon.

Notably among the markers are stones for Julian LaRose Harris (1874-1963) and Julia Collier Harris (1875-1967), the son and daughter-in-law of Joel Chandler Harris, who shared the Pulitzer Prize for public service in 1926, for editorials about the teaching of evolution and the activities of the Ku Klux Klan. (They were buried in the Rawson mausoleum at Oakland Cemetery in Atlanta.)

Augusta Jane Evans Wilson
(1835–1909)

Born 8 May 1835, Columbus GA
Died 9 May 1909, Mobile AL
Buried Magnolia, Mobile AL

Works: *Inez: A Tale of the Alamo, Beulah, Macaria, St. Elmo, Vashti, or Until Death Us Do Part, Infelice, At the Mercy of Tiberius, A Speckled Bird, Devota*

To help her family's financial trouble, Evans completed her first novel, *Inez: A Tale of the Alamo*, on Christmas Day, 1854. It was published in 1856. Her second novel, *Beulah* (1859), attracted the attention of a Northern editor, James Reed Spaulding. The two became engaged in 1860, but she broke the engagement when they realized their political differences could not be overcome.

Wilson's sentimental novels were wildly popular; she is reputed to have been the first Southern writer to earn $100,000. Her novel *Macaria*, published in 1863 and dedicated to Confederate soldiers, was banned by Gen. G. H. Thomas of the Federal Army in Tennessee for its troops, and he burned whatever copies he could find. A legend arose that a Confederate soldier was saved when a copy in his pocket stopped a bullet.

St. Elmo (1866), a best-seller, inspired a punch, a cigar, and a camellia, and a large number of girls throughout the South were named Edna Earl after its heroine. Edna Earl Ponder, the heroine of Eudora Welty's novel *The Ponder Heart* (1954), is a good example. The St. Elmo neighborhood of Chattanooga, at the base of Lookout Mountain, is named for Augusta Evans's novel.

Augusta Evans married Col. Lorenzo Madison Wilson, 28 years older than she, in 1868 at the height of her fame, and moved to Ashland, a fine house in Mobile, which became a showplace for its gardens and birds.

Wilson died in 1909 from a heart attack in Mobile, and was buried there in Magnolia Cemetery.

Frances Boyd Calhoun
(1867–1909)

Born 25 December 1867, Mecklenburg Co. VA
Died 8 June 1909, Covington TN
Buried Munford Cemetery, Covington TN

Works: *Miss Minerva and William Green Hill*

Calhoun was a schoolteacher in Covington, having been graduated from the Tipton Female Seminary there. After her husband's death, she wrote her only book, and died four months after it was published. *Miss Minerva and William Green Hill* (1909) was so popular—it went through 50 printings—that Emma Speed Sampson wrote sequels beginning with *Billy and the Major* in 1918 and continuing for 20 years, a further eleven novels with the same characters.

William Green Hill was an actual resident of Covington, buried in the same cemetery as the writer, and some of the locales of the book can be seen today.

William Green Hill, also called "Billy," is a young prankster who with his friends tests the patience of his prim Aunt Minerva. Other characters include The Major, Miss Minerva's beau and a Confederate veteran, and various members of the community.

Miss Minerva is Henry Higgins to Billy's Eliza Doolittle:

"I sho' is hongry," he remarked, as he took his seat at the breakfast table.

Miss Minerva realized that now was the time to begin her small nephew's training; if she was ever to teach him to speak correctly she must begin at once.

"William," she said sternly, "you must not talk so much like a negro. Instead of saying 'I sho' is hongry,' you should say, 'I am very hungry.' Listen to me and try to speak more correctly."

"Don't! don't!" she screamed as he helped himself to the meat and gravy, leaving a little brown river on her fresh white tablecloth. "Wait until I ask a blessing; then I will help you to what you want."

Billy enjoyed his breakfast very much. "These muffins sho' is--" he began; catching his aunt's eye he corrected himself--

"These muffins am very good."

"These muffins are very good," said Miss Minerva patiently.

Mark Twain
(1835–1910)

Born 30 November 1835, Florida MO
Died 10 April 1910, Redding CT
Buried Woodlawn, Elmira NY

Works: *The Celebrated Jumping Frog of Calaveras County, and Other Sketches, The Innocents Abroad, Mark Twain's (Burlesque) Autobiography and First Romance, Roughing It, The Gilded Age, Sketches New and Old, The Adventures of Tom Sawyer, A Tramp Abroad, The Prince and the Pauper, The Stolen White Elephant Etc., Life on the Mississippi, Adventures of Huckleberry Finn, A Connecticut Yankee in King Arthur's Court, Merry Tales, The American Claimant, The £1,000,000 Bank-Note and Other Stories, Tom Sawyer Abroad, The Tragedy of Pudd'nhead Wilson, Personal Recollections of Joan of Arc, Tom Sawyer, Detective, and Other Stories, Following the Equator, How to Tell a Story and Other Essays, A Double-Barrelled Detective Story, Extracts from Adam's Diary, A Dog's Tale, King Leopold's Soliloquy, What is Man?, Eve's Diary, The $30,000 Bequest and Other Stories, Christian Science, A Horse's Tale, Is Shakespeare Dead?, Extract from Captain Stormfield's Visit to Heaven, Mark Twain's Speeches, The Mysterious Stranger: A Romance, Mark Twain's Autobiography, Letters from the Earth*

Samuel Langhorne Clemens was an itinerant newspaper writer and columnist who ventured into several other fields before his first book was published. He began working as a newspaper apprentice and typesetter when he was 13 for the *Hannibal Journal*, which was owned by his brother, Orion Clemens. After five years he left Missouri and worked for newspapers in New York, Philadelphia, Cincinnati, and St. Louis.

He began working on a riverboat on the Mississippi River in 1857 and obtained his license as a riverboat captain in 1859. When the Civil War began, he and several friends joined the Confederate Army, but Clemens quit before seeing any combat. He joined his brother Orion for a stagecoach trip out west, to Virginia City, Nevada, where he became a miner. He failed as a miner but began writing articles for the *Territorial Enterprise*, the first publication in which he used his famous pen name, Mark Twain.

He was writing for a California newspaper when he wrote "The Celebrated Jumping Frog of Calaveras County," in 1865. The success of that article brought work as a travel writer with trips to Hawaii and Europe. The European trip provided the basis for his first book, *The Innocents Abroad* (1869). He later wrote two of the most famous works in American literature, *The Adventures of Tom Sawyer* (1876) and *Adventures of Huckleberry Finn* (1885). William Faulkner said Twain was "the father of American literature." Ernest Hemingway wrote, "All modern American literature comes from one book by Mark Twain called 'Huckleberry Finn.'"

Clemens died in 1910 in Redding, Connecticut, following a heart attack.

O. Henry
(1862–1910)

Born 11 September 1862, Greensboro NC
Died 3 June 1910, New York, NY
Buried Riverside, Asheville NC

Works: *Cabbages and Kings, The Four Million, The Trimmed Lamp, Heart of the West, The Voice of the City, The Gentle Grafter, Roads of Destiny, Options, Strictly Business, Whirligigs, Sixes and Sevens, Rolling Stones, Waifs and Strays, O. Henryana, Letters to Lithopolis, Postscripts, O. Henry Encore*

O. Henry (William Sydney Porter) was born 11 September 1862 near Polecat Creek in Guilford County, North Carolina. Porter's mother died from tuberculosis when he was three, leaving him to be reared by his father but more so by his unmarried aunt, the proprietor of a private school in Greensboro. As he grew into a young man he worked in a drug store as a bookkeeper before moving to Texas at the age of nineteen. In Texas he worked as a teller at First National Bank in Austin and also as a freelance sketch artist and writer. He briefly co-owned and edited a weekly humorous publication called *The Rolling Stone* and worked as a columnist for the *Houston Daily Post*. During his time in Houston he was indicted for having embezzled bank funds from First National in Austin. Facts came to light when the bank audited its books several years after his employment. Porter, now married, fled alone to New Orleans and later to Honduras to escape arrest, but returned to Austin a year later after learning that his wife was dying of tuberculosis.

He was a widower when he was sentenced to five years in federal prison in Ohio, where he lived and worked in the prison's hospital wing. While in prison Porter wrote his first short story, and by the time he left prison early for good behavior, he was writing consistently under the name O. Henry. In 1902 Porter moved to New York City, looking for new experiences and material for his short stories. He wrote more than 100 stories between 1904 and 1905, the vast majority of which dealt with New York-centric subjects. His stories followed ordinary people through surprise events. Some of his best known tales are "The Gift of the Magi," "A Municipal Report" and "The Ransom of Red Chief." Porter is largely responsible for growing the popularity of the "short story." And to this day the O. Henry award goes to the best short story of the year.

His works were extremely popular among his readers, yet critics saw them as too formulaic to be worthy of critical acclaim. He married a childhood friend, Sarah Lindsey Coleman, in 1907. Porter died 3 June 1910 from complications from cirrhosis of the liver, diabetes, and an enlarged heart, all spurred on by excessive drinking. He was buried in Riverside Cemetery in Asheville, North Carolina.

Thomas Cooper De Leon
(1839–1914)

Born 21 May 1839, Columbia SC
Died 19 March 1914, Mobile AL
Buried Magnolia, Mobile AL

Works: *South Songs, Cross Purposes, Coqsureus, The Soldiers' Souvenir, The Rock or the Rye, Creole and Puritan, Four Years in Rebel Capitals, Juny, Our Creole Carnivals, Society As I Have Foundered It, A Fair Blockade-Breaker, The Puritan's Daughter, Sybilla, John Holden, Unionist, Schooners That Bump on the Bar, Out of the Sulphur, The Rending of the Solid South, East, West, and South, Crag-Nest, A Novelette Trilogy, Creole Carnivals, An Innocent Cheat, The Pride of the Mercers, War Rhymes, Grave and Gay, Confederate Memories, Joseph Wheeler, Inauguration of President Watterson, Tales from the Coves, The Passing of Arle Haine, Belles, Beaux and Brains of the 60's*

Thomas Cooper De Leon was 21 years younger than his brother Edwin, who was a well-known journalist and diplomat before the Civil War began. Thomas was graduated from Georgetown College in Washington, D.C., and worked as an audit clerk for the Bureau of Topographical Engineering until 1862, when his loyalties to the Confederate states forced him to resign. He accepted a commission as a captain in the Confederate Army and later served as secretary to Confederate President Jefferson Davis. After the war he entered journalism, working for newspapers in New York and in Baltimore, where he served as editor of the magazine *Cosmopolite*.

In 1867 he became editor of the *Mobile* (Alabama) *Register*. He spent the remainder of his life in Mobile. De Leon produced 30 books, including a conciliatory trilogy about the war: *The Puritan's Daughter* (1891), *John Holden, Unionist* (1893), and *Crag-Nest* (1897). His best-known books recounted his experiences as a wartime insider: *Four Years in Rebel Capitals* (1890) and *Belles, Beaux and Brains of the 60's* (1909). He also wrote the comedic drama, *Pluck*, which was produced in 1873. In addition to his writing, De Leon also published a popular periodical, *The Gossip*, and he served as the principal organizer and for many years as the coordinator for the Mobile Mardi Gras.

In his later years his vision began to fail, and he was totally blind by 1903. He was known as the Blind Laureate for the Lost Cause.

He died in Mobile 19 March 1914.

Booker Taliaferro Washington
(1856–1915)

Born 3 April 1856, Hale's Ford, Franklin Co. VA
Died 14 November 1915, Tuskegee AL
Buried Tuskegee Institute, Tuskegee AL

Works: *The Atlanta Cotton States Exposition Address, The Future of the American Negro, Up From Slavery*

Booker T. Washington was one of the most influential black leaders of the 19th century. Born into slavery 5 April 1856 in Franklin County, Virginia, he was later able to work his way through and graduate from Hampton Institute in 1875. When Tuskegee Institute (originally called Tuskegee Normal School for Colored Teachers) was founded, on 4 July 1881, Washington was named as the first teacher. And through his close association with the Institute, he was instrumental in helping the school rise to national prominence.

Washington was a strong proponent of African-American-owned businesses, helped develop other educational opportunities for impoverished African-Americans throughout the American South, and was the first African-American to be invited to the White House as the guest of Theodore Roosevelt. Washington was viewed as a spokesperson for African-Americans, and was also known for being extremely industrious. "There was no period of my life that was devoted to play," Washington once wrote. "From the time that I can remember anything, almost every day of my life has been occupied in some kind of labor." Much of Washington's success was attributed to his institutional and political accommodation.

Despite his acclaim as an outstanding representative of the African-American community, Washington became a lightning rod for criticism within the civil rights movement. From its founding in 1909, the NAACP opposed Washington. The rift began in 1906 in what was termed the "Niagara Movement," but exploded in 1909 when W. E. B. DuBois wrote that Washington's policy was one of "non-resistance, giving up agitation, and acquiescence in semi-serfdom."

His notable works include his autobiography, *Up From Slavery* (1901), and *The Future of the American Negro* (1899). Washington died 14 November 1915 in Tuskegee, Alabama, and was buried on the campus of Tuskegee University near the University Chapel.

Christian Reid
(1846–1920)

Born 5 July 1846, Salisbury NC
Died 24 March 1920, Salisbury NC
Buried Chestnut Hill Cemetery, Salisbury NC

Works: *Valerie Aylmer, The Land and the Sky, After Many Days, Hearts of Steel, Armine, Weighed in the Balance, The Man of the Family, The Chase of an Heiress, Under the Southern Cross, The Light of Vision, Morton House, Ebb-Tide, and Other Stories, Mabel Lee, Carmen's Inheritance, Nina's Atonement, and Other Stories, A Daughter of Bohemia, Hearts and Hands, A Question of Honor, Bessie's Six Lovers, Bonny Kate, A Summer Idyl, A Gentle Bell, A Child of Mary, Roslyn's Fortune, His Victory, Miss Churchill, Philip's Restitution, A Cast for Fortune, Carmela, The Lost Lode, A Little Maid of Arcady, A Comedy of Elopement, The Land of the Sun, The Lady of Las Cruces, The Picture of Las Cruces, A Woman of Fortune, Fairy Gold, A Daughter of Sierra, Vera's Charge, Princess Nadine, The Coin of Sacrifice, The Wargrave Trust, The Daughter of a Star, A Far Away Princess, A Secret Bequest, The Child of Mary*

Christian Reid was the pen name of Frances Christine Fisher, adopted to conceal her sex. She was born in Salisbury, of distinguished North Carolina pedigree. Her father was Col. Charles F. Fisher, a director of the Western North Carolina Railroad, who was killed in the First Battle of Manassas, 21 July 1861. The family was left destitute after the Civil War, and she wrote steadily and successfully to help restore their fortunes. She began publishing in 1870.

She married a wealthy widower in 1887, and they traveled widely, to Mexico, Europe, and the West Indies. She lived for several years in Mexico. After James Tiernan died in 1898, Reid returned to North Carolina. She was active in the Daughters of the Confederacy, and proceeds from her play *Under the Southern Cross* were used to construct a monument to Jefferson Davis. The drama, performed in various cities across the South, presented the Southern view of the Constitutional Right of Secession.

Mrs. Tiernan was a devout convert to Catholicism, and had a small chapel erected in her yard. In 1909 she was awarded the Laetare Medal by Notre Dame University. The appellation "Land of the Sky" for the mountains of Western North Carolina is attributed to her, taken from a travel story she wrote about her visits there.

Mrs. Tiernan died in Salisbury and was buried in Chestnut Hill Cemetery.

Mary Noailles Murfree
(1850–1922)

Born 24 January 1850, Murfreesboro TN
Died 31 July 1922, Murfreesboro TN
Buried Evergreen, Murfreesboro TN

Works: *In the Tennessee Mountains, Where the Battle Was Fought, Down the Ravine, The Prophet of the Great Smoky Mountains, In the Clouds, The Story of Keedon Bluffs, The Despot of Broomsedge Cove, In the "Stranger People's" Country, His Vanished Star, The Mystery of Witch-Face Mountain and Other Stories, The Young Mountaineers, The Juggler, The Bushwhackers and Other Stories, The Story of Old Fort Loudon* (sic.), *The Champion, A Spectre of Power, The Frontiersmen, The Storm Centre, The Amulet, The Windfall, The Fair Mississippian, The Raid of the Guerilla and Other Stories, The Ordeal: A Mountain Romance of Tennessee, The Story of Duciehurst: A Tale of the Mississippi, The Erskine Honeymoon*

Mary Noailles Murfree was born in Murfreesboro, Tennessee, the town named for her great grandfather, and despite having had the family home destroyed in the Civil War, her family remained prominent. She attended the Nashville Female Academy and the Chegary Institute in Philadelphia, a finishing school for young women.

Her family owned a vacation home in Beersheba Springs, a resort community southeast of Nashville in the Cumberland Mountains of Middle Tennessee. A lot of Murfree's exposure to mountaineers apparently came through her family's annual vacation trips to the resort. Unfortunately, she used her modest exposure to project stereotypes of mountain life throughout the South, couched in overblown descriptions of scenery and landscape.

Murfree had published two stories under the name of R. Emmet Cembry before she published her first story using the pen name of Charles Egbert Craddock. "The Dancin' Party at Harrison's Cove" was a hit in the *Atlantic Monthly* (1878), and "Craddock" became a popular writer of the Southern mountains.

Her first book, *In the Tennessee Mountains* (1884), was a collection of eight stories previously published in the *Atlantic Monthly.* She also wrote *Where the Battle Was Fought* (1884) about her family's home that was destroyed in Murfreesboro. The following year, her first mountain novel, *The Prophet of the Great Smoky Mountains*, was published. Only after her first books had been published did her editors learn that "Craddock" was a young woman.

Murfree is regarded as the first female writer to focus on Appalachia, and despite the stereotyping, her stories and the more than 20 books she published drew national and international attention to the region. She died in Murfreesboro 31 July 1922.

Frances Hodgson Burnett (1849–1924)

Born 24 November 1849, Manchester, England
Died 29 October 1924, Plandome NY
Buried Roslyn Cemetery, Roslyn NY

Works: *That Lass o' Lowrie's, Surly Tim, Theo, Dolly, Pretty Polly Pemberton, Earlier Stories, Kathleen, Earlier Stories and Series, Miss Crespigny, A Quiet Life and The Tide on the Morning Bar, Our Neighbor Opposite, Jarl's Daughter, Natalie, Haworth's, Louisiana, A Fair Barbarian, Esmerelda, Young Folks' Ways, Through One Administration, A Woman's Will, or Miss Defarge, Sara Crewe, Editha's Burglar, The Fortunes of Philippa Fairfax, A Lady of Quality, Little Lord Fauntleroy, The Real Lord Fauntleroy, The Showman's Daughter, The One I Knew Best of All, Piccino and Other Stories, The Two Little Pilgrims Progress, His Grace Osmonde, The First Gentlemen of Europe, In Connection with the De Willoughby Claim, The Making of a Marchioness, The Methods of Lady Walderhust, In the Closed Room, That Man and I, The Dawn of a Tomorrow, The Troubles of Queen Silver-Bell, Racketty-Packetty House, The Cozy Lion, The Spring Cleaning, The Good Wolf, Barty Crusoe and His Man Saturday, The Land of the Blue Flower, My Robin, T. Tembarom, The Lost Prince, A Little Princess, A Secret Garden, The Shuttle, The White People, Little Hunchback Zia, The Head of the House of Coombe, Robin, In the Garden*

Frances Hodgson Burnett was born in 1849 in Manchester, England, where her father had been a successful businessman. He died when she was a young child, and the business failed. The family moved to New Market, Tennessee, near Knoxville, in 1865. Two years later, Frances's mother died, leaving her to care for two younger siblings.

She began submitting stories to women's magazines and had her first story published in *Godey's Lady's Book* in 1868. She subsequently had stories published in *Scribner's Monthly*, *Peterson's Ladies' Magazine*, and *Harper's Bazaar*. She married Dr. Swan Burnett of Washington, D.C., in 1873, and they had two sons, Lionel, born in 1874, and Vivian, born in 1876.

Her writing had provided a steady income over the years and favorable recognition, but her career exploded with the publication of *Little Lord Fauntleroy* (1886). The book sold more than 500,000 copies and created the stereotype for children of the rich and famous—long winsome curls and velvet suits with lace collars. She won a famous lawsuit over the dramatic rights to *Little Lord Fauntleroy* in London in 1888. Tragedy struck with the influenza death of Lionel in 1890. Burnett, who had had a series of illnesses over the years, suffered from depression following his death. Her marriage, marked by long periods of separation, ended in divorce in 1898.

She married her business manager, Stephen Townsend, in 1900, and they moved to Long Island. There she wrote *A Little Princess* (1905), a revision of an earlier short story, "Sara Crewe," and *A Secret Garden* (1911), showing her lifelong love of gardening. She died 29 October 1924 in Plandome, New York. She was buried in Roslyn Cemetery in Nassau County, New York. A stone statue of Lionel stands near the grave.

GEORGE WASHINGTON CABLE
(1844–1925)

Born 12 October 1844, New Orleans LA
Died 31 January 1925, St. Petersburg FL
Buried Bridge Street, Northampton MA

Works: *Old Creole Days, The Grandissimes, Madame Delphine, The Creoles of Louisiana, Dr. Sevier, The Silent South, Bonaventure, Strange True Stories of Louisiana, The Negro Question, The Busy Man's Bible, A Memory of Roswell Smith, John March, Southerner, Strong Hearts, The Cavalier, By-low Hill, Kincaid's Battery, "Posson Jone" and Père Raphaël, Gideon's Band, The Amateur Garden, The Flower of the Chapdelaines, Lovers of Louisiana*

George Washington Cable, a newspaper reporter, social critic, novelist, and short-story writer, served in the Confederate army during the Civil War. After taking several jobs following the war, he became a reporter and columnist for the *New Orleans Picayune*. For a time he was the sole breadwinner for his mother and her large family.

In 1869 he married Louise Stewart Bartlett, who would be his inspiration and chief assistant for the next 35 years. He had sold several local color stories to publications in the North, depicting life in the Creole community in Louisiana. However, the income from his writing was insufficient to cover the expenses of his family—four daughters and a son by 1879—so he became a bookkeeper for a short time. In 1879 he published *Old Creole Days*, a collection of some of his best stories. The book was successful in the North, but the Creole population in Louisiana was upset over his portrayals of discrimination and brutality by Creoles against African-Americans.

He published his first novel, *The Grandissimes* (1880), painting a vivid picture of plantation life in Louisiana, but drew additional scorn from the Creoles and Southern whites who were critical of his advocacy for civil rights and his insistence on equality among the races.

In 1884-85 he took a reading tour with Samuel Clemens during which he called for civil rights and legal equality for all Americans. While his initial social criticisms had drawn opposition only in the South, his continued advocacy drew sharp opposition in the Northern states as well. Following the reading tour, he moved his family to Northampton, Massachusetts, where he lived until his death. In *The Negro Question* (1890), Cable attacked racism and renewed his calls for equality among the races and civil rights for all. The opposition he encountered may have pushed his subsequent writing toward a less strident tone.

After Louise Cable died in 1904, he married Eva C. Stevenson in 1906. She died in 1923. He then wed Hannah Cowing. Cable died 31 January 1925.

Ambrose Elliott Gonzales
(1857–1926)

Born 29 May 1857, Paulo Parish, Colleton Co. SC
Died 11 July 1926, Columbia SC
Buried Elmwood, Columbia SC

Works: *The Black Border, With Aesop Along the Black Border, Laguerre: A Gascon of the Black Border, The Captain: Stories of the Black Border*

Descended from prominent Cuban and South Carolina families, Ambrose Elliott Gonzales was born in tiny Adams Run, South Carolina, in 1857. His father was the Cuban revolutionary general Ambrosio Jose Gonzales (buried in Woodlawn, the Bronx, New York City), who fought for Cuban independence from Spain.

After working as a reporter for the *Charleston News and Courier*, he and his brother Narciso Gener Gonzales founded *The State* in Columbia in an effort to combat the political influence of Benjamin Ryan Tillman. (N.G. Gonzales was later gunned down by one of Tillman's nephews.) Between 1922 and 1924 Ambrose Gonzales published four volumes in the "Black Border" series, collections of folktales rendered in the Gullah dialect he had learned in his Lowcountry childhood.

Gonzales believed that his transcriptions of Gullah speech were more authentic than those written by the literary upstart Julia Peterkin, and he refused to allow any mention of her burgeoning career in the fine arts section of *The State*. The ideal rendering of the Gullah dialect was a popular talking point among many South Carolina and Georgia writers, including Peterkin, DuBose Heyward, Gonzales and others. It was a badge of distinction that, since they had been reared by servants, Southern elites learned to speak Gullah before English.

In addition to a useful glossary, Gonzales printed in *The Black Border* (1922) renderings of the tar-baby story by Joel Chandler Harris and Charles Colcock Jones, Jr.

Severely disabled by a stroke in 1924, Gonzales nonetheless insisted upon being brought to his newspaper editor's office regularly until his death two years later. He was buried in Elmwood Cemetery in Columbia.

Sarah Bull Barnwell Elliott
(1848–1928)

Born 23 November 1848, Savannah GA
Died 30 August 1928, Sewanee TN
Buried University Cemetery, Sewanee TN

Works: *The Felmeres, A Simple Heart, Jerry, John Paget, The Durket Sperret, An Incident and Other Happenings, Sam Houston, The Making of Jane*

Sarah Bull Barnwell Elliott was born in Savannah, Georgia, in 1848, but spent most of her life at Sewanee, Tennessee. Her father, Bishop Stephen Elliott, was one of the founders of the University of the South at Sewanee, and her mother was a member of the socially and politically prominent Bull family of South Carolina.

Elliott had private tutors for most of her education, but studied at Johns Hopkins University in 1886.

She was the author of six novels, a collection of short stories, a biography of Sam Houston (1900), a play, and dozens of essays on behalf of women's suffrage. She also wrote book reviews and gave detailed accounts of her travels in Europe in a series of 16 letters published by the Louisville *Courier-Journal* in 1887.

Her novels were celebrated for her use of local dialect, particularly the dialect of the Cumberland Plateau region in Middle Tennessee. But she also depicted the prejudice and discrimination of city residents against mountain people.

Jerry (1891) is her best-known work. It opens in a Tennessee mountain town, but takes place principally in a western mining area. It was originally published as a serial in *Scribner's Magazine* (1890).

Elliott's short story collection, *An Incident and Other Happenings* (1899), deals with racial and social problems of the Cumberland Plateau and the surrounding area.

Her play, *His Majesty's Servant*, was produced in London in 1904.

In Tennessee, Elliott was best known as an advocate for the women's right to vote. She was elected president of the Tennessee Equal Suffrage Association and penned a famous petition to the state lawmakers printed in the Nashville *Banner* 17 August 1912.

She died in Sewanee 30 August 1928 and was buried at University Cemetery.

Frances Newman
(1883–1928)

Born 11 September 1883, Atlanta GA
Died 22 October 1928, Decatur GA
Buried Westview, Atlanta GA

Works: *The Short Story's Mutations, The Hard-Boiled Virgin, Dead Lovers are Faithful Lovers, Six Moral Tales from Jules Laforgue, Frances Newman's Letters, The Gold-Fish Bowl*

Frances Newman was born in Atlanta in 1883, the daughter of a Confederate war hero who became a U.S. District Court Judge. She attended the Calhoun Street School and Washington Seminary in Atlanta as well as finishing schools in Washington, D.C., and New York. She completed a library science degree at the Carnegie Library in Atlanta in 1912.

She wrote reviews for the Atlanta *Journal* and the Atlanta *Constitution* and drew favorable notice from H. L. Mencken and Virginia's James Branch Cabell.

She wrote her first novel, *The Gold Fish Bowl* (1921), but had no success in getting it published. She left the Carnegie Library in 1923 to study at the Sorbonne in Paris and to complete *The Short Story's Mutations* (1923), a collection of stories she had translated from five languages. She returned to Atlanta in 1924 and accepted a position as librarian at the Georgia Institute of Technology.

The following year, she asked for a leave of absence to attend the MacDowell Colony in Peterborough, New Hampshire. There, she completed her best-known novel, *The Hard-Boiled Virgin*, in two months. Published in 1926, the book became an immediate best-seller. Though she had used satire and a biting wit to discuss such topics as sexual arousal, menstruation, and birth control, the book was sufficiently scandalous to earn a "banned in Boston" fly-leaf notice.

Her novels were labeled "experimental," though she showed the conflicts for the feelings of Southern women restricted by the social mores in the early 20th Century. Her strident feminist writings were opposed by the Southern Agrarians, who could not abide any challenge to the sexism and racism of the patriarchal South.

She returned to the MacDowell Colony in 1927, where she worked on *Dead Lovers Are Faithful Lovers* (1928). She completed the manuscript in January 1928 and left for Europe, to complete her research on Jules LaForgue's short fiction. But she had to return to the United States after developing a serious eye ailment. She could not see well enough to write, but completed her translation by dictation.

She was found unconscious in her hotel room in New York 19 October 1928, and she died three days later. The death was attributed to a cerebral hemorrhage initially, but later reports indicated that she may have died from an overdose of barbiturates. She was buried in Westview Cemetery in Atlanta.

John Trotwood Moore
(1856–1929)

Born 26 August 1856, Marion AL
Died 10 May 1929, Nashville TN
Buried Mt. Olivet, Nashville TN

Works: *Tennessee Tales, Songs and Stories from Tennessee, A Summer Hymnal: A Romance of Tennessee, The Bishop of Cottontown: A Story of the Southern Cotton Mills, Ole Mistis, and Other Songs and Stories from Tennessee, The Old Cotton Gin, Uncle Wash: His Stories, The Gift of the Grass: Being the Autobiography of a Famous Racing Horse, Jack Ballington, Forester, Hearts of Hickory: A Story of Andrew Jackson and the War of 1812, Tom's Last Forage*

John Moore was born in Marion, Alabama, in 1856 and he appropriated the middle name Trotwood from the character Aunt Betsy Trotwood in Charles Dickens's semi-autobiographical novel, *David Copperfield*.

He moved to Maury County, Tennessee—the center of Tennessee's Blue Grass region—in 1885 and became involved in the breeding of cattle and standard bred horses. Moore began writing about horse breeding and training with the goal of developing a natural pacing horse for harness racing. He developed a following for his writings about horses and the encouragement led him to further his career as a writer. In 1905 he founded *Trotwood's Monthly*.

Moore moved to Nashville in 1906 and for several years was associated with the colorful Sen. Robert Love "Bob" Taylor. Their association resulted in the establishment of a new publication, the *Taylor-Trotwood Magazine*.

Moore wrote of local color and historical events. His best-known novel, *Hearts of Hickory: A Story of Andrew Jackson and the War of 1812* (1926), was warmly received.

However, although his local color and historical writings were widely read and respected, it was through his tireless work as Tennessee's state librarian and archivist that he became best known.

Moore developed a questionnaire that was sent to 5000 Civil War veterans (with 1650 returns) that formed the basis of a priceless collection at the Tennessee State Library and Archives.

He undertook a similar project through the Tennessee History Committee to obtain data from Tennesseans who had fought in World War I. Moore also acquired the Tennessee Historical Society's holdings for the State Library and Archives. He lived to see his son, Merrill Moore, achieve recognition as one of the most revered "Fugitive" poets.

John Trotwood Moore died in Nashville in 1929, and was buried at Mt. Olivet Cemetery.

Grace Elizabeth King
(1851–1932)

Born 29 November 1851, New Orleans LA
Died 14 January 1932, New Orleans LA
Buried Metairie, New Orleans LA

Works: *Monsieur Motte, Balcony Stories, New Orleans: The Place and its People, Tales of a Time and Place, Stories from Louisiana History, The Pleasant Ways of St. Medard, La Dame de Sainte Hermine, Memories of a Southern Woman of Letters*

Grace Elizabeth King was born into a socially and financially prominent New Orleans family that was reduced to poverty by the Civil War and Reconstruction. Her father was an attorney and landowner before the war, but he fled with his family to St. Martin Parish near Lafayette when Federal troops occupied New Orleans in 1862.

When the family returned to the city after the war, the financial ruin and harsh Reconstruction edicts forced a new way of life for Grace, who was a teenager. She could still associate with her socially elite peer group, but the lack of money pushed her toward a French Creole education.

Encouraged by Charles Dudley Warner, she began writing local color pieces and short stories, frequently telling of women confronting patriarchal society. She believed in equal rights for women and racial minorities, but Twentieth Century critics have accused her of stereotyping African-American and Creole minorities and of defending the segregated caste system. A common theme for her writings was the hardships faced by women of mixed races and their children.

King also wrote several histories, primarily focusing on New Orleans and southern Louisiana.

She authored a biography of Bienville, the governor of French Louisiana, and a history of New Orleans. Her novel *The Pleasant Ways of St. Medford* (1916) is a fictional rendering of her family's experiences during Reconstruction.

Tulane University granted her an honorary doctorate in 1915, and in her final years she offered encouragement to younger writers, particularly Lyle Saxon and Sherwood Anderson. Her autobiography, *Memories of a Southern Woman of Letters*, was published the year of her death.

She died in New Orleans 14 January 1932, and was buried in Metairie Cemetery.

Charles Waddell Chesnutt
(1858–1932)

Born 20 June 1858, Cleveland OH
Died 15 November 1932, Cleveland OH
Buried Lake View, Cleveland OH

Works: *The Conjure Woman, The Wife of His Youth and Other Stories of the Color Line, Frederick Douglass, The House Behind the Cedars, The Marrow of Tradition, The Colonel's Dream, The Short Fiction of Charles W. Chesnutt*

Charles W. Chesnutt was born in 1858 in Cleveland, Ohio, to parents who were designated as "free persons of color" from Fayetteville, North Carolina. Chesnutt could claim, among other white ancestors, his paternal grandfather. Although he could have "passed" as a white writer, he made a conscious decision to be identified as an African-American. Growing up in postwar North Carolina, he worked hard to keep his struggling family solvent.

He became assistant principal of a normal school in Fayetteville. Chesnutt married in 1878 and moved to New York City, then back to Cleveland, where he prepared for and passed the bar exam. In his native city he subsequently launched a successful legal stenography service. His first short story, a local color piece set in North Carolina, "The Goophered Grapevine," was published in *The Atlantic Monthly* in 1887. *The Conjure Woman* (1899) was a popular collection of dialect tales. Although his short fiction was widely read and admired, his novels garnered comparatively little notice.

Nevertheless, by the early twentieth century Chesnutt had made a name for himself in literary circles, and was invited, along with other high-profile authors, to attend Mark Twain's seventieth birthday observance in New York City in 1905. In his later years he became an active member of the NAACP and wrote articles for its official organ, *The Crisis*.

In 1917 Chesnutt lobbied to prevent screenings in Ohio of the pro-Ku Klux Klan film, *Birth of a Nation*. He died in Cleveland in 1932, and was buried in that city's Lake View Cemetery.

Corra Mae White Harris
(1869–1935)

Born 17 May 1869, Elbert Co. GA
Died 7 February 1935, Atlanta GA
Buried Pine Log, Bartow Co. GA

Works: *The Jessica Letters, A Circuit Rider's Wife, Eve's Second Husband, The Recording Angel, In Search of a Husband, Justice, The Co-Citizen, A Circuit Rider's Widow, Making Her His Wife, From Sun-up to Sun-down, Happily Married, My Son, The Eyes of Love, A Daughter of Adam, The House of Helen, My Book and Heart, As a Woman Thinks, Flapper Ann, The Happy Pilgrimage*

Corra Mae White married Lundy Harris, her former teacher, when she was 17 and he was 29. He became a Methodist minister, a circuit-riding preacher at various places in Georgia. He died in Bartow County where he had gone to take a "cure" from alcohol and drug addiction, but committed suicide before the cure took. He is buried in Oxford, the original home of Emory College.

Harris's first book of fiction, *A Circuit-Rider's Wife* (1910), was a best-seller, and she eventually wrote 19 books. She bought 350 acres in Bartow County when she visited to see where her husband had died. The property included the log cabin of Cherokee Chief Pine Log, built in the 1820s, and she expanded the house with log additions to 17 rooms, the timber coming from the property. She added a library and planned a chapel, where she intended to be buried. This is where she is said to have entertained many famous people, including U.S. Sen. Rebecca Felton, Martha Berry, and Margaret Mitchell, who regarded her as her mentor.

She died before the chapel was completed, and her funeral was conducted in the original room of the cabin, per her request. She had had a door enlarged to allow her coffin to be moved in and out. The funeral—a three-minute service, according to Harris's wishes—was conducted by Bishop Warren Candler, who had known her husband.

The autobiographical novel *A Circuit-Rider's Wife* was the basis for the 1950 film *I'd Climb the Highest Mountain*, in which Harris was portrayed by Susan Hayward. The movie was filmed nearby in Helen, Georgia. Her estate, including the chapel, was donated by Jamie Hill to the University System of Georgia in 2009.

Mary Johnston
(1870–1936)

Born 21 November 1870, Buchanan VA
Died 9 May 1936, Warm Springs VA
Buried Hollywood, Richmond VA

Works: *Prisoners of Hope, To Have and To Hold, Audrey, Sir Mortimer, The Goddess of Reason, Lewis Rand, The Long Roll, Cease Firing, Hagar, Witch, Fortunes of Garin, Wanderers, Foes, Michael Forth, Sweet Rocket, Pioneers of the Old South, 1492, Silver Cross, Croatan, Slave Ship, The Great Valley, Exile, Hunting Shirt, Miss Delicia Allen, Drury Randall*

Born the daughter of a former Confederate soldier, Mary Johnston grew up in post-Civil War Virginia, surrounded by books and schooled by tutors. She is best remembered for authoring twenty-three romantic histories and novels. *Prisoners of Hope* (1898), *To Have and to Hold* (1900, originally serialized in *The Atlantic Monthly*), *Pioneers of the Old South* (1920), and *Sir Mortimer* (1904) are all set in her native state.

She was honored to see several of her books adapted for the then-new medium of silent film. Miss Johnston also wrote narrative verse, short stories, and a play, *The Goddess of Reason* (1907), during her long career. Her popularity as a writer gave her a platform to champion women's rights, especially the crusade for female suffrage. She was a founder of the Equal Suffrage League of Virginia in 1909. She died at sixty-five and was buried in Hollywood Cemetery in Richmond.

Hollywood is one of the most striking cemeteries in the South. It was established in 1849 on a high bluff overlooking the James River. Two Presidents are buried there, James Monroe and John Tyler, as well as Jefferson Davis, president of the Confederate States of America (relocated from Metairie Cemetery in New Orleans, where he died). Twenty-five Confederate generals are buried there, along with 18,000 other soldiers, memorialized with a granite pyramid.

Robert Ervin Howard
(1906–1936)

Born 22 January 1906, Peaster TX
Died 11 June 1936, Cross Plains TX
Buried Greenleaf, Brownwood TX

Works: *The Valley of the Worm, Trails in Darkness, Crimson Shadows, Conan: The Tower of the Elephant, The Vultures, The Last Ride, Always Comes Evening, Bloodstar, Wings in the Night, The Return of Skull Face, Mayhem on Bear Creek, Iron Man Adventure, Dorgan, The Essential Conan, The End of the Trail: Western Stories, The She Devil, Queen of the Black Coast, The Hills of the Dead, Black Hounds of Death, Red Shadows, The Pool of the Black One, Red Blades of Black Cathay, Blood of the Gods, Black Colossus, Echoes from an Iron Harp, The Ultimate Triumph, The Hunter of the Ring, Conan of the Isles, Shadows of Dreams, The Haunter of the Ring, Kings of the Night, The Return of Conan, Singers in the Shadows,, When Death Birds Fly, The Hills of the Dead, Conan the Buccaneer, The Gold and the Grey, A Song of the Naked Lands, Rogues in the House*

Robert Ervin Howard was born in Peaster, Texas, on 22 January 1906. He was the only child of Dr. Mordecai and Hester Jane Howard. He spent most of his childhood in the small central Texas town of Cross Plains. After having been graduated from Brownwood High School, Howard attended Howard Payne University for a year, beginning in 1925. He began writing for local Daniel Baker College's school newspapers and sold his first story to a popular pulp magazine, *Weird Tales*. The result was electric. Howard decided to dedicate himself to writing as his only source of income. In the years that followed he would write prolifically from his childhood home in Cross Plains. He was so prolific that he made $500 in one month at a penny a word during the Great Depression. Ultimately, he became known as the creator of the "sword and sorcery" genre of pulp fiction.

He created Conan the Barbarian, an epic character he described as being "too stupid to do anything but cut, shoot, or slug" his way out of a jam. Conan was featured in 18 novels and feature-length stories. But Howard's fantasies were not limited to Conan. He spun tales of heroic adventures, exotic locales, and horrific drama—basically anything his publishers would buy. Much of Howard's success came after his death.

Although he enjoyed recognition in having his works published, he was not a happy young man. His relationship with his mother was perhaps too close, one of neurotic dependence on the part of each. Sadly, on 11 June 1936, a nurse told Howard that his mother would never recover from a coma. He reportedly said nothing, walked out of the house, got into his car, and fatally shot himself. His mother died only a few hours later, and the two were buried in a service in Greenleaf Cemetery in Brownwood. Howard is the subject of a film entitled *The Whole Wide World* (1996).

James Weldon Johnson
(1871–1938)

Born 17 June1871, Jacksonville FL
Died 26 June 1938, Wiscasset ME
Buried Green-Wood Cemetery, Brooklyn NY

Works: *God's Trombones: Seven Negro Sermons in Verse,* "Lift Ev'ry Voice and Sing," *The Autobiography of an Ex-Coloured Man, Fifty Years and Other Poems, Self-Determining Haiti,* ed. *The Book of American Negro Poetry,* ed. *The Book of American Negro Spirituals,* ed. *Second Book of Spirituals, Black Manhattan, Saint Peter Relates an Incident of the Resurrection Day, Along the Way, Negro Americans, What Now?*

James Weldon Johnson (James William Johnson) was born in Jacksonville, Florida, 17 June 1871. He was interested in reading and music from a young age and was encouraged by his father, a headwaiter, and his mother, the first female African-American to be a public school teacher in Florida. After graduating from the school where his mother taught, Johnson traveled to both Nassau and New York before attending Atlanta University. He earned his degree in 1894 and then taught poor, rural African-Americans, a group with whom he was unfamiliar given his middle-class upbringing in Jacksonville.

He returned to Jacksonville as principal of the school where his mother taught, and in 1895 founded *The Daily American*, a newspaper aimed at educating the adult African-American community, but funding problems made the paper short lived. He studied law as well, and was the first African-American in Florida to pass the bar exam. In 1897 he and his brother began a successful musical theater career in New York that continued for several years. "Lift Every Voice and Sing," which they wrote, became known as the "Negro National Anthem." In New York he attended Columbia, which led him to studies in Venezuela and Nicaragua, where he married and finished his first novel, *The Autobiography of an Ex-Coloured Man* (published anonymously in 1912). Johnson returned to New York and worked as an editor for *New York Age*, and published poetry, including *Fifty Years and Other Poems* in 1917.

He worked for the NAACP as well, finding time between his duties as general secretary to publish numerous poetic works later in life. Tragically, in 1938, the car he was driving near his summer home in Maine was struck by a train. He died 26 June 1938. A funeral held in Harlem was attended by more than 2000 people.

Thomas Wolfe
(1900–1938)

Born 3 October 1900, Asheville NC
Died 15 September 1938, Baltimore MD
Buried Riverside, Asheville NC

Works: *The Return of Black Gavin: The Tragedy of a Mountain Outlaw, Look Homeward, Angel, Of Time and the River, From Death to Morning, The Story of a Novel, A Note on Experts: Dexter Vespasian Joyner, The Face of a Nation: Poetic Passages from the Writing of Thomas Wolfe, The Web and the Rock, You Can't Go Home Again, The Hills Beyond, Gentlemen of the Press, Thomas Wolfe's Letters to His Mother, Julia Elizabeth Wolfe, Mannerhouse, The Years of Wandering in Many Lands and Cities, A Western Journal: A Daily Log of the Great Parks Trip, June 20-July 2, 1938, The Correspondence of Thomas Wolfe and Homer Andrews Watt, The Letters of Thomas Wolfe, The Short Novels of Thomas Wolfe, The Thomas Wolfe Reader, Thomas Wolfe's Purdue Speech: "Writing and Living," The Mountains: A Play in One Act, The Mountains: A Drama in Three Acts and a Prologue, The Notebooks of Thomas Wolfe, A Prologue to America, Welcome to Our City, K-19: Salvaged Pieces, Beyond Love and Loyalty: The Letters of Thomas Wolfe and Elizabeth Nowell, My Other Loneliness: Letters of Thomas Wolfe and Aline Bernstein, The Train and the City, Holding on for Heaven: The Cables and Postcards of Thomas Wolfe and Aline Bernstein, The Hound of Heaven, The Complete Stories of Thomas Wolfe, The Starwick Episodes, Thomas Wolfe's Composition Books: The North State Fitting School, 1912-1915, The Autobiographical Outline for "Look Homeward, Angel" by Thomas Wolfe, The Good Child's River, The Lost Boy: A Novella, Thomas Wolfe's Notes on Macbeth, The Party at Jack's, Antaeus: or, A Memory of Earth, Passage to England: A Selection, O Lost: A Story of the Buried Life, To Loot My Life Clean: The Thomas Wolfe-Maxwell Perkins Correspondence, The Medical Students*

Wolfe was born to a stonecutter father and a businesswoman mother. She ran a boardinghouse, now the Thomas Wolfe House—a museum—in Asheville.

Wolfe was graduated from the University of North Carolina in 1920. His first novel, *Look Homeward, Angel* (1929), annoyed people in Asheville when it was published, particularly his mother's family, the Penlands. They weren't very well disguised as "Pentlands" in the novel, set in Altamont, North Carolina.

Wolfe's novels, notably *Look Homeward, Angel*, were largely autobiographical. In Asheville there is a pillar with a collection of stonecutting tools on the corner where his father's tombstone shop stood. Down the street is a bronze replica of the marble angel of the title of the book. The marble angel itself is in Oakdale Cemetery in nearby Hendersonville, North Carolina, according to an historical marker on U.S. 64 just west of town, but some have argued that a competing angel in Bryson City is likelier.

Wolfe's writings were voluminous; his editor Max Perkins and later Edward Aswell carved the novels out of the manuscripts. Wolfe died 15 September 1938 in Baltimore of tubercular meningitis.

Abbie Mandana Holmes Christensen (1852–1938)

Born 28 January 1852, Westborough MA
Died 21 September 1938, Greenville SC
Buried Baptist Church of Beaufort, Beaufort SC

Works: *Afro-American Folk Lore Told Round Cabin Fires on the Sea Islands of Georgia*

Abbie Mandana Holmes was born in Westborough, Massachusetts, to abolitionist parents. The family moved to Beaufort, South Carolina, in 1864 as missionaries, when Abbie was twelve. They joined the Port Royal Experiment, an abolitionist effort begun in 1861 to educate African-Americans.

After studying at Ipswich Female Seminary in Massachusetts, she returned to Beaufort, and taught school to African-Americans from 1870 to 1872. Then she returned to the North to study at Mount Holyoke. When she was graduated, she gave a public reading of "The Tar Baby," and in 1874 she published "De Wolf, de Rabbit an' de Tar Baby" in the *Springfield Daily Republican*.

She permanently settled in Beaufort and married Niels Christensen, a Dane who had come to the United States in 1864 and served in the Union Army as captain of the 44th U.S. Colored Infantry. When they married, he was superintendent of the Federal cemetery in Beaufort. They had six children. Mrs. Christensen continued publishing her folk-tales in Northern publications, gathering them from local African Americans and writing them down "verbatim."

Her transcription of the Gullah dialect has been praised for its accuracy, but is considered difficult by scholars, compared with those written by Joel Chandler Harris, DuBose Heyward, Julia Peterkin, E.C.L. Adams, and Ambrose Gonzales.

Gullah, a common dialect among African-Americans living in the Low Country of the Carolinas, Georgia, and the Sea Islands, was an interesting challenge and a point of contention for Southern writers. The inability of the reading public to interpret Christensen's rendering of the Gullah patois denied her commercial success. Her collection of folk-tales was published in 1892, several years after Harris's Uncle Remus tales had become famous. Christensen's Northern friends called her "the original Uncle Remus."

In addition to her work as a writer and teacher, Christensen was active in temperance and suffragist movements, the NAACP, the Rosicrucians, and the Socialist Party. In 1932, she was a presidential elector for the Socialist candidate Norman Thomas.

She died in Greenville, South Carolina, in 1938 at the age of eighty-six, but was entombed in her beloved Low Country, at the Baptist Church of Beaufort.

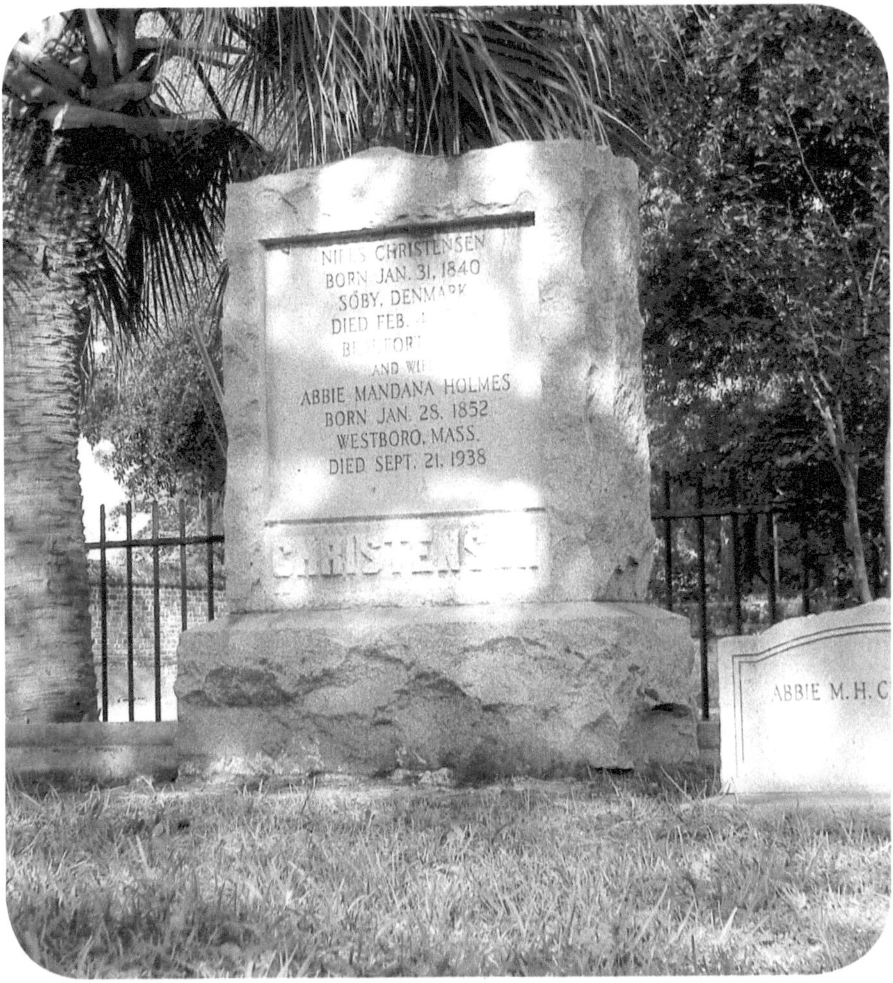
BORN JAN. 31, 1840
ABBIE MANDANA HOLMES
BORN JAN. 28, 1852
WESTBORO, MASS.
DIED SEPT. 21, 1938

ABBIE M. H. CHRISTENSEN

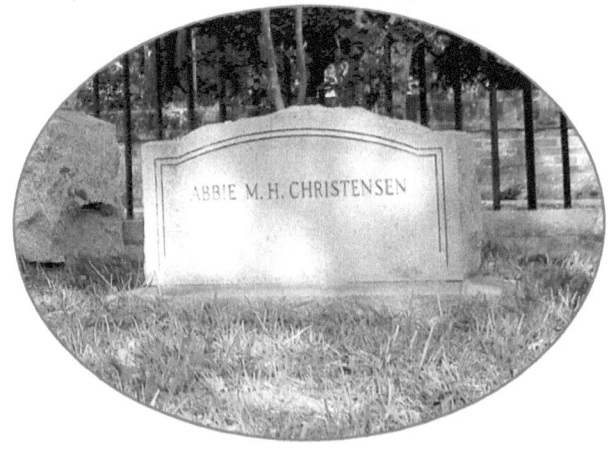

Harry Stillwell Edwards
(1855–1938)

Born 23 April 1855, Macon GA
Died 22 October 1938, Macon GA
Buried Rose Hill, Macon GA

Works: *The Two Runaways and Other Stories, Sons and Fathers, The Marbeau Cousins, His Defense and Other Stories, The Fifth Dimension, Bypaths in Dixie: Folk Tales of the South, Eneas Africanus, The Adventures of a Parrot, Brother Sim's Mistake, Isam's Spectacles, Just Sweethearts, Eneas Africanus, Defendant, The Blue Hen's Chickens, The Tenth Generation, Little Legends of the Land*

Although his early education was interrupted by the Civil War, Harry Stillwell Edwards devoted long hours to study in the reading rooms of the Library of Congress while he was employed by the U.S. Treasury Department. In 1874 he returned to Macon, Georgia. Edwards attended Mercer University in his home city, having been graduated with a degree in law in 1877, although he never practiced.

He was editor of the *Macon Telegraph* (1881-1887), and wrote a popular column, "What Comes Down My Creek." Edwards was later co-editor of the *Macon Evening News*. He published two popular mystery novels, *Sons and Fathers* (1895) and *The Marbeau Cousins* (1897).

Although he penned many works and was a high-profile journalist of long standing, his literary reputation today rests almost exclusively upon a slender volume, *Eneas Africanus* (1920), the local-color account of a peripatetic, tall tale-telling ex-slave, Eneas Tommey.

In the story, Eneas's master sends him on a mission to take family valuables to a different plantation, as Federal troops threaten near the end of the Civil War. Eneas embarks on a seven-year odyssey, during which he acquires a new wife and makes a lot of money racing Tommey's racehorse, Lightning. The book, reprinted many times, has sold over two million copies.

Edwards died at eighty-three and was buried in Macon's historic Rose Hill Cemetery. His restored home, called Kingfisher Cabin, has been relocated to the grounds of the Museum of Arts and Sciences in Macon.

Virginia Frazer Boyle
(1863–1938)

Born 14 February 1863, Chattanooga TN
Died 13 December 1938, Memphis TN
Buried Elmwood, Memphis TN

Works: *The Other Side, Devil Tales: Black Americana Folk-Lore, Love Songs and Bugle Calls, Brokenburne: A Southern Auntie's War Tale, Songs From the South*

Virginia Frazer Boyle allegedly was dubbed the "poet laureate of the Confederacy" by former Confederate President Jefferson Davis. The story goes that she read a poem to Davis in 1873 while on a trip to the Mississippi Gulf Coast and that he was so impressed that he bestowed a garland of jessamine on her head and called her the poet laureate of the Confederacy.

Her literary career began four years later when *Harper's Weekly* accepted a poem for publication.

She worked for many years in her father's law firm, helping research cases for him. He had been a colonel in the Confederate Army and she remained close to him until his death in 1897. Her first book, *The Other Side* (1893), detailed the causes for the Civil War from a Southern perspective. She wrote a number of pieces for various publications, including some stories in the African-American dialects of the Mid-South.

She was prolific as a poet, particularly on poems about the South and the various states. Her "Ode to Tennessee" was selected by state officials as the winning entry for the state's centennial celebration in 1896. For a number of years, she wrote an "Ode to the Confederate Dead." She wrote one novel, *Serena* (1905), that drew some praise, and her best-known poetry collection was *Love Songs and Bugle Calls* (1906).

The United Confederate Veterans removed all doubt about her standing in 1910 when the organization officially recognized her as the "poet laureate of the Confederacy."

As the Great War in Europe drew ever greater attention from the United States, her writing showed more patriotic fervor, and her poems "Union," and "Christmas in Argonne" were translated into several different languages.

She was honored by France for her work in support of the Red Cross, the Women's Committee on National Defense, and the Writer's Bureau on Public Information.

She died in Memphis 13 December 1938. At the time of her death she was writing a novel about Hernando de Soto.

DuBose Heyward
(1885–1940)

Born 31 August 1885, Charleston SC
Died 16 June 1940, near Tryon NC
Buried St. Philip's, Charleston SC

Works: *Angel, Porgy, Mamba's Daughters, Carolina Chansons, The Half-Pint Flask, Peter Ashley, The Country Bunny and the Little Gold Shoes, Jasbo Brown and Selected Poems, Lost Morning, Skylines and Horizons, Star Spangled Virgin, Brass Ankle, Porgy and Bess, Lost Morning*

DuBose Heyward, a descendant of a signer of the Declaration of Independence, was a genuine Charleston aristocrat but born into impoverished circumstances in 1885. An early bout with polio left his health compromised, and the family's modest resources ruled out a college education. Heyward entered the insurance business but discovered his real passion in writing, which he shared with his friend and mentor, John Bennett.

Bennett introduced Heyward to Hervey Allen, a wounded World War I veteran who was teaching high school English, and the Poetry Society of South Carolina thus came into being. Heyward and Allen collaborated on *Carolina Chansons*, a slender volume of poetry, in 1922.

But Heyward achieved lasting fame with the appearance of his novel *Porgy* in 1925. A play version, written in conjunction with his wife, Dorothy Kuhns Heyward, became the basis for George Gershwin's renowned folk opera *Porgy and Bess* (1935), to which Heyward contributed a number of lyrics.

He published other novels, including *Angel, Peter Ashley, Mamba's Daughters*, and *Star-Spangled Virgin*, but none garnered the attention of his earlier work.

Heyward succumbed to a heart attack while vacationing at his summer residence in the western North Carolina mountains on 16 June 1940. He was buried in the graveyard across the street from Charleston's St. Philip's Episcopal Church. His widow was buried at his side in 1961.

Wilbur Joseph Cash
(1900–1941)

Born 2 May 1900, Gaffney SC
Died 1 July 1941, Mexico City, Mexico
Buried Sunset, Shelby NC

Works: *The Mind of the South*

 W. J. Cash was an indifferent student at Wofford College and then at Valparaiso in Indiana, but a summer job with the *Charlotte Observer* gave him a desire for a career in newspapers. When he enrolled in Wake Forest College he was recognized for his outstanding scholarship. He excelled as first managing editor and then the editor of the campus newspaper, *Old Gold & Black*.
 After having been graduated, he entered the Wake Forest law school, but he quit after two years, later explaining that law school "required too much mendacity." He wrote for the old *Chicago Post* and the *Charlotte News* before accepting the editorship of the *Cleveland Press*, a weekly in Shelby, North Carolina. When that newspaper folded, he freelanced several articles for the *American Mercury* magazine. The *Mercury* was edited by the legendary H. L. Mencken, who appreciated Cash's writing style. One of Cash's articles, "The Mind of the South," published in October 1929, drew particular praise. Blanche and Alfred Knopf, publishers of the *Mercury*, asked Cash to expand the article into a book.
 In addition to the articles for the *Mercury*, Cash was also writing weekly book reviews and occasional editorials as a freelancer for *The Charlotte News*. He used the reviews and the editorials to attack Nazism under Hitler and fascism under Mussolini in Italy. Worsening conditions in Europe brought more focus on Hitler and Mussolini, and in 1937 Cash was named associate editor of *The Charlotte News*. Meanwhile, he continued on his book manuscript, finally completing it in July 1940.
 It was published in February 1941. The book drew rave reviews from the *New York Times*, *Time* magazine, *Atlantic Monthly*, the *Saturday Review of Literature*, the NAACP, the *Dallas Morning News*, and the *Baltimore Evening Sun*, and most major Southern newspapers.
 Cash was nominated for a Pulitzer Prize for his editorials criticizing Hitler and Mussolini in 1940. He was on a roll. He won a Guggenheim Fellowship, allowing him a year of study in Mexico. It was a fateful trip.
 He and his new wife, Mary Ross Northrop, went to Mexico City. Shortly afterwards, he told her that he believed he was being followed by Nazi spies. He left the hotel where his wife was staying and checked into another hotel. He was found hanged by a necktie in his hotel room on 1 July 1941. Mexican authorities ruled the death a suicide.

William Alexander Percy
(1885–1942)

Born 14 May 1885, Greenville MS
Died 21 January 1942, Greenville MS
Buried Greenville Cemetery, Greenville MS

Works: *Sappho in Levkes, and Other Poems, In April Once, and Other Poems, Enzio's Kingdom, and Other Poems, Selected Poems, Collected Poems, Lanterns on the Levee*

William Alexander Percy was the son of LeRoy Percy, the last Mississippi senator who was elected by the Legislature. He entered the University of the South at Sewanee, Tennessee at 15 and after having been graduated, earned a law degree at Harvard. He returned to his home in Greenville, Mississippi and worked in his father's law firm. He traveled extensively in Europe and claimed personal friendships with a number of Southern writers, including William Faulkner.

Percy served in the Army in World War I, rising to the rank of captain and earning a *Croix de Guerre* from France. From 1925 to 1932 he edited the Yale Young Poets series and also published collections of his own poetry. For a time he served as a godfather to the Fugitives, the group of poets and writers in Nashville that became known as the Southern Agrarians—principally John Crowe Ransom, Allen Tate, Robert Penn Warren and Donald Davidson. Percy had met Herbert Hoover during his service in World War I and Hoover had Percy named as the head of relief efforts during the Great Flood of 1927—one of the greatest floods in American history.

Percy had planned to evacuate large numbers of African-Americans from the bluffs at Greenville to Vicksburg to escape the flood, but the boats left empty when Percy acceded to his father's fears that the victims might not return if they ever left the Delta. His decision resulted in scathing attacks from newspapers across the South. In 1931 when his cousin's widow was killed in a car wreck, Percy, who never married, adopted her three young sons—Walker, LeRoy and Phinizy Percy—and raised them as his own. Walker Percy became a far better known writer than his adoptive father. Percy finished his autobiography, *Lanterns on the Levee: Recollections of a Planter's Son* (1941), months before his death 31 January 1942.

The armored knight statue, designed by William Aleaxander Percy, is a memorial to his father.

Ben Robertson
(1903–1943)

Born 22 June 1903, Calhoun SC
Died 22 February 1943, Lisbon, Portugal
Buried Westview, Liberty SC

Works: *Red Hills and Cotton, Travelers' Rest, I Saw England*

Benjamin Franklin (Ben) Robertson, Jr., was born in Calhoun (now Clemson), South Carolina, in 1903. After earning a bachelor's degree in botany at Clemson College, "Class of 1923," he studied journalism at the University of Missouri, and subsequently took writing positions at the *Anderson* (SC) *Independent*, the *Greenville* (SC) *News*, the *Charleston News and Courier*, *The News* (Adelaide, Australia), the *Honolulu Star-Bulletin*, and the Associated Press. At the outset of World War II, Robertson served as a regular contributor to the New York-based, politically liberal periodical *P.M.*

Apart from his journalistic endeavors, Robertson found time to author *Travelers' Rest* (1938), a historical novel that he published at his own expense. *I Saw England*, his eyewitness account of the Battle of Britain, appeared in 1941. But Robertson is best known for *Red Hills and Cotton: An Upcountry Memory*, an almost-lyrical tribute to the rural South Carolina Piedmont region and its people. Issued in 1942, it still enjoys a faithful readership.

In February 1943, as Robertson traveled to assume new duties at the *New York Herald-Tribune*'s London bureau, the plane in which he was a passenger, a Pan American Boeing 314 flying boat dubbed the *Yankee Clipper*, crashed near Lisbon, Portugal. Friends and colleagues, including Clemson classmate Strom Thurmond and CBS Radio's North Carolina-born Edward R. Murrow, lamented his untimely passing. Robertson's body was eventually recovered from the Tagus River and returned to his family in South Carolina. Many mourners turned out for his committal rites at Westview Cemetery in Liberty, South Carolina. An imposing granite monument bears this inscription: "I rest in thy bosom, Carolina, thy skies over me, thy earth and air above and around me. Among my own, in my own country, I sleep."

A Liberty cargo ship, *S.S. Ben Robertson*, built by the Southeastern Shipyard Corporation in Savannah, Georgia, was christened on 4 January 1944 by Robertson's sister, Mrs. Julian Longley of Dalton, Georgia. The ship joined a line of vessels named in memory of war correspondents who had died in action.

John Peale Bishop
(1892–1944)

Born 21 May 1892, Charles Town WV
Died 4 April 1944, Hyannis MA
Buried Evergeen, Harwich MA

Works: *Green Fruit, The Undertaker's Garland, Many Thousands Gone, Now With His Love, Minute Particulars, Act of Darkness, Selected Poems, Collected Essays, Collected Poems*

John Peale Bishop was born on 21 May 1892 in Charles Town, West Virginia. Although born in a relatively "young" state, the Bishop family always considered themselves wholly Southerners. At the age of 18, Bishop fell ill, which caused him to delay his start at Princeton University until 1913, at the age of 21. It was here that he became close friends with Edmund Wilson and F. Scott Fitzgerald. Bishop would later become the model for the character of Tom D'Invilliers in Fitzgerald's *This Side of Paradise*.

Bishop was graduated from Princeton in 1917, and in the same year published his first volume of verse, *Green Fruit*. After serving as an officer in the American Expeditionary Forces in Paris for two years, Bishop moved to New York and became editor for *Vanity Fair* from 1920–1922. He married Margaret Hutchins in 1922 and shortly after departed for France.

Other than a brief relocation to New York from 1925-1926, when he worked for Paramount Pictures, the couple lived in France until 1933 and had three sons. Despite Bishop's strong admiration for French culture, his written collections still focused on stories about his native South, such as *Many Thousands Gone* (1931) and *Now with His Love* (1933).

Bishop's stories of Southern heritage were given an edge because of his lengthy immersion in French culture, yet he never forgot his Southern roots. In 1940, Bishop became chief poetry reviewer for *The Nation,* and in the same year published his poem, "The Hours," an elegy on the death of F. Scott Fitzgerald, notably his finest poem.

Bishop died on 4 April 1944 in Hyannis, Massachusetts.

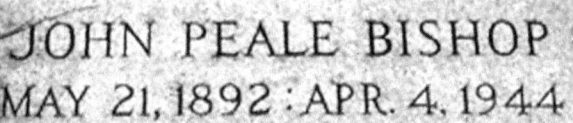

Henry Bellamann
(1882–1945)

Born 28 April 1882, Fulton MO
Died 16 June 1945, New York NY
Buried Church of the Heavenly Rest, New York NY

Works: *Kings Row, Victoria Grandolet, A Music Teacher's Notebook (verse), Petenera's Daughter, Crescendo, The Richest Woman in Town, The Gray Man Walks, Floods of Spring, Red Shoes Run Faster (novella), Cups of Illusion (verse), The Upward Pass (verse)*

A musician, educator, poet, critic, and novelist, Henry Bellamann (born Heinrich Hauer Bellaman) is remembered principally as the early champion of the avant-garde American composer Charles Ives and as the author of the popular novel *Kings Row* (1940), made into a 1942 motion picture. He grew up in Fulton, Missouri, reared by his maternal grandmother, in whose household he spoke only German. In 1900 he enrolled at Westminster College in Fulton, but left after a year.

He subsequently studied music at the University of Denver's conservatory. After teaching appointments in Tennessee, Alabama, and Texas, Bellamann in 1907 married singer and voice teacher Katherine McKee Jones of Carthage, Mississippi, and began with her a life devoted to the fine arts. For the next 17 years, the couple taught at Chicora College in South Carolina, during which time they studied abroad, and Bellamann published two volumes of poetry.

He also joined the Poetry Society of South Carolina and was an initial encourager of Julia Peterkin. In 1924 Bellamann accepted a post at the Juilliard Musical Foundation in New York; other teaching jobs at Vassar College and Philadelphia's Curtis Institute of Music followed. At the same time, his literary output increased: he served as book reviewer and fine arts editor for newspapers in the Carolinas, and produced another poetry collection and seven novels.

A keen critic—he was among the first to recognize in print the Southern Literary Renaissance—and an eclectic writer, Bellamann authored numerous articles on a variety of topics and published many poems in journals and little magazines in the 1920s and 1930s. He died at his New York apartment on 16 June 1945. Two days later his funeral was conducted in the Chapel of the Beloved Disciple in the Episcopal Church of the Heavenly Rest at Manhattan. Following cremation, his ashes were entombed in the church's columbarium, downstairs from the narthex.

Ellen Glasgow
(1873–1945)

Born 22 April 1873, Richmond VA
Died 21 November 1945, Richmond VA
Buried Hollywood, Richmond VA

Works: *The Descendant, Phases of an Inferior Planet, The Voice of the People, The Battle-Ground, The Freeman and Other Poems, The Deliverance, The Wheel of Life, The Ancient Law, The Romance of a Plain Man, The Miller of Old Church, Virginia, Life and Gabriella, The Builders, One Man in His Time, The Shadowy Third and Other Stories, Barren Ground, The Romantic Comedians, They Stooped to Folly, The Sheltered Life, Vein of Iron, In This Our Life, A Certain Measure, The Woman Within, Letters of Ellen Glasgow, The Collected Stories of Ellen Glasgow, Beyond Defeat*

Ellen Anderson Gholson Glasgow was born in Richmond, Virginia, on 22 April 1873, the ninth of ten children, to Francis Thomas and Anne Jane Gholson Glasgow. She began writing as a child and composed her first poem at the age of seven. Poor health prevented her from attending public school; however, she read voraciously on subjects such as philosophy, social and political theory, and European literature. Early on, a spirit of rebellion against both the Southern aristocratic order and conventional perceptions of the female's role in society began to appear.

Brought up in an aristocratic home, Glasgow was determined to portray democratic values rarely found in the works of other Southern writers. She rejected the Victorian definition of femininity and, through her works, stressed the changing social order with the emergence of a dominant middle class and independent women. Realism and irony were the tools she used to begin a "literary revolution against the romantic treatment of Southern life."

Glasgow published her first novel, *The Descendant,* in 1897. Over the next four and a half decades, she would write 20 novels, a volume of poems, a collection of stories, and a book of literary criticism. In 1931, Glasgow presided over the Southern Writers Conference at the University of Virginia. She received honorary degrees from Duke University and the University of Richmond and was the first Virginian elected to the American Academy of Arts and Letters.

Glasgow found her works on the best-seller list five times, and in 1942 she received the Pulitzer Prize for her last published novel, *In This Our Life* (1941), which was later made into a film. Ellen Glasgow died in her Richmond home on 21 November 1945. She was buried with her beloved dog Jeremy, who had died in 1929.

Thomas Dixon, Jr. (1864–1946)

Born 11 January 1864, Cleveland Co. NC
Died 3 April 1946, Raleigh NC
Buried Sunset, Shelby NC

Works: *What is Religion? An Outline of Vital Ritualism, Dixon on Ingersoll: Ten Discourses Delivered in Association Hall, New York, The Failure of Protestantism in New York and Its Causes, Dixon's Sermons, Delivered in the Grand Opera House, 1898-1899, Living Problems in Religion and Social Science, The Leopard's Spots: A Romance of the White Man's Burden—1865-1900, The One Woman: A Story of Modern Utopia, The Clansman: An Historical Romance of the Ku Klux Klan, The One Woman: A Drama, The Traitor: A Story of the Fall of the Invisible Empire, Comrades: A Story of Social Adventure in California, The Root of Evil: A Novel, The Sins of the Father: A Romance of the South, The Southerner: A Romance of the Real Lincoln, , The Victim: A Romance of the Real Jefferson Davis, The Life Worth Living: A Personal Experience, The Foolish Virgin: A Romance of Today, The Fall of a Nation: A Sequel to The Birth of a Nation, The Way of a Man: A Story of the New Woman, A Man of the People: A Drama of Abraham Lincoln, The Man in Gray: A Romance of North and South, The Black Hood, The Love Complex, The Hope of the World: A Story of the Coming War,*

Thomas F. Dixon, Jr., was a lawyer and legislator who became a Baptist minister before joining the lecture circuit. He later became a playwright and novelist. He was a son of former slave-owning parents, and his family encountered hardships in coping with the Reconstruction period in the South during Dixon's childhood.

He was graduated from Shelby Academy and entered Wake Forest College in 1879. In four years he earned his master's degree and established what then was the most outstanding academic record ever at Wake Forest. He received a scholarship to Johns Hopkins University, where he met future President Woodrow Wilson. Despite pleas from Wilson, Dixon dropped out of Johns Hopkins and went to New York to the Frobisher School to study drama. He had dreamed of becoming an actor, but his gaunt appearance (he stood 6 feet, 3 inches tall, and weighed 150 pounds) scuttled his chances. He returned to North Carolina in shame. He enrolled in the Greensboro Law School and was graduated in 1884.

Even though Dixon was not old enough to vote for himself, he campaigned and won election to the North Carolina General Assembly. After a term in the legislature, he withdrew from politics, disgusted by the corruption and shady dealing. He described politicians as "prostitutes of the masses."

His first novel was *The Leopard's Spots* (1902), followed by *The Clansman* (1905) and *The Traitor* (1907). Dixon termed the three novels his "trilogy of the Reconstruction." *The Clansman* was used by D. W. Griffith as the basis for *The Birth of a Nation* (1915). While he opposed the institution of slavery, Dixon believed African-Americans were an inferior race, and he was an ardent segregationist. Dixon wrote 22 novels. Over the years he had earned millions of dollars, but he was working as court clerk in Raleigh when he died 3 April 1946.

Lyle Saxon
(1891–1946)

Born 4 September 1891, Bellingham WA
Died 9 April 1946, New Orleans LA
Buried Magnolia, Baton Rouge LA

Works: *Father Mississippi, Fabulous New Orleans, Old Louisiana, Lafitte the Pirate, Children of Strangers, A Collection of Folk Tales: Gumbo Ya-Ya, The Friends of Joe Gilmore*

Lyle Chambers Saxon was a reporter for the New Orleans *Times-Picayune* who gained literary notice while writing book reviews and fiction for the newspaper. He had aspired to an education at an elite Eastern university, but attended Louisiana State University in Baton Rouge because of limited family finances. He withdrew one course short of his degree.

While with the *Times-Picayune*, he lived in the Vieux Carré, the French Quarter. The area was regarded by most residents of New Orleans as a place of squalor, fit only for thieves and prostitutes. But Saxon personally restored two buildings there and led the preservationist movement that eventually rehabilitated much of the French Quarter.

His home on Rue Royale drew important literary visitors, including William Faulkner, John dos Passos, John Steinbeck, Dorothy Dix, Edmund Wilson, and Sherwood and Elizabeth Anderson. His hospitality was legendary, and he seemed always to have on hand quantities of Prohibition-era liquor. Saxon left the newspaper in 1926, but then wrote four very popular books: *Father Mississippi* (1927), *Fabulous New Orleans* (1928), *Old Louisiana* (1929), and *Lafitte the Pirate* (1930). He became known as Mr. New Orleans.

In 1935, in the depths of the Great Depression, he was named the head of the Works Progress Administration's Federal Writer's Project for the state of Louisiana. In that role he helped compile two important guidebooks and *Gumbo Ya-Ya* (1945), a collection of Louisiana folklore that is still used as resource material for the state and its cultural vagaries.

Saxon died in New Orleans 9 April 1946.

George Madden Martin
(1866–1946)

Born 3 May 1866, Louisville KY
Died 30 November 1946, Louisville KY
Buried Cave Hill, Louisville KY

Works: *The Angel of the Tenement, Emmy Lou: Her Book and Her Heart, [6 more books about Emmy Lou], Abbie Ann, Children in the Mist, Made in America*

Georgia May Madden Martin was born in Louisville, Kentucky, in 1866 and received most of her education from private tutors. She taught at Wellesley School for two years before her marriage to Attwood Reading Martin, who became a prominent Louisville businessman. In the 1890s, she joined the Author's Club in Louisville, along with Annie Fellows Johnston, Alice Hegan Rice, and Eva Madden, her sister. Club members would take a situation, write a treatment for the situation, and then criticize the work of fellow writers.

Her professional career as a writer began with the publication of *Teckla's Lilies* (1895) as a serial in *Harper's Weekly*. In *The Angel of the Tenement* (1897) Martin, who had chosen the George Madden Martin pseudonym, spun experiences of a child through the eyes of adults. In *Emmy Lou: Her Book and Heart* (1902), she wrote from the perspective of the child, struggling with the concept of the need to learn letters and numbers. *Emmy Lou* became her best-known work. The novel had first appeared as a serial in *McClure's Magazine* in 1900.

Three other Martin novels, *The House of Fulfillment* (1904), *Abbie Ann* (1907), and *Letitia: Nursery Corps, U.S. Army* (1907), were first published serially. *Selina* (1914) was her first novel concerning the development of the "new woman," a woman actively concerned about political and social ills. Martin held a number of appointive and elective posts in the 1920s and 1930s. In 1920, she became a board member on the Committee for Interracial Cooperation, a position she would hold for 14 years.

She wrote a children's book of Shakespeare's early life, *A Warwickshire Lad* (1916), and a collection of short stories, *Children in the Mist* (1920), which related the oppression of African-American children in the South. In *March On* (1921), she took up the political and social issues arising from World War I, urging her new woman to help prevent war.

In a series of articles in *Atlantic Monthly* (1924-1925), Martin explored her paradoxical political views: she was an ardent supporter of states' rights, but she was repulsed by lynchings and the mistreatment of African-Americans and other minorities. In the 1930s, she became the chairwoman of the Association of Southern Women for the Prevention of Lynching. She died in Louisville 30 November 1946.

Margaret Mitchell
(1900–1949)

Born 8 November 1900, Atlanta GA
Died 16 August 1949, Atlanta GA
Buried Oakland, Atlanta GA

Work: *Gone With the Wind*

Margaret Mitchell embraced Atlanta in *Gone With the Wind* (1936) with a fervor unequaled by any other author. She was, in all respects, a child of the city. She grew up in a stately house on Peachtree, worked as a features writer under Ralph McGill at the *Atlanta Journal*, and lived in a small apartment she called "The Dump" just off Peachtree.

She wrote her epic novel in the apartment over a 10-year period, but swirled to instant fame and astonishing fortune in the year after it was published. *Gone With the Wind* won the Pulitzer Prize for fiction in 1937, but Mitchell's depictions of the city crystallized her affection, from the mindless pomp of the citizens advocating secession at the outbreak of the Civil War to the torment of the soldiers in the grimy hospital as the battle for the city raged. The cast of *Gone With the Wind* included brothel owner Belle Watling with a heart of gold, and saintly Melanie Wilkes, who represented the "good women" of Atlanta—doing the right thing in every circumstance.

Mitchell, known to her friends as Peggy Marsh, moved to a house just off Peachtree after selling the film rights to her book. The rights contract, up to $50,000, was the largest amount that had been paid for a movie at that time. The movie won 10 Academy Awards after its release in 1939, and it became the largest- grossing movie of its era. Mitchell subsequently retired from her writing career. Crossing Atlanta's busy Peachtree Street, she was struck by a taxi and died five days later, on 16 August 1949.

She was buried in the city's Oakland Cemetery, established in 1855. The cemetery contains the graves of 6,000 Civil War soldiers. Among them is Scarlett O'Hara's first husband, Charles Hamilton. Mitchell included mention of that burial in *Gone With the Wind*, but the reference was anachronistic because the cemetery was not named Oakland until 1876. Confederate General John Bell Hood observed Sherman's assault on Atlanta on 22 July 1864 from high ground now within the cemetery. The Mitchell family plot, featuring a classical design landscaped with zoysia, fairy roses, and conifers, is nearby.

Hervey Allen
(1889–1949)

Born 8 December 1889, Pittsburgh PA
Died 28 December 1949, The Glades FL
Buried Arlington National Cemetery, Arlington VA

Works: *Anthony Adverse, Carolina Chansons, Wampum and Old Gold, Israfel, Is It Like This?, The Forest and the Fort, Bedford Village, Toward the Morning*

Allen grew up in Pittsburgh, Pennsylvania, and was graduated from the University of Pittsburgh, but moved to Charleston, South Carolina, after serving as an Army first lieutenant in World War I. He had been wounded and gassed during the war, and as a result suffered from "shell shock" (later called "combat fatigue" and now known as Post-Traumatic Stress Disorder). His war poetry is admired by many.

Because his health was delicate, a doctor had recommended his moving to a milder climate, which Charleston readily provided him. While teaching at Porter Military Academy he met John Bennett, Laura Bragg, Josephine Pinckney, and DuBose Heyward, and became with them a founder of the Poetry Society of South Carolina. With Heyward he published *Carolina Chansons* (1922), poems set in the Lowcountry. In 1924 he left South Carolina.

He taught at Columbia University and at Vassar. His marriage to Annette Andrews, his former student from Vassar and 19 years his junior, created a scandal.

His most famous work, *Anthony Adverse*, appeared in 1933. The sprawling historical novel of the Napoleonic period sold over three million copies, and was made into a popular Warner Brothers film produced by David O. Selznick, starring Frederic March and Olivia de Havilland.

With Carl Carmer and Stephen Vincent Benét he edited the "Rivers of America" series. This series was begun in 1937, eventually reaching 65 volumes, and was intended to be written by novelists and poets rather than by historians or geographers. Allen asked his friend Marjory Stoneman Douglas to write a volume for the series, and she produced the influential *The Everglades: River of Grass* (1947). Allen moved to Florida in the 1940s. He had great affection for the Everglades, and was interested in environmentalism.

Allen continued writing until his death from heart disease at age sixty in The Glades, Florida. He was buried with military honors at Arlington National Cemetery. (In 2007, Allen's burial record at Arlington wrongly identified him as William Harvey Allen.)

John Gould Fletcher
(1886–1950)

Born 3 January 1886, Little Rock AR
Died 20 May 1950, Little Rock AR
Buried Mount Holly Cemetery, Little Rock AR

Works: *Irradiations: Sand and Spray, Goblins and Pagodas, Selected Poems, Arkansas*

The independent wealth of John Gould Fletcher allowed him to travel extensively in Europe after dropping out of Harvard. He settled in London in 1913 and came under the influence of poets Ezra Pound and Amy Lowell. Fletcher began a liaison with Florence Emily "Daisy" Arbuthnot, a recent divorcée, in 1915, and they were married the following year.

His early works included *Irradiations: Sand and Spray* (1914) and *Goblins and Pagodas* (1916), in the Imagist free-verse style, but his later works were more traditional poetry. In the 1920s, his poems aimed at shaking readers from complacency with attacks on industrialization.

He joined the Southern Agrarians in 1927—John Crowe Ransom, Allen Tate, and Donald Davidson—but his anti-democratic essay on education in the Agrarians' manifesto, *I'll Take My Stand* (1930) signaled the onset of a depressive crisis. Fletcher suffered from bi-polar disorder.

He returned to his home town of Little Rock after a suicide attempt in England in 1932. He divorced his first wife but married Charlie May Simon, a well-known author of children's books, in 1936. Friends credited the marriage to Simon for providing Fletcher with the stability needed to continue writing successfully.

His *Selected Poems* (1938) earned him the Pulitzer Prize for poetry in 1939. The well-crafted *Arkansas* (1947) was considered the definitive history of the state, though it drew little notice elsewhere. Fletcher was becoming increasingly arthritic, and his drift toward obscurity exacerbated a deepening bout with depression.

Fletcher drowned himself in a shallow pond near his home in Little Rock 20 May 1950.

Douglas Southall Freeman
(1866–1953)

Born 16 May 1866, Lynchburg VA
Died 13 June 1953, Richmond VA
Buried Hollywood, Richmond VA

Works: *Lee, Washington, Lee's Lieutenants*

Douglas Southall Freeman was born in Lynchburg, Virginia, on 16 May 1886. The son of a Confederate general, Freeman was a newspaperman who would go on to become one of America's most important and significant biographers. Freeman graduated from Richmond College in 1904; he then attended Johns Hopkins, where he earned a doctorate in history at the age of 22. He returned to Richmond, where he began writing for local newspapers.

In 1915, Freeman became the editor of the *News Leader*, and he commenced research on what would become the pivotal book of his career, a biography of Robert E. Lee (four volumes, 1934-1935).

For this biography, Freeman was awarded the Pulitzer Prize in 1935. The accolades he garnered resulted in Freeman's being named Visiting Professor of Journalism at Columbia University from 1936 to 1945. He then began the exhaustive task of writing the biography of George Washington.

When Freeman died in Richmond on 13 June 1953, he had completed only six of the proposed seven volumes of the Washington biography. John Alexander Carroll and Mary Wells Ashworth finished the last volume of *George Washington: A Biography*, which was awarded the Pulitzer Prize in 1958.

Freeman was buried at Hollywood Cemetery in Richmond.

Emily Clark
(1891–1953)

Born 8 September 1891, Richmond VA
Died 22 July 1953, Philadelphia PA
Buried Hollywood, Richmond VA

Works: *Stuffed Peacocks, Innocence Abroad*

Emily Tapscott Clark began writing book reviews for the Richmond *Evening-Journal*, but when the newspaper stopped publishing its book page, she became the founding editor for *The Reviewer*, an experimental literary journal (1921).

She continued as a staff writer for the *Evening-Journal* until 1923, supplementing her pay from *The Reviewer*.

She used her impeccable social connections—she hailed from one of the First Families of Virginia and was a member of the Daughters of the American Revolution—to draw submissions from an eclectic mix of writers, including Ellen Glasgow, Allen Tate, Gertrude Stein, and DuBose Heyward. With assistance from H. L. Mencken, she also helped promote a new writer, Julia Peterkin, who became the first Southern author to win a Pulitzer Prize (1929), for *Scarlet Sister Mary*).

While traveling in Baltimore, Clark met Edwin Balch. Balch agreed to finance several issues of *The Reviewer*, and put $3,000 of the publication's stock in his name. Clark married Balch, more than 30 years her senior, 1 November 1924, and they moved to Philadelphia.

She published *Stuffed Peacocks* (1927), a collection of satirical character sketches drawn from Richmond society. She subsequently wrote *Innocence Abroad* (1931) about her experiences with *The Reviewer* and her colleagues. She occasionally wrote reviews in various magazines, including *The Virginia Quarterly Review*, published by the University of Virginia, but she was known primarily as a patron of the arts.

She died in Philadelphia 2 July 1953.

Marjorie Kinnan Rawlings
(1896–1953)

Born 8 August 1896, Washington DC
Died 14 December 1953, near St. Augustine FL
Buried Antioch, Island Grove FL

Works: *South Moon Under, The Yearling, Cross Creek, The Secret River*

Born in Washington, D.C., in 1896, Marjorie Kinnan earned a degree in English in 1918 from the University of Wisconsin, where she met her first husband, Charles Rawlings. They wed in 1919, and after a brief flirtation with print journalism, purchased a 72-acre orange grove near Hawthorne, Florida, in a hamlet known as Cross Creek.

Her first novel, the Pulitzer-nominated *South Moon Under*, was published in 1933. Soon thereafter, the idyllic rural existence that the Rawlingses had planned for themselves fell apart, and the couple divorced. Charles left Cross Creek, but Marjorie remained, studying the area and continuing to write. Her next book, *Golden Apples* (1935), was poorly received. But with the appearance of *The Yearling* in 1938—a best-selling coming-of-age novel that won the Pulitzer fiction prize in 1939—Marjorie Kinnan Rawlings became a well-known name in literary circles. A subsequent film version of *The Yearling* brought the author international recognition.

With her earnings from this successful novel, Rawlings acquired a cottage at Crescent Beach, south of St. Augustine. In 1941 she married Nathan Baskin, owner of a hotel in Ocala. They agreed to pursue separate careers.

Rawlings published *Cross Creek*, a memoir of her years in the Florida wilderness, and *Cross Creek Cookery*, a volume of her favorite recipes, in 1942. The following year Zelma Cason, a close friend, sued her for invasion of privacy, contending that the depiction of the Zelma character in *Cross Creek* had made her seem "like a hussy." Rawlings won the initial lawsuit, only to lose on appeal. A judge ordered her to pay Cason one dollar in damages.

As a writer, she formed friendships with Ernest Hemingway, Thomas Wolfe, F. Scott Fitzgerald, Robert Frost, Margaret Mitchell, and fellow Florida resident Zora Neale Hurston. Although Rawlings opposed racial injustice, she treated Hurston as her inferior. When Hurston visited Cross Creek, Rawlings assigned Hurston quarters in the "tenant house" where her maid resided, not in the main house where Rawlings lived.

Rawlings suffered a fatal cerebral hemorrhage on 14 December 1953 in St. Augustine, and was buried at Antioch Cemetery in nearby Island Grove, Florida. *The Secret River* (1955), a children's book, won a posthumous Newbery Honor in 1956.

James Street
(1903–1954)

Born 15 October 1903, Lumberton MS
Died 28 September 1954, Chapel Hill NC
Buried Old Chapel Hill Cemetery, Chapel Hill NC

Works: *Look Away—A Dixie Notebook, Oh, Promised Land, In My Father's House, The Biscuit Eater, Tap Roots, By Valour and Arms, Short Stories, The Gauntlet, Tomorrow We Reap, Mingo Dabney, The High Calling, The Velvet Doublet, The Civil War, Good-bye, My Lady, The Revolutionary War, James Street's South, Captain Little Ax*

James Street began his newspaper career at the age of 14, reporting for the *Laurel Daily Leader*. Five years later, he took a job with the *Hattiesburg American*.

In 1923 he married Lucy Nash O'Briant, the daughter of a Baptist minister. Although he had been reared as a Catholic, he decided to become a minister and studied at Southwestern Baptist Theological Seminary in Fort Worth. He was appointed as minister at St. Charles, Missouri, and later served as pastor of a Baptist church in Lucedale, Mississippi. He began attending Howard University in Birmingham and became pastor of a Baptist church in Bayles, Alabama.

He gave up the ministry and returned to journalism in 1926, working briefly for the Pensacola, Florida, *Journal*, and then accepting a position with the Associated Press. The Associated Press transferred Street to New York. He was hired by the New York *World-Telegram* in 1937.

Street then began writing fiction. One of his short stories was sold to *Cosmopolitan* magazine ("A Letter to the Editor"). Film producer David O. Selznick turned the short story into a feature movie, *Nothing Sacred* (1937). The success of the movie, a comedy hit starring Carole Lombard, allowed Street to begin writing fiction full time.

In 1939 he sold "The Biscuit Eater" to the *Saturday Evening Post*. The novel-length story began a theme on racial injustice in the South that Street explored more deeply later.

Through the 1940s, he wrote on the pentalogy of the Dabney family: *Oh, Promised Land* (1940), *Tap Roots* (1942), *By Valor and Arms* (1944), *Tomorrow We Reap* (1949), and *Mingo Dabney* (1950). *Tap Roots* was made into a successful film.

The Biscuit Eater was made into a movie, as was *Good Bye, My Lady* (1954). Both books dealt with boys and dogs. Street's *The Gauntlet* (1945) and *The High Calling* (1951) were autobiographical novels about a Baptist minister. Street was set to become the advisor for filming *Good Bye, My Lady*, when he died 28 September 1954. The movie was a smash hit featuring Walter Brennan, Brandon De Wilde, and Sidney Poitier.

JAMES AGEE (1909–1955)

Born 27 November 1909, Knoxville TN
Died 16 May 1955, New York NY
Buried Agee Farm, Hillsdale NY

Works: *Permit Me Voyage, Let Us Now Praise Famous Men, The Morning Watch, A Death in the Family, Agee on Film, Letters of James Agee to Father Flye, Collected Poems of James Agee, Collected Short Prose of James Agee*

A rough, unlettered boulder marks James Agee's grave on the Agee farm near Hillsdale, New York. Agee's son John, who was only eight months old when his father died, lives there part of the year.

Agee was born on Highland Avenue in Knoxville, Tennessee, in 1909. After his father's death when he was six, he attended an Episcopal boys' school, St. Andrew's, in Sewanee, Tennessee. He formed a liflong friendship with a teacher there, Father Harold Flye. Later Agee attended Philips Exeter Academy and Harvard. At Harvard he edited a parody of *Time* magazine, which attracted the attention of Henry Luce, the publisher. He wrote for *Time, The Nation,* and *Fortune*. His poetry was published in the *Yale Younger Poets Series, Permit Me Voyage* (1934), with an introduction by Archibald MacLeish. His sonnets and lyrics show a command of form and a preoccupation with religion and his Tennessee roots.

In 1936 he and photographer Walker Evans were sent to Alabama to write a *Fortune* article about the condition of Alabama sharecroppers during the Great Depression. The result was too long for the magazine, so Agee reworked the material into a 600-page book, with a portfolio of Evans's photographs, *Let Us Now Praise Famous Men* (1941). The book was a commercial failure, but was highly praised when it was reissued 20 years later, after Agee's death. The novella *The Morning Watch* (1951) tells the story of boys in a high-church boarding school during Holy Week.

Agee's film criticism is highly esteemed; he is credited with being the first to regard film as an art form, not just entertainment for the masses. He began writing screenplays in the 1950s, and was nominated for an Academy Award for his adaptation of *The African Queen* (1951).

He drank and smoked heavily throughout his life. After a series of heart attacks, he died from a heart attack in 1955 in a New York taxicab. At that time all of his books were out of print.

Agee's posthumous novel, *A Death in the Family* (1957), was constructed from his manuscript by his friend David McDowell and won the Pulitzer Prize for fiction in 1958. It was adapted for theater and film by Tad Mosel as *All The Way Home* (1960, 1963). After the success of *A Death in the Family*, McDowell published two volumes of Agee's film criticism and screenplays, and in the 1960s Robert Fitzgerald edited volumes of his poetry and short prose.

Beatrice Witte Ravenel
(1870–1956)

Born 24 August 1870, Charleston SC
Died 15 March 1956, Charleston SC
Buried Magnolia, Charleston SC

Works: *Arrow of Lightning, The Yemassee Lands*

Beatrice Witte was the third of six daughters born to her well-to-do German immigrant father and a mother of French Huguenot ancestry. In addition to his business interests, her father also served as the Norwegian consul in Charleston.

She was educated privately, then attended Miss Kelly's Female Seminary in Charleston and Radcliffe College, the women's division of Harvard University. She was known for her encyclopedic memory and as a great storyteller. At Radcliffe she began publishing verse and short stories. Returning to Charleston, she married Francis Ravenel, and after a series of financial setbacks, resumed writing, submitting work to *Ainslie's*, the *Atlantic Monthly*, *Harper's*, and the *Saturday Evening Post*.

In 1919 she began writing editorials for *The State*, a Columbia, South Carolina, newspaper of which her brother-in-law, William Watts Ball, was editor. Francis Ravenel died in 1920. Newly widowed, Mrs. Ravenel joined the Poetry Society of South Carolina and was elected to its first executive committee. Her one book of poetry, *The Arrow of Lightning*, was published in 1925. Many of her poems concerned exotic themes related to the voodoo culture of the Caribbean.

The following year she married Samuel Prioleau Ravenel, an affluent, Paris-born lawyer and a distant kinsman of her first husband. They took a three-year honeymoon trip to the Middle East and Europe and were accompanied by Beatrice St. Julian (Kitty) Ravenel, Mrs. Ravenel's daughter from her first marriage. Her improved financial situation led to her abandoning a commercial literary career, although she continued to write verse and to read contemporary literature (she especially favored Faulkner's work).

She maintained interest in literature among her contemporaries and carried on correspondence with such writers as Amy Lowell, Hervey Allen, Josephine Pinckney, Norman Hapgood, Edwin Markham, and DuBose Heyward. She was also involved in the visual arts and devoted effort to both charcoals and watercolors. She had compiled a series of sketches of birds near Lake Maggiore in Italy during her honeymoon. A sketch book of her art works is held by the Wilson Library at the University of North Carolina at Chapel Hill.

She died in 1956 and was buried at Magnolia Cemetery.

John Bennett
(1865–1956)

Born 17 May 1865, Chillicothe OH
Died 28 December 1956, Charleston SC
Buried Magnolia, Charleston SC

Works: *Master Skylark: A Story of Shakespeare's Time; Barnaby Lee; The Treasure of Peyre Gaillard; Madame Margot: A Grotesque Legend of Old Charleston; The Pigtail of Ah Lee Ben Loo; The Doctor to the Dead: Grotesque Legends and Folk Tales of Old Charleston*

Although he numbered native southerners among his ancestors, John Bennett was born in Chillicothe, Ohio, in 1865. He dropped out of high school in Ohio, but began a career as a writer-illustrator, focusing primarily on children's stories. His *Master Skylark* (1897) is a classic children's book on the Shakespearean Age, with vivid descriptions of harsh conditions, straw mattresses, and British accents.

During a visit to Charleston, South Carolina, Bennett encountered the Smythe family and was smitten by Susan Smythe. He moved to Charleston in 1898 and married Susan in 1902. As a Southerner-by-choice, Bennett began a study of the servants working for the Smythe family, some of whom had previously been slaves or were descendants of slaves. He also undertook research about the African-American culture, focusing on the Gullah-speaking African-Americans in Charleston.

In conducting his inquiries, Bennett had spoken with Walter Mayrant and Cesar Grant, two African-Americans who had been paid by a white man to "move" some lumber for him. Actually, he was paying to have them steal the lumber. When the two were caught and taken to trial, Bennett intervened, saving both men from almost certain conviction.

The story is told in *The Doctor to the Dead* (1946), a collection of short stories and sketches about strange characters and paranormal happenings in the vicinity of his adopted city. His affection for Charleston, the Carolina Low Country and its folklore—both white and African-American—is clearly evident in the collection.

Bennett deserves credit as a key founder of the Poetry Society of South Carolina, especially for his early encouragement of Hervey Allen and DuBose Heyward. From the Poetry Society's creation in October 1920, Bennett kept the organization a viable and visible fixture in Charleston's artistic community for many years until deafness and other infirmities curtailed his active involvement.

In his ninety-first year he died and was buried at Magnolia Cemetery.

Josephine Pinckney
(1895–1957)

Born 25 January 1895, Charleston SC
Died 4 October 1957, Charleston SC
Buried Magnolia, Charleston SC

Works: *Sea-Drinking Cities, Hilton Head, Three O'Clock Dinner, Great Mischief, My Son and Foe, Splendid in Ashes*

Best remembered for her comedy of Charleston manners, *Three O'Clock Dinner* (1945), Josephine Pinckney was born in 1895 into a distinguished family of South Carolina planters and politicians. The family included two signers of the Constitution and two governors of South Carolina. The century from 1730 to 1830, Charleston's finest, is known as the "Age of the Pinckneys." Her female ancestors were equally famous, including the planter Eliza Lucas Pinckney, who promoted indigo, and Rebecca Motte, who sacrificed her plantation house to help Francis Marion capture British officers in 1781.

She studied at the College of Charleston, Columbia, and Radcliffe. A close friend and encourager of DuBose Heyward, she was one of the unsung founders of the Poetry Society of South Carolina. This group, both in conjunction and rivalry with literary societies in Richmond and Nashville, gave birth to the Southern Renaissance of the 1920s and 1930s.

Her poetry was published in the *Yearbook of the Poetry Society of South Carolina* and other magazines, including *Poetry*, but in the 1930s she turned to fiction. Her first novel, *Hilton Head* (1941), tells the life story of the South Carolina colonist Henry Woodward.

Three O'Clock Dinner was optioned for $125,000 by MGM, but the novel's treatment of adultery and divorce was considered too daring. *Great Mischief* (1948) was a popular success and a Book-of-the-Month-Club selection. Reviewers compared her to Nathaniel Hawthorne.

Her other works include novels *My Son and Foe* (1952) and *Splendid in Ashes* (1958), and a poetry collection, *Sea-Drinking Cities* (1927), for which she received the Caroline Sinkler Award for Poetry in 1928.

She acquired a national reputation as the last Southern lady, and entertained extensively. She was noted for her family antiques and heirlooms and her hospitality, and she remained active in the cultural affairs of her native city until her death from cancer in 1957.

Miss Pinckney was buried at Magnolia Cemetery.

James Branch Cabell
(1879–1958)

Born 14 April 1879, Richmond VA
Died 5 May 1958, Richmond VA
Buried Hollywood, Richmond VA

Works: *The Eagle's Shadow, The Line of Love, Branchiana, Gallantry, Chivalry, The Cords of Vanity, Branch of Abingdon, The Soul of Melicent, The Majors and Their Marriages, The Rivet in Grandfather's Neck, The Certain Hour, From the Hidden Way, The Cream of the Jest, Beyond Life, Jurgen, Domnei, The Judging of Jurgen, Figures of Earth, The Jewel Merchants, Joseph Hergesheimer, The Lineage of Litchfield, The High Place, Straws and Prayer-Books, Retractions, The Silver Stallion, The Music from Behind the Moon, Something About Eve, Ballades from the Hidden Way, The White Robe, Sonnets from Antan, The Way of Echen, Some of Us, Townsend of Litchfield, Between Dawn and Sunrise, These Restless Heads, Special Delivery, Ladies and Gentlemen, Smirt, Smith, Preface to the Past, The Nightmare Has Triplets, Smire, The King Was in His Counting House, Of Ellen Glasgow, Hamlet Had an Uncle, The First Gentleman of America, The St. Johns, There Were Two Pirates, Let Me Lie, The Witch-Woman, The Devil's Own Dear Son, Quiet, Please, As I Remember It, Between Friends, The Letters of James Branch Cabell*

James Branch Cabell was a well-born Virginian whose neatly crafted fantasy fiction novels entertained the escapist reading public of the 1920s. He entered the College of William and Mary at the age of 15 and taught French and Greek at the college. He was dismissed from the school for becoming "too intimate" with a professor, but then was reinstated.

He was graduated in 1898 and worked as a reporter for the New York *Herald*, but returned home to his native Richmond in 1901. His first three short stories were accepted for publication in 1901, but his budding success as a writer was countered by family scandal. He was suspected of the murder of John Scott, his mother's first cousin.

His first novels concerned the Virginia gentry, drolly spoofing their troubles and efforts to maintain appearances. His eighth book, *Jurgen, A Comedy of Justice* (1919), was attacked by the New York Society for the Suppression of Vice. The society filed suit against the publication of the novel, claiming it was obscene. The society suit dragged through the courts for two years before Cabell and his publishers won.

The court ruled that the book's "indecencies" were double entendres that could also have decent interpretations. As the suit progressed, Cabell was supported by H. L. Mencken, Theodore Dreiser, and other well-known personalities. His major work was the biography of Manuel, a total of 25 books written over a 23-year period. It traces Dom Manuel and his descendants through many generations, also reflecting his life-long fascination with genealogy.

Cabell died 5 May 1958 of a cerebral hemorrhage.

Byron Herbert Reece
(1917–1958)

Born 14 September 1917, Blood Mountain GA
Died 3 June 1958, Young Harris GA
Buried Old Union Baptist Church, Young Harris GA

Works: *Ballad of the Bones, Bow Down in Jericho, Better a Dinner of Herbs, A Song of Joy, The Season of Flesh, The Hawk and the Sun*

The hardscrabble life of Byron Herbert Reece improved when he was "discovered" by author Jesse Stuart. Stuart read Reece's poem "Lest the Lonesome Bird" in the *Prairie Schooner* and persuaded E. P. Dutton to publish a collection of Reece's poems.

The first collection, *Ballad of the Bones and Other Poems* (1945,) drew critical notice and enjoyed multiple printings. But Reece had been writing for years before his discovery, mainly on themes of nature, love, death, and religion.

His second collection, *Bow Down in Jericho* (1950), brought a nomination for a Pulitzer Prize and a feature story in *Newsweek* magazine (1 January 1951). The acclaim earned him a position as poet-in-residence at the University of California at Los Angeles. He later served as poet-in-residence at Emory University in Atlanta, and at Young Harris College, a small North Georgia school he had attended. The Georgia Writers' Association presented him its literary achievement award five times, though his earnings from writing were meager.

He published the first of two novels, *Better a Dinner of Herbs* (1950) and drew favorable support from Ralph McGill, the executive editor of the Atlanta *Constitution*. His second novel, *The Hawk and the Sun* (1955), evolves around a lynching in a small North Georgia town.

Reece continued his poetry with *A Song of Joy* (1952) and *The Season of Flesh* (1955), but he had contracted tuberculosis, the disease that had killed his parents. He was treated in a sanatorium in 1954.

He held a teaching post at Young Harris College on 3 June 1958 when he committed suicide, shooting himself in the chest. His most recently graded students' papers were stacked neatly in a desk drawer, and Mozart's *Piano Sonata in D* was playing on his record player.

Zora Neale Hurston
(1891–1960)

Born 7 January 1891, Notasulga AL
Died 28 January 1960, Ft. Pierce FL
Buried Garden of Heavenly Rest, Ft. Pierce FL

Works: *Sweat, How It Feels to Be Colored Me, The Gilded Six-Bits, Jonah's Gourd Vine, Mules and Men, Tell My Horse, Their Eyes Were Watching God, Moses, Man of the Mountain, Dust Tracks on a Road, Seraph on the Suwanee, Sanctified Church, Mule Bone, Spunk: Selected Stories, The Complete Stories, Novels and Stories, Folklore, Memoirs, and Other Writings, Barracoon*

Zora Neale Hurston was a novelist and anthropologist, a member of the Harlem Renaissance. Her most popular novel is *Their Eyes Were Watching God* (1937). By the time she died her books were out of print and she was destitute, living in a poorhouse in Ft. Pierce, Florida. She was buried in an unmarked grave in a little cemetery, the Garden of Heavenly Rest.

The tomb remained unmarked for thirteen years until Georgia-born novelist Alice Walker located it and had a tombstone erected 15 August 1973. The epitaph on her grave in Ft. Pierce, Florida, reads

> Zora Neale Hurston
> A Genius of the South
> 1901 — — —1960
> Novelist Folklorist Anthropologist

(The birth date on the tombstone is wrong.)

Walker's action of placing a tombstone at Hurston's grave led to a revival of interest in Hurston's work. She published the essay "In Search of Zora Neale Hurston" in *Ms.* magazine in March 1975. Walker wrote that she went into the snaky cemetery and shouted, "Zora!" and decided that she had found the right spot when her shoe sank into the soil. This article did much to revive interest in Hurston's work.

Julia Peterkin
(1880–1961)

Born 31 October 1880, near Gray Court, Laurens County SC
Died 1 August 1961, Orangeburg SC
Buried: Peterkin, Fort Motte SC

Works: *Scarlet Sister Mary, Green Thursday, Black April, Roll, Jordan, Roll, Bright Skin, A Plantation Christmas, The Collected Stories of Julia Peterkin*

Julia Alma Mood Peterkin possessed a sure gift of storytelling, although she was educated in music—she had earned two degrees by the time she was 17 at Converse College in Spartanburg, South Carolina. In 1903, she married planter William George Peterkin of Fort Motte, South Carolina, and settled down as mistress of Lang Syne Plantation. When boredom set in, Peterkin turned again to music; she began piano lessons with Henry Bellamann, dean of fine arts at Chicora College, forty miles away in Columbia. She alternately amused and startled Bellamann with her tales of plantation life.

Encouraged by Bellamann, Carl Sandburg, and H.L. Mencken, she began writing and submitting sketches for publication. Mencken accepted her work for his own little magazine, *Smart Set* (1921). Peterkin also in 1921 published short pieces in *The Reviewer*, and in 1924 issued a short story collection, *Green Thursday*, an assortment of realistic glimpses into the lives of Gullah-speaking African-Americans who inhabited South Carolina's plantations. Gullah is a dialect common in the Lowcountry of the Carolinas, Georgia, and the Sea Islands.

Peterkin's success with *Green Thursday* prompted three full-length novels: *Black April* (1927), *Scarlet Sister Mary* (1928, which won the 1929 Pulitzer Prize in fiction), and *Bright Skin* (1932). A sociological study of the Gullah-speaking people, with photographs by Doris Ulmann, *Roll, Jordan, Roll*, appeared in 1933. In 1934, Peterkin's last major literary effort, *A Plantation Christmas*, was published. All her works ignited controversy in the South in the 1920s and 1930s. In some areas, her books were banned from public libraries.

Peterkin taught briefly at Bennington College and maintained her association with several literary societies, but she published nothing more after 1937. Her husband's death in 1938 and the suicide of her daughter-in-law in 1941, coupled with farming's tribulations and her own declining health, drastically reduced her public activities. She died in Orangeburg, South Carolina, in 1961, and was buried in the Peterkin family plot across the road from St. Matthew's Episcopal Church in Fort Motte.

William Faulkner
(1897–1962)

Born 25 September 1897, New Albany MS
Died 6 July 1962, Byhalia MS
Buried St Peter's, Oxford MS

Works: *Soldiers' Pay, Mosquitoes, Sartoris (Flags in the Dust), The Sound and the Fury, As I Lay Dying, Sanctuary, Light in August, Pylon, Absalom, Absalom!, The Unvanquished, The Wild Palms (If I Forget Thee, Jerusalem), The Hamlet, Go Down, Moses, Intruder in the Dust, Requiem for a Nun, A Fable, The Town, The Mansion, The Reivers, Knight's Gambit, Big Woods, Dr. Martino and Other Stories, These Thirteen, Collected Stories, Uncollected Stories, Essays, Speeches, and Public Letters*

William Cuthbert Falkner (later Faulkner) was born in 1897 in New Albany, Mississippi. In 1902 the family moved to Oxford, seat of the state's flagship university. A high school dropout, he enlisted in the Royal Air Force of Canada, but World War I ended before he could see combat. He briefly attended the University of Mississippi. His friend Phil Stone encouraged Faulkner to read the works of Freud, Proust, Mann, Joyce, Pound, Stein, and Eliot. A short tour of Europe in 1925 further acquainted him with modern tendencies in art, music, and literature. In 1929 Estelle Oldham Franklin and Faulkner wed, although the marriage was an unhappy one.

The year 1929 also marked the beginning of a golden period in Faulkner's career with the appearance of *The Sound and the Fury*. Other masterpieces ensued, including *As I Lay Dying* (1930), *Sanctuary* (1931), *Light in August* (1932), *Absalom, Absalom!* (1936), *The Unvanquished* (1938), *The Wild Palms* (1939), *The Hamlet* (1940), and *Go Down, Moses* (1942). Only *Sanctuary* was a commercial success, and Faulkner spent long stretches in Hollywood churning out screenplays he considered a waste of his talent. In 1950 Faulkner was awarded the Nobel Prize for Literature. He continued to write, earning the 1955 Pulitzer Prize for *A Fable* (1954). *The Town* (1957) and *The Mansion* (1959), sequels to *The Hamlet*, followed. During this period he also served as writer-in-residence at the University of Virginia. His last novel, the Pulitzer Prize-winning *The Reivers* (1962), was published just weeks before his death.

In pain after a June, 1962, horseback-riding accident, Faulkner resorted to binge-drinking. He entered Wright's Sanitarium in Byhalia, Mississippi, to undergo treatment, but suffered a fatal heart attack only hours later. Following funeral rites at his restored antebellum mansion, Rowan Oak, Faulkner was buried at St. Peter's Cemetery in Oxford.

Stark Young
(1891–1963)

Born 11 October 1891, Como MS
Died 6 January 1963, New York NY
Buried Friendship, Como MS

Works: *So Red the Rose, Heaven Trees, The Torches Flare, River House, Feliciana, Pavilion*

Stark Young was a playwright, novelist, essayist, and painter, but he was best known as the pre-eminent drama critic of the 1920s and 1930s, when he was the drama critic for *The New Republic*. He was born in Como, Mississippi, and entered the University of Mississippi at the age of 15. He was graduated at 19 and earned a master's from Columbia University in New York at 20 in 1902. He joined the faculty at the University of Mississippi in 1905, but after three years there, he left to go to the University of Texas in Austin.

He started the *Texas Review* and became involved with local theater in Austin. In 1915 he left Texas to teach English at Amherst College. At the age of 40 he decided to pursue a new career as a writer and drama critic. He resigned from Amherst and returned to New York.

He was named editor of *Theater Arts Magazine* and the drama critic for *The New Republic*. His popularity as a drama critic led Adolph Ochs, the owner of the *New York Times*, to offer him the job as the newspaper's lead drama critic in 1924. Young took the job, but quickly soured on the idea of producing his reviews under deadline pressure—often the night of the play's opening. He resigned from the *Times* and returned to *The New Republic*.

In 1923 he wrote *The Flower in Drama*, followed by *Theater Practice* (1926) and *The Theater* (1927). The three books have become standard texts at several schools for actors. Between 1926 and 1934 he wrote four novels about life in Mississippi: *Heaven's Trees* (1926), *The Torches Flare* (1928), *River House* (1929), and *So Red the Rose* (1934). *So Red the Rose* was a best-seller and was considered the best novel about the Civil War until *Gone With the Wind* (1936) swept across the South and the rest of the country.

Young also wrote an essay included in *I'll Take My Stand* (1930), the book published by the Southern Agrarians. In "Not in Memoriam, but in Defense," Young strongly defended Southern culture, its sensitivity, respect for law, fairness to others, and respect for social order. He continued as chief drama critic at *The New Republic* until 1947, when he retired. He wrote his autobiography, *The Pavilion*, in 1951. In 1959 he suffered a stroke while visiting his sister in Austin. Although he recovered partially, his activities were severely curtailed. He died in New York 6 January 1963.

John Faulkner
(1901–1963)

Born 24 September 1901, Ripley MS
Died 28 March 1963, Oxford MS
Buried St. Peter's, Oxford MS

Works: *Men Working, Dollar Cotton, Chooky, Cabin Road, Uncle Good's Girls, The Sin Shouter of Cabin Road, Ain't Gonna Rain No More, Uncle Good's Weekend Party, My Brother Bill: An Affectionate Reminiscence*

William Faulkner's younger brother John Wesley Thompson Faulkner III was born in Ripley, Mississippi, in 1901. After graduating from the University of Mississippi with a civil engineering degree, he served as assistant city engineer in Greenville, Mississippi, and was later employed in Greenwood by the Mississippi State Highway Department. Leaving that position, John Faulkner became a Memphis-based commercial airline pilot.

In 1938 he assumed management of Greenfield, William Faulkner's 320-acre farm located seventeen miles outside Oxford. As another means of income to help support himself and his family, John Faulkner turned to writing. From 1941 until his death, he authored essays, short stories, and novels noted for their use of local color. The novels *Men Working* (1941) and *Dollar Cotton* (1942) are among his best-regarded titles. *My Brother Bill: An Affectionate Reminiscence* (1963), a memoir that chronicles his relationship with his Nobel-laureate sibling, and another novel, *Cabin Road* (1969), appeared posthumously.

He also earned recognition as a lecturer and as a self-taught landscape painter.

John Faulkner died in Oxford on 28 March 1963 and was buried near the old Falkner family plot in St. Peter's Cemetery. His tombstone acknowledges the original spelling of the family name, "FALKNER," on one side, and the spelling that he and his more famous brother adopted, "FAULKNER," on the reverse.

For many years John Faulkner and his family occupied a stately Victorian mansion at 406 University Avenue in Oxford. Built in 1837, Memory House is one of north Mississippi's architectural treasures. Faulkner's sons, Jimmy and Murry (known as "Chooky"), sold the property to the University of Mississippi Foundation in 1992.

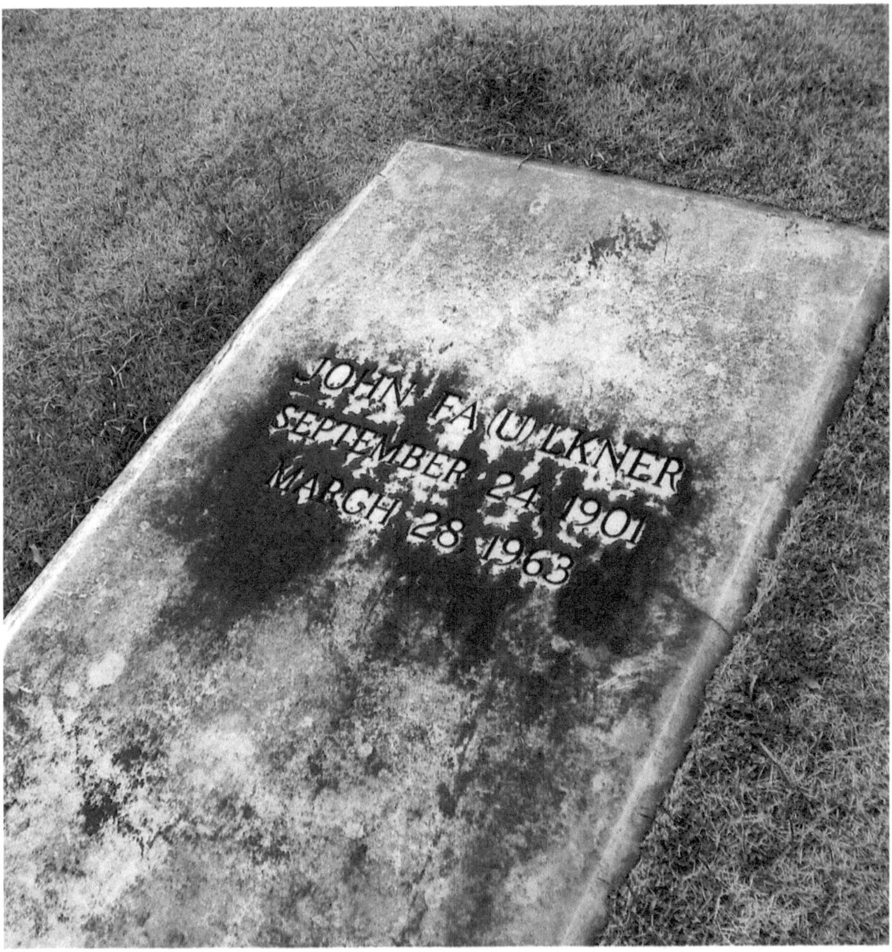
JOHN FA(U)LKNER
SEPTEMBER 24 1901
MARCH 28 1963

Hamilton Basso
(1904–1964)

Born 5 September 1904, New Orleans LA
Died 13 May 1964, New Haven CT
Buried Lyons Plains Cemetery, Weston CT

Works: *Relics and Angels, Beauregard: The Great Creole, In Their Own Image, Courthouse Square, The View from Pompey's Head, A Touch of the Dragon, The Light Infantry Ball, The Greenroom, Sun in Capricorn, Days Before Lent, Wine of the Country, Cinnamon Seed, A Quota of Seaweed, Mainstream, The World From Jackson Square*

Born into an Italian-American family in New Orleans, Hamilton Basso dropped out of Tulane University just shy of an undergraduate degree in Pre-law. Early involvement with his native city's eminent "little magazine," the *Double Dealer*, drew him into a circle of such writers as Oliver LaFarge, Sherwood Anderson, and William Faulkner. A caricature of him, dancing the Charleston with his muse, is included in William Spratling's and Faulkner's book *Sherwood Anderson and Other Famous Creoles* (1927).

After a short career as a newspaperman in New Orleans, Basso later wrote for such magazines as *Time*, the *New Republic, Holiday, Life, Saturday Review*, and *The New Yorker*. In the 1930s he lived in Western North Carolina, then traveled and lived in Europe. In 1955 he was elected to the National Institute of Arts and Letters.

Unlike many Southern authors of his generation, Basso was a left-of-center, anti-Agrarian, pro-civil rights figure throughout his adulthood. From 1929 until his death in 1964 he prolifically turned out substantive novels and other prose works. *The View from Pompey's Head* (1954), set in South Carolina, was a best-seller and the basis for a successful movie. A prequel, *The Light Infantry Ball* (1959), was a finalist for the 1960 National Book Award.

Basso died on 13 May 1964 in New Haven, Connecticut, and was interred at Emmanuel Episcopal Church in nearby Weston.

Flannery O'Connor (1925–1964)

Born 25 March 1925, Savannah GA
Died 3 August 1964, Milledgeville GA
Buried Memory Hill, Milledgeville GA

Works: *Wise Blood, A Good Man is Hard to Find, The Violent Bear It Away, Everything that Rises Must Converge, Mystery and Manners: Occasional Prose, The Complete Stories, The Habit of Being, A Memoir of Mary Ann*

Mary Flannery O'Connor was born into a devout Irish Catholic family in Savannah, Georgia, in 1925. In her native city she attended parochial school before the O'Connors moved to Atlanta and then to Milledgeville. Upon being graduated from Baldwin County High School, she entered Georgia State College for Women ("GSCW," as it was known for many years, now Georgia College and State University), earning her bachelor's degree in 1945. She had already decided upon a literary career. Accordingly, Miss O'Connor enrolled in the Writer's Workshop at the University of Iowa, where she studied under Paul Engle and her fellow Southerner, Andrew Nelson Lytle, and received in 1947 the Master of Fine Arts diploma.

She moved to the Northeast, with the idea that being close to the publishing industry in New York would be beneficial to her professionally. But a mysterious illness—later identified as disseminated lupus erythematosus, the disease that had taken her father's life in 1941—struck her down in the early 1950s, and she was forced to move back to Georgia and live on the family farm, Andalusia, with her mother. There she remained for the rest of her life. But it was a productive life; she lived to see two novels (*Wise Blood* [1952] and *The Violent Bear It Away* [1960]), a short story collection (*A Good Man is Hard to Find* [1955]), and a number of essays and sketches published. She was an inveterate reader—every subject from history to politics to theology captured her interest—and a brilliant letter-writer. As long as her health permitted, she traveled throughout the United States to present lectures at literary conferences, and even made a pilgrimage to the shrine at Lourdes in France. Miss O'Connor died on 3 August 1964.

After the requiem mass at Milledgeville's Sacred Heart Church, she was buried under an imposing white marble slab in her family's plot at Memory Hill Cemetery. Another short story collection, *Everything That Rises Must Converge*, was issued in 1965, and *The Collected Stories* (1971) won the National Book Award. Her excellent letters are collected in *The Habit of Being* (1979).

T. S. Stribling
(1881–1965)

Born 4 March 1881, Clifton TN
Died 8 July 1965, Florence AL
Buried Clifton, Clifton TN

Works: *The Cruise of the Dry Dock, Birthright, East is East, Fombombo, Red Sand, Teeftallow, Bright Metal, Strange Moon, Clues of the Caribees, Backwater, The Forge, The Store, The Unfinished Cathedral, The Sound Wagon, These Bars of Flesh, Laughing Stock: The Posthumous Autobiography of T. S. Stribling*

Thomas Sigismund Stribling was born in Clifton, Tennessee, on 4 March 1881. Although raised in Clifton, he often visited his maternal grandparents on their farm in Gravelly Springs, Alabama. These formative years in northern Alabama were very influential on Stribling, who used the setting and the characters he encountered there to help create his written view of Southern life.

He first attended school at the Clifton Masonic Academy. There, at the age of 12, he became a "professional" writer, earning the sum of $5 for writing and selling his first story, "The House of Haunted Shadows." He received further education at Huntingdon Southern Normal University in Huntingdon, Tennessee, for one year. He completed his education at the Florence Normal School (now the University of North Alabama) in 1903. After graduation, he moved to Tuscaloosa to teach high school, and he later was graduated from the University of Alabama Law School. His law career was brief, and after a move to Nashville, he began working as a writer full-time.

His notable works include his first novel, *The Cruise of the Dry Dock* (1917), *Birthright* (1922), and *Teeftallow* (1926). *The Store* (1932), Stribling's tale of life in post-Reconstruction South, received the 1933 Pulitzer Prize. Stribling continued to write for the rest of his life; it was even rumored that he wrote some of the episodes for the *Little Rascals*. He died 8 July 1965, at Mitchell-Hollingsworth Annex in Florence. He was buried in his hometown of Clifton, where the inscription on his tombstone reads, "Through This Dust These Hills Once Spoke."

Randall Jarrell
(1914–1965)

Born 6 May 1914, Nashville TN
Died 14 October 1965, Chapel Hill NC
Buried New Garden Friends Cemetery, Greensboro NC

Works: *Blood from a Stranger, Little Friend, Little Friend, Losses, Poetry and the Age, The Woman at the Washington Zoo, The Lost World, Pictures from an Institution, The Bat-Poet. The Animal Family*

Randall Jarrell attended Vanderbilt University in his hometown, where he was a student of John Crowe Ransom. When Ransom took a teaching position at Kenyon College, Jarrell followed.

At Kenyon Jarrell roomed with poet Robert Lowell.

Jarrell later befriended Peter Taylor, and the two writers and their wives bought a duplex together in Greensboro when they taught together at Greensboro Women's Institute, which later became the University of North Carolina at Greensboro.

In 1965, Jarrell accepted a visiting professorship at the University of North Carolina at Chapel Hill. Family members, friends, and biographers have speculated whether his death, as a result of being struck by a car in Chapel Hill, was a suicide, since he had made previous attempts and was being treated for depression.

The driver reported that Jarrell had lurched in front of the car, making it impossible to miss him, but his death was ruled accidental.

Jarrell's grave is situated between those of his wife and mother-in-law, three ledger stones under a large tree. It features a crescent and stars motif that was also used on his wife's grave. Jarrell drew the stars-within-crescent image on envelopes of letters to his wife, "physically impossible though spiritually so."

In this peaceful, bucolic setting in a Quaker cemetery in Greensboro, visitors may find it ironic to recall that Jarrell's best-known work is "The Death of the Ball-Turret Gunner," a graphic reminder of the gruesome nature of aerial combat during World War II.

Hubert Creekmore
(1907–1966)

Born 16 Jan 1907, Water Valley MS
Died 23 May 1966, New York, NY
Buried Lakewood, Jackson MS

Works: *Personal Sun: The Early Poems of Hubert Creekmore*, "The Stone Ants," *The Fingers of Night, The Long Reprieve, and Other Poems of New Caledonia, Formula, The Welcome,* translator of *Erotic Elegies of Albius Tibulus, with Poems of Sulpicia Arranged as a Sequence Called No Harm to Lovers,* ed., *A Little Treasury of World Poetry: Translations from the Great Poems of Other Languages, The Chain in the Heart,* ed. and trans., *Satires of Decimus Junius Juvenalis, Daffodils are Dangerous*

Hiram Hubert Creekmore, Jr., grew up in Water Valley, Mississippi, and was graduated from the University of Mississippi. He studied drama at the University of Colorado and playwriting at Yale University. He obtained a master's degree from Columbia University in New York.

He was related to Eudora Welty by marriage and was known as her friend and advisor. Both Creekmore and Welty were involved with the Federal Writers' Project in Mississippi during the Great Depression, collecting folklore and history about the state and its culture.

He published a volume of poems, *Personal Sun, the Early Poems of Hubert Creekmore* (1940), but the collection drew little notice.

He served in the Navy during World War II, spending most of his time in the Pacific Theater. He continued writing during his military service, including one of his better-known poems, "The Long Reprieve" (1946). After his release from military service, Creekmore returned to New York. He was prolific as a translator, but he also wrote of poor white Mississippians and poor African-Americans battered daily by a Jim Crow South.

His first novel, *Fingers of the Night* (1946), depicted a young Southern girl's tormented experience with religious fundamentalism. *The Welcome* (1948) portrayed the psychological crises for outsiders attempting to cope with Southern culture.

Creekmore also enjoyed success as a book reviewer and occasional critic for the *New York Times*.

He was a life-long gardener, and his last book, *Daffodils Are Dangerous* (1966), surveyed plants and flowers known for their surface beauty but which contain deadly toxins. For Creekmore, the flowers were analogous to the South and its culture.

He collapsed and died in a taxi on his way to catch a flight to Spain on 23 May 1966.

Lillian Smith
(1897–1966)

Born 12 December 1897, Jasper FL
Died 28 December 1966, Atlanta GA
Buried Lillian E. Smith Center, Clayton GA

Works: *Strange Fruit, Killers of the Dream, The Journey, Now Is the Time, One Hour, Memory of a Large Christmas, Or Faces, Our Words*

Lillian Eugenia Smith was born on 12 December 1897 in Jasper, Florida. In 1915, she moved to Clayton, Georgia, after her father's sudden death. There she left a profound effect on the young girls she taught at the Laurel Falls Camp her family owned. Smith was a pioneer activist against segregation and racism.

Her career as a writer began with *Pseudopodia*, the small literary magazine she co-edited. Her national fame came after the publication of *Strange Fruit* (1944), which has been translated into 15 languages. She continued to oppose racism through her non-fiction work, which included *Killers of the Dream* (1949), *Now Is the Time* (1955), and *Memory of a Large Christmas* (1962).

In May 1960, Dr. Martin Luther King, Jr., was stopped by a DeKalb County policeman when he was driving Smith back to Emory University, where she was being treated for cancer. He was charged with driving without a license and placed on probation. That October King was arrested for refusing to leave a restaurant in Rich's department store in Atlanta. Because he was still on probation, he was placed in solitary confinement in the state prison in Reidsville until U. S. Senator John F. Kennedy intervened on his behalf.

In an acceptance speech for the Charles S. Johnson Award at Fisk University in 1966, Smith stated, "Segregation is evil; there is no pattern of life which can dehumanize men as can the way of segregation."

Lillian Smith died on 28 September 1966 at the age of 68. A stone fireplace, rescued from a barn fire, now serves as Smith's grave marker. A bronze plaque beside the chimney bears her epitaph: "Death can kill a man; that is all it can do to him; it cannot end his life, because of memory – "

Carson McCullers
(1917–1967)

Born 19 February 1917, Columbus GA
Died 29 September 1967, Nyack NY
Buried Oak Hill Cemetery, Nyack NY

Works: *The Heart is a Lonely Hunter, Reflections in a Golden Eye, Clock Without Hands, The Member of the Wedding, The Ballad of the Sad Café and Other Works, The Member of the Wedding* (play), *The Ballad of the Sad Café and Collected Short Stories, The Square Root of Wonderful, Sweet as a Pickle and Clean as a Pig, The Mortgaged Heart*

Born Lula Carson Smith in Columbus, Georgia, she lost $500 on arriving in New York City to study music at the Juilliard School. She then enrolled in creative writing classes at Columbia University, and enjoyed early success. *The Heart is a Lonely Hunter* was published to widespread acclaim in 1940.

She became the darling of writers' workshops at Bread Loaf and Yaddo, and befriended such fellow Southern writers as Tennessee Williams. At these writers' retreats, McCullers would sometimes cause scenes, upsetting the serenity of the enterprise; her tomboyish appearance and disrespectful behavior generated some resentment, especially with Katherine Anne Porter and Eudora Welty.

During the 1940s McCullers shared a literary salon in Brooklyn, New York, at 7 Middagh Street, variously with W. H. Auden, Paul and Jane Bowles, Benjamin Britten, Richard Wright, and Gypsy Rose Lee.

Her own adaptation of her novel *The Member of the Wedding* (1946) enjoyed a very successful Broadway run beginning in 1949, followed by a national tour.

Her personal life was troubled.

She twice married Reeves McCullers, who committed suicide in 1953, and she was involved in several extramarital relationships. From the 1950s on, the increasingly chemically-dependent McCullers suffered a number of strokes, and spent her final years bedridden, cared for by her mother at the home they shared in Nyack, New York.

Donald Davidson
(1893–1968)

Born 18 August 1893, Campbellsville TN
Died 25 April 1968, Nashville TN
Buried Calvary, Nashville TN

Works: *An Outland Piper, The Tall Men, British Poetry of the Eighteen-Nineties, The Attack on Leviathan, American Composition and Rhetoric, Readings for Composition from Prose Models, The Tennessee, Twenty Lessons in Reading and Writing Prose, Still Rebels, Still Yankees, Southern Writers in the Modern World, The Long Street, The Spyglass: Views and Reviews, Poems 1922-1961, Selected Essays and Other Writings of John Donald Wade*

Donald Grady Davidson was a veteran of World War I and a faculty member at Vanderbilt University when he became a founder of the Fugitives, a group of students and faculty members who met regularly to discuss and critique poetry and writing.

As one of the older Fugitives, he took a lead role as the group evolved into what became the Southern Agrarians, who bemoaned the loss of Southern culture and the industrialization of the country. A leader in the publication of *I'll Take My Stand* (1930), a defense of the Southern way of life, he was a staunch segregationist. He believed that African-Americans were genetically inferior to white people. In the 1950s, after several of the original Southern Agrarians had repudiated their former views supporting segregation, he formed the Tennessee Federation for Constitutional Government, somewhat patterned on the White Citizens Council in other states.

Davidson spent his entire teaching career at Vanderbilt, and from 1923 to 1930 he also edited the book page for the *Tennessean*, Nashville's largest daily newspaper. His critical reviews were syndicated by the newspaper. Davidson's masterwork was his two-volume history of the Tennessee River, *The Tennessee*, in the *Rivers of America* series. The volumes were published in 1946 and 1948. In the second volume, he leveled strong criticisms against the Tennessee Valley Authority, which had transformed much of Tennessee's old economic base from one principally defined by agriculture to one of a highly diversified industrial state.

Though the history was superb, Davidson's importance has been adversely affected by his segregationist mindset and racist views.

He died 25 April 1968 in Nashville.

Katherine Drayton Mayrant Simons
(1890–1969)

Born 21 January 1890, Charleston SC
Died 31 March 1969, Charleston SC
Buried Magnolia, Charleston SC

Works: *Shadow Songs, The Patteran, Stories of Charleston Harbor, A Sword from Galway, The Running Thread, First the Blade, White Horse Leaping, Courage is not Given, The Red Doe, Always a River, Lamp in Jerusalem, The Land Before the Tempest*

The family of Katherine Drayton Mayrant Simons had its roots in the Carolina Lowcountry for at least 170 years before she was born in 1890. She was the oldest of four children born to Sedgewick Lewis Simons and Katherine Drayton Mayrant Simons. Her mother was descended from generations of French Huguenots.

She was graduated from Converse College, a college for women in Spartanburg, South Carolina, and began what would become a prolific career as a writer. She wrote nine historical novels under the pen names of Drayton Mayrante and Drayton Mayrant. She also wrote a large volume of poetry exotically signed, "Kadra Maysi."

Simons did not explain why she had chosen her pen names, but apparently favored Drayton Mayrant for her historical novels to mask her gender as a writer about soldiers and conflicts. Two of her novels won national book club awards.

In her later years, she wrote poems under her own name. She also wrote at least one play, *Bewley's Bewitched*, a ghost-story comedy set along a waterway in Georgia.

Miss Simons was an early subscriber to the Poetry Society of South Carolina (and its first female president, elected in 1964), and an active member of Charleston's John Doyle Writing Group, through which she offered generous encouragement to younger poets. In addition, she published many articles on local history, particularly the lineage of old families of the Lowcountry and the homes from which the families ruled their estates. She was a contributing editor to the journal *Names in South Carolina*.

She was not noted as an activist, but she was a staunch defender of Charleston "as it is," and opposed re-zonings and new construction in the city's historic district. In 1948 Simons wrote a letter to the editor of the *News and Courier*, Charleston's daily newspaper, in which she threatened to leave the city if a large apartment building was approved for construction on Meeting Street.

Her death in 1969 marked the end of a notable literary epoch in the artistic chronicle of Charleston. She was buried at Magnolia Cemetery.

John Kennedy Toole
(1937–1969)

Born 17 December 1937, New Orleans LA
Died 26 March 1969, New Orleans LA
Buried Greenwood, New Orleans LA

Works: A *Confederacy of Dunces*, *The Neon Bible*

John Kennedy Toole was born 17 December 1937, and lived a sheltered childhood in New Orleans. Toole's father worked as an automobile salesman and a mechanic, and his mother was a dominating woman who was convinced that her son was a genius and rarely let him play with other children.

After high school, Toole attended Tulane and graduated with a degree in English. He later earned a master's degree from Columbia University. He then taught at both Hunter College in New York and the University of Southwestern Louisiana. In 1961, while pursuing a doctorate at Columbia, he was drafted into the Army, where he served for two years as an English teacher to Spanish-speaking recruits. During this time he began a novel that would, in its final form, become *A Confederacy of Dunces*.

Post-Army, Toole returned to his parents' home in New Orleans and taught at Dominican College. In New Orleans he completed *A Confederacy of Dunces* and considered it a masterpiece, sending it to Simon and Schuster, hoping for publication, only to meet rejection. This perceived failure, combined with the stress of caring for his elderly parents, caused Toole to drink heavily and deteriorate in health. He disappeared after arguing with his mother in late January 1969. On 26 March 1969 he committed suicide on the way home to New Orleans after a month-long cross-country road trip that included a stop at the former home of Flannery O'Connor.

Following his death, Toole's mother and author Walker Percy campaigned for the publication of *A Confederacy of Dunces* (1980). In 1981, Toole was posthumously awarded the Pulitzer Prize. One other Toole novel, written when the author was only 16, appeared in print in 1989; titled *The Neon Bible*, it was adapted for a film version in 1995.

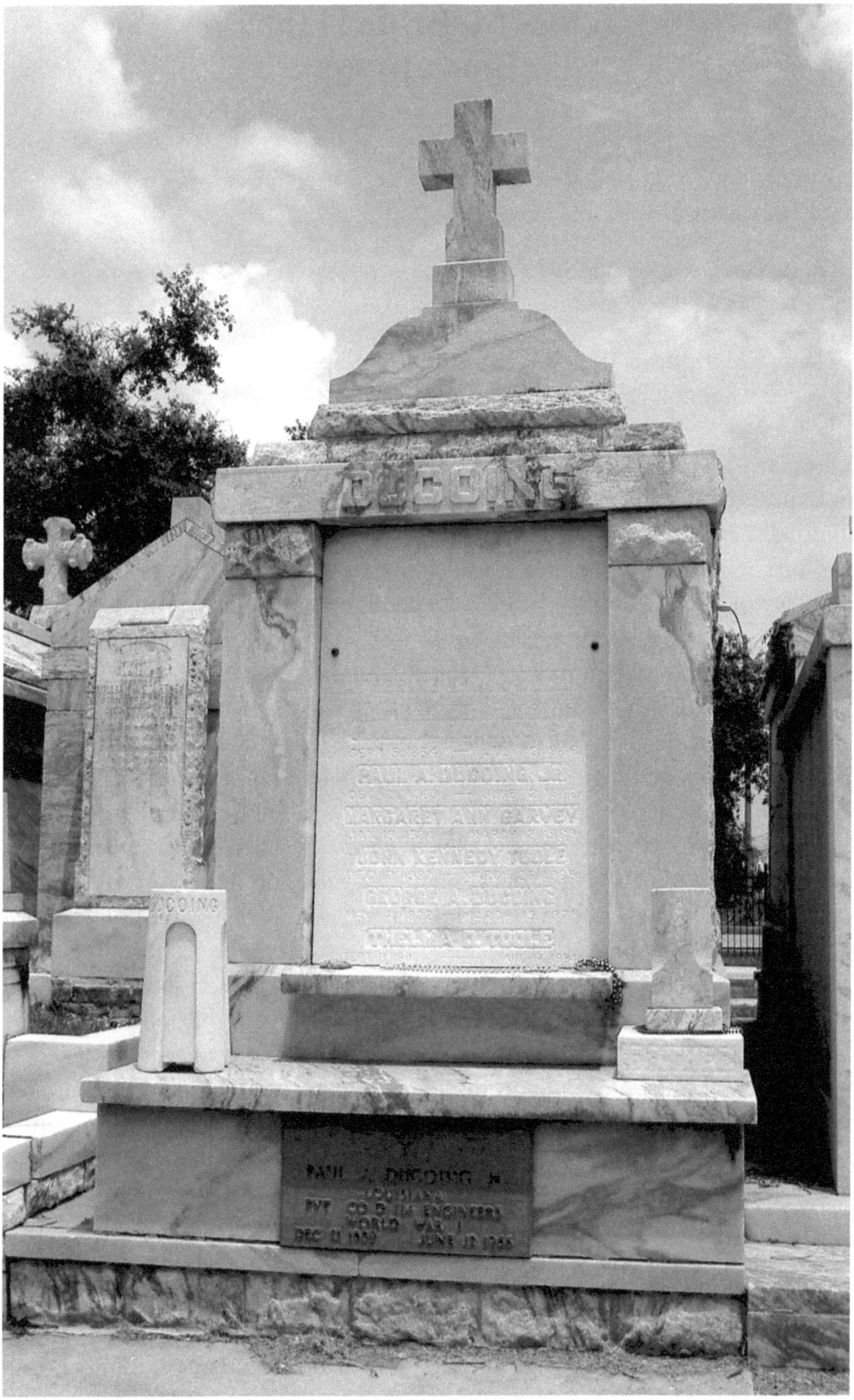
DUCOING
MARGARET ANN GARVEY
JOHN KENNEDY TOOLE
THELMA D. TOOLE
DUCOING

James McBride Dabbs
(1896–1970)

Born 8 May 1896, Mayesville SC
Died 30 May 1970, Mayesville SC
Buried Salem Black River, near Mayesville SC

Works: *Pee Dee Panorama, Who Speaks for the South?, The Southern Heritage, Haunted by God, Pee Dee Panorama Revisited, The Road Home, Civil Rights in Recent Southern Fiction*

James McBride Dabbs was born at Rip Raps, his family's plantation near Mayesville, Sumter County, South Carolina, in 1896. He was educated at the University of South Carolina, Clark University (Worcester, Massachusetts), and Columbia University. During World War I he served in France with the American Expeditionary Force, and afterwards was briefly a student at the University of Edinburgh. He returned to the U.S. in the summer of 1919. Dabbs directed the Farm Life School in Vass, North Carolina, before taking a teaching position at the University of South Carolina. In 1925 he became chair of the Department of English at Coker College in Hartsville, South Carolina, a post he held until 1937. In 1942 he retired from teaching and spent the rest of his life at Rip Raps Plantation.

Dabbs's years away from the college classroom were hardly idle. He reared a family, farmed, lectured, read widely, published prolifically, and maintained a correspondence with religious leaders, civil rights activists, and such fellow Southern authors as Eudora Welty, Hodding Carter, and Paul Green. Committed to progressive causes, he joined the Delta Ministry of Mississippi, served as chair of the South Carolina Council on Human Relations, presided over the Southern Regional Council, and headed the board of trustees of Penn Community Services. The National Conference of Christians and Jews conferred on Dabbs its Brotherhood Award for his book *Southern Heritage* in 1958. In recognition of his writings calling for social and economic justice and racial equality in the South, he received honorary degrees from Morehouse College and Tuskegee University.

In his well-known "Letter from a Birmingham Jail" (1963), the Reverend Martin Luther King, Jr., wrote, "I am thankful that some of our white brothers in the South have grasped the meaning of this social revolution and committed themselves to it. They are still all too few in quantity, but they are big in quality. Some—such as Ralph McGill, Lillian Smith, Harry Golden, James McBride Dabbs, Ann Braden, and Sarah Patton Boyle—have written about our struggle in eloquent and prophetic terms."

Dabbs died shortly after his seventy-fourth birthday in 1970. He was buried near his home, at picturesque Salem Black River Presbyterian Church, a historic congregation he had faithfully served as ruling elder and Sunday school teacher. His epitaph reads as follows (beneath the photograph on the facing page):

A gentle man of uncommon strength and urbanity.
Born at Salem Black River, where he spent much of his
life and served this church as clerk of the Session
from 1937 until his death.
He was a scholar and poet, known for devotion
to the South and dedication to making it better.
He loved the time in which he lived, and while he
knew perfection unattainable, championed justice
and truth. He was a writer and farmer, his home
a home to students and leaders in human affairs.
He was a Southerner, one who belonged to all mankind,
who traveled far and returned.
He was understanding and love, and love, like God, endures forever.

Hodding Carter
(1907–1972)

Born 3 February 1907, Hammond LA
Died 4 April 1972, Greenville MS
Buried Greenville Cemetery, Greenville MS

Works: *The Winds of Fear, Southern Legacy, John Law Wasn't So Wrong: The Story of Louisiana's Horn of Plenty, Where Main Street Meets the River, Robert E. Lee and the Road of Honor, So Great a Good, Marquis de Lafayette: Bright Sword for Freedom, The Angry Scar: The Story of Reconstruction, First Person Rural, The Ballad of Catfoot Grimes and Other Verses, So the Heffners Left McComb, The Commandos of World War II, Their Words Were Bullets: The Southern Press in War, Reconstruction, and Peace*

Hodding Carter was principally known as a crusading journalist. In his hometown of Hammond, Louisiana, he edited the *Daily Courier*, and railed against the abuses of Huey Long.

Later, backed by Greenville, Mississippi, investors including William Alexander Percy, he became the editor of the Greenville *Delta Democrat-Times*, noted for its progressive views, and opposition to Senator Theodore Bilbo and the White Citizens Council.

He received the Pulitzer Prize in 1946 after writing a series of editorials complaining of the mistreatment of the Nisei, Japanese-American soldiers returning after World War II.

Carter was censured by the Mississippi legislature in 1955 for his criticism of the White Citizens Council in *Look* magazine. He responded with a front-page editorial in the *Democrat-Times,* telling the 89 legislators who had voted for the censure to "go to hell collectively or singly and wait there until I back down."

Carter also started a small press with Ben Wasson and Kenneth Haxton, called the Levee Press, which produced signed, limited editions of stories by William Faulkner, Eudora Welty, William Alexander Percy, and Shelby Foote.

Carter died from a heart attack at the age of 65, and was buried at Greenville Cemetery.

Arna Wendell Bontemps
(1902–1973)

Born 13 October 1902, Alexandria LA
Died 4 June 1973, Nashville TN
Buried Greenwood, Nashville TN

Works: *God Sends Sunday, Popo and Fifina: Children of Haiti* with Langston Hughes, *You Can't Pet a Possum, Black Thunder, Sad-Faced Boy, Drums at Dusk,* ed. *Golden Slippers: An Anthology of Negro Poetry for Young People, Father of the Blues: The Autobiography of William C. Handy* with Handy, *The Fast Sooner Hound* with Jack Conroy, *We Have Tomorrow, They Seek a City* with Jack Conroy, *Anyplace But Here, Slappy Hooper: The Wonderful Sign Painter* with Jack Conroy, *The Story of the Negro, The Poetry of the Negro: 1746-1949* with Langston Hughes, *George Washington Carver, Chariot in the Sky, Sam Patch, the High, Wide, and Handsome Jumper* with Jack Conroy, *Lonesome Boy, Frederick Douglas: Slave Fighter, The Book of American Negro Folklore* with Langston Hughes, *100 Years of Negro Freedom, American Negro Poetry, Personals, Famous Negro Athletes,* ed. *Hold Fast to Dreams,* ed. *Great Slave Narratives,* ed. *The Harlem Renaissance Remembered, The Old South: 'A Summer Tragedy" and Other Stories of the Thirties*

Best known for the widely anthologized short story "A Summer Tragedy," Arnaud Wendell "Arna" Bontemps was born in Alexandria, Louisiana, in 1902. The Bontemps family subsequently moved to California. Following graduation from Union Pacific College, Arna Bontemps secured a teaching position in New York, and was soon involved in the Harlem Renaissance.

He numbered among his literary friends Langston Hughes, Countee Cullen, and Jack Conroy. His first novel, *God Sends Sunday*, appeared in 1931, and was the basis for *St. Louis Woman*, a stage musical produced in 1946 in which Pearl Bailey made her debut.

Following a teaching stint in Alabama and graduate work at the University of Chicago, Bontemps was employed as a librarian at Fisk University in Nashville for 22 years. He later taught at the University of Illinois and at Yale, where he also oversaw the James Weldon Johnson archives. Throughout his adulthood he maintained a steady regimen of writing and editing (including W.C. Handy's autobiography, *Father of the Blues* [1941]).

Retiring to Nashville, he died in 1973, and was buried in that city's Greenwood Cemetery.

Conrad Aiken
(1889–1973)

Born 5 August 1889, Savannah GA
Died 17 August 1973, Savannah GA
Buried Bonaventure, Savannah GA

Works: *The Great Circle, Earth Triumphant, The Charnel Rose, And In the Hanging Gardens, Selected Poems, Ushant, Scepticisms: Notes on Contemporary Poetry, The Jig of Forslin, King Coffin, Collected Short Stories, A Reviewer's ABC: Collected Criticism of Conrad Aiken from 1916 to the Present, Nocturne of Remembered Spring*

Conrad Aiken was ten years old when he found the bodies of his parents. They died in a murder-suicide at their home in Savannah, Georgia, 27 February 1901. Young Conrad was sent to live with his mother's family in Massachusetts. Educated at Harvard, where he co-edited the *Advocate* with T. S. Eliot, he spent most of his productive years as a poet, critic, and short-story writer in New England and Great Britain.

Two of Aiken's best stories are "Strange Moonlight" (set in Savannah) and "Silent Snow, Secret Snow"; the latter was the basis of a memorable episode on NBC-TV's *Night Gallery*. His *Selected Poems* (1929) won the Pulitzer Prize for poetry in 1930. He also received the Bollingen Prize, the National Medal for Literature, the Gold Medal for Poetry from the National Institute of Arts and Letters, and the National Book Award. He was a champion of the poetry of Emily Dickinson.

In his final years he returned to his native city, occupying a residence next door to the house where he had discovered his parents' bodies. Aiken was awarded the National Medal for Literature in 1969. Gov. Jimmy Carter named Aiken Poet Laureate of Georgia shortly before his death in 1973.

He was buried in Section H of Bonaventure Cemetery beside the graves of his mother and father. Aiken is said to have wanted visitors to have a drink "on him," and a stone bench at the site—inscribed "COSMOS MARINER / DESTINATION UNKNOWN"—awaits them. The grave marker is mentioned in John Berendt's Savannah novel, *Midnight in the Garden of Good and Evil* (1994), and is a local landmark.

Archibald Rutledge
(1883–1973)

Born 23 October 1883, McClellanville SC
Died 15 September 1973, McClellanville SC
Buried Camellia garden, Hampton Plantation SC

Works: *The Heart's Quest, Under the Pines, and Other Poems, The Banners of the Coast, Spirit of Mercersburg, New Poems, Tom and I on the Old Plantation, Songs from a Valley, Old Plantation Days, Plantation Game Trails, South of Richmond, Days Off in Dixie, Heart of the South, Collected Poems, A Monarch of the Sky, Children of Swamp and Wood, Life's Extras, Bolio and Other Dogs, The Flower of Hope, Peace in the Heart, Veiled Eros, When Boys Go Off to School, Wild Life in the South, Brimming Chalice, An American Hunter, My Colonel and His Lady, It Will be Daybreak Soon, The Sonnets of Archibald Rutledge, Rain on the Marsh, Christ is God, Home by the River, Love's Meaning, Hunter's Choice, The Beauty of the Night, God's Children, The Angel Standing; or, Faith Alone Gives Poise, The Everlasting Light and Other Poems, A Wildwood Tale: A Drama of the Open, Beauty in the Heart, The Heart's Citadel and Other Poems, Brimming Tide and Other Poems, Those Were the Days, Bright Angel and Other Poems, Santee Paradise, From the Hills to the Sea: Fact and Legend of the Carolinas, Deep River: The Complete Poems of Archibald Rutledge, The World Around Hampton, The Ballad of the Howling Hound and Other Poems, Willie Was a Lady, How Wild Was My Village, I Hear America Singing, Poems in Honor of South Carolina's Tricentennial, The Woods and Wild Things I Remember, Voices of the Long Ago: Bible Stories Retold*

Although born into South Carolina's aristocracy—an ancestor signed the Declaration of Independence—Rutledge maintained modest ways throughout his long life. After passing his early years at his family's Hampton Plantation, he entered Porter Military Academy in Charleston, where he began writing poetry and essays. At sixteen he enrolled at Union College in New York, from which he was graduated in 1904. Following stints in sales and journalism, he taught at Mercersburg Academy in Pennsylvania. Acclaimed for his nature writing, poetry, and devotional literature, Rutledge was named South Carolina's first poet laureate in 1934.

Leaving Pennsylvania in 1937, he returned to Hampton Plantation, laboring to restore its eighteenth-century grandeur and writing prolifically. During his career Rutledge authored nearly sixty books. At his death in 1973, the twice-widowed Rutledge was deeply mourned. Currently his books are little read outside South Carolina. While his devotional writings still inspire readers and his meditations on Southern landscapes are vividly detailed, the racial attitudes that surface in some of his works belong to a bygone era. Nonetheless, the lyrical beauty Rutledge's poetry and prose exude in depicting his beloved native state attests to his unquestionable literary gifts. Rutledge died just shy of 90 years at Summer Place, the house where he had been born.

John Crowe Ransom
(1888–1974)

Born 30 April 1888, Pulaski TN
Died 3 July 1974, Gambier OH
Buried Kenyon College Cemetery, Gambier OH

Works: *Poems About God, Chills and Fever, Grace After Meat, Two Gentlemen in Bonds, God Without Thunder, The World's Body, The New Criticism, Selected Poems, Poems and Essays, Selected Poems, Beating the Bushes*

Born on 30 April 1888 in Pulaski, Tennessee, the son of a Methodist minister, John Crowe Ransom was the third of five children. He was reared in a strongly religious, yet open-minded household. Ransom entered Vanderbilt University in Nashville, Tennessee, at 15. After having been graduated in 1909, he studied as a Rhodes Scholar at Oxford from 1910-1913, and was appointed an instructor in Vanderbilt's English department in 1914. His first book, *Poems about God*, was completed in 1919 while serving as an artillery officer in France during World War I.

He married Robb Reavill in 1920, and later they had three children. During the years of 1922-1927, Ransom produced several poetic works, including his best-known poem, "Bells for John Whiteside's Daughter" (1924). Although he continued to write and critique poetry throughout his long career, the output of his work from 1922-1925, as publisher of *The Fugitive* magazine, legitimized his status as a poet and theoretical literary critic. As a guiding member of the Fugitives, he sought to preserve a traditional aesthetic ideal, as portrayed by a collection of essays called *I'll Take My Stand: The South and the Agrarian Tradition*, written by Ransom and 11 other Southern poets in 1930.

He later retreated from his agrarian position. Ransom remained at Vanderbilt until 1937, at which time he moved to Kenyon College in Ohio. There he became editor of *The Kenyon Review* from 1939-1959. His book of essays called *The New Criticism*, published in 1941, explained to readers how they should critique literature. Ransom won the Bollingen Prize in Poetry in 1951 and the National Book Award in 1964 for *Selected Poems* (1963). He died in his sleep on 3 July 1974 in Gambier, Ohio.

A memorial more picturesque than his grave marker is Ransom Hall on the Kenyon College campus, with sculpted black crows on the eaves.

Allen Tate
(1899–1979)

Born 19 November 1899, Winchester KY
Died 9 February 1979, Sewanee TN
Buried University Cemetery, Sewanee TN

Works: *The Golden Mean and Other Poems, Mr. Pope and Other Poems, Stonewall Jackson, the Good Soldier: A Narrative, Jefferson Davis, His Rise and Fall: A Biographical Narrative, Poems: 1928-1931, The Mediterranean and Other Selected Poems, Reactionary Essays on Poetry and Ideas, Who Owns America? Another Declaration of Independence, Selected Poems, The Fathers, Reason in Madness: Critical Essays, Sonnets at Christmas, The Winter Sea, Poems: 1920-1945, Poems: 1922-1947, On the Limits of Poetry: Selected Essays, 1928-1948, The Hovering Fly and Other Essays, The Forlorn Demon: Didactic and Critical Essays, The Man of Letters in the Modern World: Selected Essays 1928-1955, Collected Essays, Collected Poems, Essays of Four Decades, The Swimmers and Other Selected Poems, The Literary Correspondence of Donald Davidson and Allen Tate, Memoirs and Opinions, 1926-1974, Collected Poems: 1919-1976, The Poetry Reviews of Allen Tate, 1924-1944, The Lytle-Tate Letters: The Correspondence of Andrew Lytle and Allen Tate, Cleanth Brooks and Allen Tate: Collected Letters, 1933-1976.*

John Orley Allen Tate studied violin at the Cincinnati Conservatory of Music, but left a possible career as a musician to attend Vanderbilt University, where he became the editor of *The Fugitive*. The Fugitives evolved into the Southern Agrarians, concerned with preserving the agrarian traditions in the South and opposing industrialization. Tate contributed to *I'll Take My Stand* (1930), the manifesto of the Southern Agrarians.

In 1924 he moved to New York where he published his most famous poem, "Ode to the Confederate Dead" (1928), and the first two installments of what had been planned as a trilogy on Confederate heroes: *Stonewall Jackson: The Good Soldier* (1928) and *Jefferson Davis: His Rise and Fall* (1929). Tate also contributed to *I'll Take My Stand* (1930), the manifesto of the Southern Agrarians. He published his only novel, *The Fathers*, tracing activities of his mother's family in Fairfax County, Virginia, in 1938. He was named a consultant in poetry to the Library of Congress in 1943. In the early 1940s he was also helping Andrew Lytle shape *The Sewanee Review* into one of the most prestigious literary quarterlies in the country. In 1948 he began a three-year teaching stint at New York University.

In 1951 he moved to the University of Minnesota, where he remained until he retired in 1968. He received the Bollingen Prize in 1956. Tate was a notorious womanizer. He married Caroline Gordon in May 1925. They divorced in 1945, but re-married the following year. He divorced Gordon a second time in 1959 and married poet Isabella Gardner. Tate began an affair with a student and divorced Gardner in 1966. He then married Helen Heinz, a former nun who had been one of his students at the University of Minnesota. After his retirement, he and his family moved to Sewanee, the geographic nirvana for Southern Agrarians.

Tate died in Nashville 9 February 1979.

John Jacob Niles
(1892–1980)

Born 28 April 1892, Louisville KY
Died 1 March 1980, Lexington KY
Buried St. Hubert's, Winchester KY

Works: *One Man's War, The Story of the Lafayette Escadrille, Songs My Mother Never Taught Me, Songs of the Hill Folk, The Shape Note Study Book, The Ballad Book of John Jacob Niles, Singing Soldiers*

Born into a musically gifted family, Niles was already composing music by his teenage years. During World War I he served as a reconnaissance pilot for the U.S. Army Signal Corps in France, and afterwards undertook the study of music at the University of Lyon and the *Scola Cantorum* in Paris. Upon his return to the United States, he attended the Cincinnati Conservatory of Music, sang with Chicago's Lyric Opera, and became an early radio star.

After moving to New York in 1925, he issued his first music anthologies and then toured America and Europe with contralto Marion Kerby, performing an eclectic repertoire. Niles left New York and returned to his native Kentucky. He took a job with the old Burroughs Adding Machine Co. The job required him to visit stores that used the Burroughs adding machines, check and calibrate the machines, and offer a line of office products such as rubber stamps, note pads, and the like.

His sales area was Eastern Kentucky, so he used his sales trips to call on clients while also collecting folk songs from the miners and mountain communities throughout the region. This "Dean of American Balladeers" gained wide recognition as a collector of folk tunes and other forms of primitive music during his journeys through lower Appalachia in the 1930s.

He is probably best known for "discovering" and popularizing an old mountain carol, "I Wonder as I Wander," a song he captured during a stay in Murphy, North Carolina, in 1933.

Niles's relationship with photographer Doris Ulmann—Julia Peterkin's collaborator on *Roll, Jordan, Roll* (1933)—precipitated a scandal after Ms. Ulmann's sudden death in 1934. In 1936 he wed Rena Lipetz and settled in his native Kentucky, where he began a long-term recording career. He remained active in musical circles until his death in 1980.

Niles was buried in St. Hubert's Episcopal churchyard in Clark County, Kentucky.

Katherine Anne Porter
(1890–1980)

Born 15 May 1890, Indian Creek TX
Died 18 September 1980, College Park MD
Buried Indian Creek Cemetery, Indian Creek TX

Works: *Flowering Judas and Other Stories, Katherine Anne Porter's French Song Book, Hacienda, Noon Wine, Pale Horse, Pale Rider: Three Short Novels, The Leaning Tower and Other Stories, The Days Before, Ship of Fools, Collected Stories, Collected Essays and Occasional Writings of Katherine Anne Porter, The Never-Ending Wrong*

Katherine Anne Porter (originally Callie Russell Porter) was born in Indian Creek, Texas, on 15 May 1890. She was two years old when her mother died during childbirth. Her father left her (and her four siblings) to be reared by their paternal grandmother, a capable storyteller. At 16 she sought escape from her family's poor situation and past and was married to John Henry Koontz. The marriage, the first of four, would last until 1915. Porter went to work as a journalist, first for Fort Worth's *Critic* in 1917, and then at Denver's *Rocky Mountain News* in 1918. She worked as a society gossip columnist and music, movie, drama, and vaudeville critic. She moved to New York in October 1919, but left for Mexico a year later. Her goal in Mexico was to help reform educational and arts curriculums. The time spent in Mexico served as the inspiration for the story she later claimed had launched her career—"Mariá Concepción" (1922). Her experiences in Mexico also served as grist in perhaps her best short story, "Flowering Judas" (1929).

Upon returning to the United States, Porter continued to write. She became comfortable with the idea that her past, though tinged with poverty and hardship, was not a liability but rather a source of inspiration. As she matured in age, she matured as a writer and wrote more prolifically. She also traveled and lived abroad. Her travels would later serve as fodder for the novel *Ship of Fools* (1962), which she had worked on for more than two decades. By 1939 Porter was receiving rave reviews for her literary works. She presented workshops for writers and made public appearances as a Southern lady of literature. She also taught at both the University of Texas at Austin and the University of Michigan. She won both the National Book Award and the Pulitzer Prize for Fiction in 1966 for *The Collected Stories of Katherine Anne Porter* (1965). Porter was nominated three times for the Nobel Prize for Literature.

While she enjoyed great success as a writer, her personal life was tragic. She endured severe illnesses including tuberculosis, and went through four marriages and stormy relationships. She died in Maryland at the age of 90 on 18 September 1980. Her ashes were buried next to her mother's grave in Indian Creek, Texas.

Paul Green
(1894–1981)

Born 17 March 1894, Lillington NC
Died 4 May 1981, Chapel Hill NC
Buried Old Chapel Hill Cemetery, Chapel Hill NC

Works: *Salvation on a String, Contemporary American Literature, The Lord's Will and Other Carolina Plays, Lonesome Road: Six Plays for the Negro Theater, The Field God and In Abraham's Bosom, In the Valley and Other Carolina Plays, Wide Fields, The House of Connelly and Other Plays, The Laughing Pioneer, Fixin's, This Body the Earth, Shroud My Body Down, Johnny Johnson, The Lost Colony, The Southern Cross, The Lost Colony Song-Book, The Critical Year, Franklin and the King, Out of the South, The Enchanted Maze, The Highland Call, The Hawthorne Tree, Forever Growing, Song of the Wilderness, The Common Glory, Dog on the Sun, The Common Glory Song-Book, Dramatic Heritage, Wilderness Road, The Founders, Drama and the Weather, The Confederacy, Wings for to Fly: Three Plays of Negro Life, The Stephen Foster Story, Five Plays of the South, Plough and Furrow, Cross and Sword, Texas, Texas Song-Book, Words and Ways, Home to My Valley, Honeycomb, Trumpet in the Land, The Land of Nod, Paul Green's War Songs: A Southern Poet's History of the Great War, 1917-1920, A Southern Life: Letters of Paul Green, 1916-1981*

Paul Eliot Green began his playwriting career as an undergraduate student at the University of North Carolina at Chapel Hill. His play, *In Abraham's Bosom* (1926), won the Pulitzer Prize for Drama in 1927. He is best remembered as the author of *The Lost Colony* (1937), still performed in Manteo, North Carolina; and *The Stephen Foster Story* (1960), a major tourist draw in Bardstown, Kentucky. Both works belong to the "symphonic drama" genre which Green launched. At least two other Green symphonic dramas remain in production: *Texas* (1967) at Canyon, Texas, and *Trumpet in the Land* (1972) at Schoenbrunn, Ohio.

Green's symphonic drama genre involved real historical figures and actual events, surrounded by the daily lives of the supporting cast members, some of whom might also have been real personages though not of historical acclaim. There is homespun humor and a musical score, dancing girls, and usually some romantic involvement among the supporting cast.

The genre was adapted by Kermit Hunter, who wrote more than 40 outdoor dramas, most notably *Unto These Hills* (1950) and *Horn in the West* (1952). Hunter received a graduate degree from the University of North Carolina, from which Green had launched the genre.

In addition to the Pulitzer Prize, Green received two Guggenheim Fellowships, nine honorary degrees, and the National Theater Conference Award. He died at the age of 87 in Chapel Hill in 1981. The University of North Carolina memorialized him with the Paul Green Theater on campus, near Old Chapel Hill Cemetery.

Harry Golden
(1902–1981)

Born 6 May 1902, Milulintsky, Ukraine
Died 2 October 1981, Charlotte NC
Buried Hebrew Cemetery, Charlotte NC

Works: *Only in America, The Right Time, For 2 Plain, You're Entitle', Ess, Ess Mein Kind, The Best of Harry Golden, The Greatest Jewish City in the World, Carl Sandburg, Mr. Kennedy and the Negroes, The Israelis*

Born Herschel Goldhirsch in Ukraine, Golden emigrated in childhood to Canada, and then to the lower East Side of New York City. After having been graduated from City College of New York, he became a stockbroker, and served a five-year prison sentence in Atlanta for mail fraud.

In 1941 he settled in North Carolina, the next year founding *The Carolina Israelite*. This newspaper drew subscribers from throughout the country, and Golden's humorous but socially and politically liberal essays and speeches appealed to a wide audience.

He was an outspoken opponent of racial and religious prejudice. Golden's well-known collection of *Israelite* essays, *Only in America* (1958), became the basis for a Jerome Lawrence-Robert E. Lee play.

Cajoling white Southerners, he proposed a "Vertical Negro Plan," in which integrated classrooms would not be equipped with chairs: white Southerners were opposed to sitting with African-Americans, but had no objections to standing together in grocery stores and other places. Another suggestion was a "White Baby Plan" to help integrate Southern theaters by arranging for African- Americans to enter them while carrying white babies.

He developed close relationships with two other prominent North Carolina residents, poet Carl Sandburg and evangelist Billy Graham. Granted a presidential pardon by Richard Nixon in 1974, Golden died in his adopted city of Charlotte, and was interred in the Hebrew Cemetery there.

Tennessee Williams
(1911–1983)

Born 29 March 1911, Columbus MS
Died 25 February 1983, New York NY
Buried Calvary, St. Louis MO

Works: *A Streetcar Named Desire, Cat in a Hot Tin Roof, The Glass Menagerie, Night of the Iguana, Summer and Smoke, Baby Doll & Tiger Tail, Battle of Angels, Camino Real, Clothes for a Summer Hotel, Dragon County: A Book of Plays, Eccentricities of a Nightingale, The Gnadiges Fraulein, In the Bar of a Tokyo Hotel, I Rise in Flame Cried the Phoenix, Kingdom of Earth, A Lovely Summer for Creve Coeur, The Milk Train Doesn't Stop Here Anymore, The Mutilated, Not About Nightingales, A Notebook of Trigorin, A Perfect Analysis Given by a Parrot, Period of Adjustment, The Red Devil Battery Sign, The Rose Tattoo, Small Craft Warnings, Something Cloudy, Something Clear, Suddenly Last Summer, Sweet Bird of Youth, 27 Wagons Full of Cotton, Two-Character Play, Vieux Carre, Ten 10-minute Plays, Collected Stories, Hard Candy: A Book of Stories, One Arm and Other Stories, The Roman Spring of Mrs. Stone, Stopped Rocking and Other Screenplays, Tennessee Williams: Memoirs*

Thomas Lanier "Tennessee" Williams—a collateral descendant of poet Sidney Lanier—was born in Columbus, Mississippi, in 1911. His morbidly dysfunctional family life affected much of his literary output. After three years of study at the University of Missouri, his father withdrew him for failing ROTC. Soon thereafter the younger Williams suffered an emotional trauma.

Eventually he resumed his college education, being graduated from the University of Iowa in 1938. He read and wrote almost ceaselessly. His first play, *Battle of Angels* (1940), had a short, disappointing run, but *The Glass Menagerie* (1944) four years later brought Williams widespread acclaim. *A Streetcar Named Desire* (1947), *The Rose Tattoo* (1951), *Cat on a Hot Tin Roof* (1955), *Sweet Bird of Youth* (1959), and *Night of the Iguana* (1962) were among his most popularly-lauded efforts. Williams received the Pulitzer Prize and the Drama Critics Circle Award for *A Streetcar Named Desire*. He won the same two awards for *Cat on a Hot Tin Roof*.

In his later years Williams suffered from the effects of alcohol, prescription-drug dependencies, and numerous breakdowns. Always he remained loyal to his sister, Rose, long institutionalized after undergoing a pre-frontal lobotomy in an ill-conceived scheme to cure her of schizophrenia and other aberrant behaviors. (The central character in *The Glass Menagerie* was based upon Rose Williams.) Ridiculed by critics and even by his peers for his final Broadway productions in the late 1960s and 1970s, he nonetheless continued to write, hoping for a significant comeback. Williams died in a New York City hotel in 1983 after choking on a medicine bottle cap. In his will he left a sizeable fortune to Sewanee, the University of the South, for creative writing scholarships, a tribute to his maternal grandfather, an Episcopal priest. He was buried at Calvary Cemetery in St. Louis, a city he had grown to despise in his young adulthood, a decision taken as an insult from his younger brother, Dakin, from whom he was estranged.

Lillian Hellman
(1905–1984)

Born 20 June 1905, New Orleans LA
Died 30 June 1984, Martha's Vineyard MA
Buried Abel's Hill, Chilmark MA

Works: *Toys in the Attic, The Children's Hour, Pentimento, Maybe, Days to Come, Watch on the Rhine, Four Plays, The North Star, The Searching Wind, Another Part of the Forest, Montserrat, The Autumn Garden,* ed. *The Selected Letters of Anton Chekov, The Lark, Candide, My Mother, My Father, and Me, An Unfinished Woman, Scoundrel Time*

Lillian Florence Hellman lived in New Orleans as a child, but moved to New York with her family when she was eleven. She attended New York University for three years, but dropped out before completing her degree. She began reading manuscripts for Horace Liveright and met a number of theatrical people. In 1925 she married Arthur Kober, an aspiring dramatist. In 1930 the Kobers moved to Hollywood, where she became a scenario reader for Metro-Goldwyn-Mayer. At MGM she met Dorothy Parker and Dashiell Hammett. Parker became one of her best friends; Hammett became her lover and her companion until his death in 1961.

Her first play, *The Children's Hour* (1934), created a sensation by introducing lesbianism to the Broadway stage. She returned to Hollywood and adapted the play for a movie, *These Three* (1936), but the homosexual triangle from the play was re-written as a conventional triangle. Her next play, *Days to Come* (1936), failed, and she left for Europe, visiting Russia and Spain during the Spanish Civil War, in which she strongly supported the loyalists.

Hellman wrote *The Little Foxes* (1939), her best-known play. Keyed to the German army's race across Europe, she wrote *Watch on the Rhine* (1941), a play about the treachery and dangers of Nazism. The play hit Broadway before the attack on Pearl Harbor. *Watch on the Rhine* won the Drama Critics Circle Award. She wrote the movie, *The North Star* (1943), detailing the struggles of the Russian people attacked by Germany, and *The Searching Wind* (1944) on the failures of diplomacy before World War II. In 1948 she learned that her name was on a secret blacklist in Hollywood.

Toys in the Attic (1960), her longest-running play since *The Children's Hour*, earned a Drama Critics Circle Award. Her successful return as a playwright was dimmed by the worsening health of Hammett, who died of lung cancer in 1961. She published *An Unfinished Woman* (1969), the first of four memoirs, which won a National Book Award. *Pentimento* (1973) was also very successful, but *Scoundrel Time* (1976) was shorter and less inviting, and *Maybe* (1980) was criticized for what was generously termed shading the truth. Mary McCarthy said on *The Dick Cavett Show* that "every word she writes is a lie, including 'and' and 'the.'"

Hellman died 30 June 1984 of heart failure.

Walter Tevis
(1928–1984)

Born 28 February 1928, San Francisco CA
Died 8 August 1984, New York NY
Buried Richmond Cemetery, Richmond KY

Works: *The Hustler, The Color of Money, The Man Who Fell to Earth, The Queen's Gambit, Mockingbird, The Steps of the Sun, Far From Home*

Walter Tevis was born on 28 February 1928 in San Francisco. At the age of ten, he was placed in the Stanford Children's Convalescent Home due to heart problems. His family moved to Kentucky during this time and left him in the hospital for a year. At age eleven, Tevis traveled by train to rejoin his family in Madison County, Kentucky.

At age 17, he joined the Navy and served for two years. He then studied at the University of Kentucky, where he received both a bachelor's and a master's in English literature. Upon graduation, he taught many different subjects in several Kentucky high schools and also began to write short stories, which made their way to major publications. Tevis' first novel, *The Hustler*, was published in 1959 and was made into a movie in 1961.

His second novel, *The Man Who Fell to Earth*, was published in 1963 and, too, became a movie. Tevis drew on his own life experiences when writing his novels, as when he called *The Man Who Fell to Earth* "a very disguised autobiography." For the next 14 years, Tevis taught English literature and creative writing at Ohio University, where he was a distinguished professor.

There was a 17-year gap in his writing, after which he moved to New York and created four more literary works between 1979 and 1983. His books have been translated into many different languages.

His novel *Mockingbird* (1980) is set in New York in the 25th Century, a bleak cityscape with an illiterate, drug-addicted populace on the brink of extinction. The book was nominated for a Nebula Award for Best Novel by the Science Fiction and Fantasy Writers of America.

He was a member of the Authors Guild and died of lung cancer in 1984.

Truman Capote
(1924–1984)

Born 30 September 1924, New Orleans LA
Died 25 August 1984, Los Angeles CA
Buried Westwood, Los Angeles CA (partly)

Works: *Other Voices, Other Rooms, A Tree of Night, Local Color, The Grass Harp, The Muses are Heard, Breakfast at Tiffany's, Observations, In Cold Blood, A Christmas Memory, The Thanksgiving Visitor, The Dogs Bark, Music for Chameleons, One Christmas, Answered Prayers*

Truman Capote, born Truman Streckfus Persons, was one of America's most controversial authors, known as much for his extravagant lifestyle as he was for his writing. Murder and the effects of death are the central themes of Capote's most famous novel, *In Cold Blood* (1965). Capote claimed that he had launched a new genre—a "non-fiction novel." The novel deals with the grisly quadruple murder of a Kansas wheat farmer and his family. Capote was inspired to write the story after reading an account of the ghastly killings in the *New York Times*.

Capote traveled to Kansas to research the event, and while he was there, the killers were captured. Richard Eugene Hickock and Perry Edward Smith were then tried and convicted of the murders. Capote spent hours with Smith and Hickock while they were on death row, to learn more about the killers and to present a more complete version of the crimes for his book.

On 15 April 1965, Capote witnessed the executions of Hickock and Smith. Being an observer at the hangings left a strong impression on Capote. "I came to understand that death is the central factor of life," he told *Playboy* magazine in 1982. "And the simple comprehension of this fact alters your entire perspective.... The experience served to heighten my feeling of the tragic view of life."

However, had Capote never written *In Cold Blood*, he still would have enjoyed an enviable reputation among Southern writers, most notably for another masterwork, *Breakfast at Tiffany's* (1958). His characterization of Holly Golightly, a poor Arkansas girl who transforms into a New York socialite, struck a resonance with the reading public in America and Europe. Capote's depictions of the Manhattan social scene in the 1950s emerged from his own way of life.

The controversy about Capote continued even after his death. While official records show that he died at the home of Joanne Carson, the ex-wife of late night television icon Johnny Carson, and that his ashes were entombed at Westwood in Los Angeles, friends contended that at least a portion of his ashes were scattered at Crooked Pond, near Sagaponack, New York, with those of his partner, Jack Dunphy. No one would have loved the controversy more than Capote.

William Bradford Huie
(1910–1986)

Born 13 November 1910, Hartselle AL
Died 20 November 1986, Guntersville AL
Buried City Cemetery, Hartselle AL

Works: *Mud on the Stars, The Revolt of Mamie Stover, The Execution of Private Slovik, The Americanization of Emily, Hotel Mamie Stover, The Klansman, In the Hours of the Night, A Fight for Air Power, Seabee Roads to Victory, Can DO! The Story of the Seabees, The Case Against the Admirals, Wolf Whistle and Other Stories, The Hiroshima Pilot: The Case of Major Claude Eatherley, Three Lives for Mississippi, He Slew the Dreamer: My Search with James Earl Ray for the Truth about the Murder of Martin Luther King, A New Life to Live: Jimmy Putnam's Story, It's Me, O Lord!*

This prolific and controversial author grew up in the northern Alabama town of Hartselle. Valedictorian of his high school class, Huie was graduated with honors from the University of Alabama in 1930. He was a veteran of World War II, a print and broadcast journalist, and a novelist who wrote during and about the civil rights era. He served as editor of *The American Mercury*, where he hired William F. Buckley as a staff writer.

He lectured during the 1950s, and appeared on the television talk show *Longines Chronoscope*, where guests included John F. Kennedy and Joseph McCarthy. He covered the murders of Emmet Till and of the "Freedom Summer" workers James Chaney, Andrew Goodman, and Michael Schwerner, and wrote about them in *Wolf Whistle and Other Stories* (1959) and *Three Lives for Mississippi* (1965), respectively. His book about the assassination of Martin Luther King, Jr., *He Slew the Dreamer* (1970), had the initial cooperation of James Earl Ray.

Mud on the Stars (1942), his first book, is an autobiographical *bildungsroman*. *The Execution of Private Slovik* (1954), focusing on the only U.S. serviceman convicted of treason during World War II, was made into a well-received television movie in 1975. But his best-known work, *The Americanization of Emily* (1959), became a major Hollywood film (1964).

Huie died in Guntersville, Alabama, and was buried in the Hartselle City Cemetery. The local public library today bears his name and houses a permanent shrine dedicated to his literary career.

Huie's house in Hartselle is a landmark of modern design. The Ku Klux Klan burned a cross on his lawn in 1967.

Robert Penn Warren
(1905–1989)

Born 24 April 1905, Guthrie KY
Died 15 September 1989, West Wardsbury VT
Buried Willis Cemetery, Stratton VT

Works: *John Brown: The Making of a Martyr, Thirty-Six Poems, An Approach to Literature,* ed. *A Southern Harvest: Short Stories by Southern Writers, Understanding Poetry: An Anthology for College Students, Night Rider, Eleven Poems on the Same Theme, At Heaven's Gate, Understanding Fiction, All the King's Men, The Circus in the Attic and Other Stories, Modern Rhetoric, Fundamentals of Good Writing: A Handbook of Modern Rhetoric, World Enough and Time: A Romantic Novel,* ed. *An Anthology of Stories from the "Southern Review," Brother to Dragons: A Tale in Verse and Voices,* ed. *Short Story Masterpieces, Band of Angels,* ed. *Six Centuries of Great Poetry, Segregation: The Inner Conflict in the South, A New Southern Harvest: An Anthology, Promises: Poems 1954-56, Remember the Alamo!, Selected Essays, The Cave, The Gods of Mount Olympus, How Texas Won Her Freedom: The Story of Sam Houston and the Battle of San Jacinto, All the King's Men: A Play, The Scope of Fiction, You, Emperors, and Other Poems 1957-60, The Legacy of the Civil War: Meditations on the Centennial, Wilderness: A Tale of the Civil War, Flood: A Romance of Our Time, Who Speaks for the Negro?,* ed. *Faulkner: A Collection of Critical Essays,* ed. *Randall Jarrell, 1914-1965, Incarnations: Poems, 1966-1968, Audubon: A Vision, Homage to Theodore Dreiser, August 27, 1871-December 28, 1945, on the Centennial of His Birth,* ed. *Selected Poems of Herman Melville,* ed. *John Greenleaf Whittier's Poetry: An Appraisal and a Selection, Meet Me in the Green Glen, Or Else—Poem/Poems 1968-1974,* ed. *American Literature: The Makers and the Making, Democracy and Poetry, Selected Poems 1923-1975, A Place to Come To*

Robert Penn Warren is the only writer ever to win Pulitzer Prizes in poetry and fiction. He was a novelist, a poet, a literary critic, and a college professor. He was born in Guthrie, Kentucky, a small town near the Tennessee state line. He was educated at Vanderbilt and the University of California at Berkeley and later studied at Yale. He was a Rhodes Scholar, studying at New College at Oxford, and won a Guggenheim Fellowship that allowed him to study in Italy during the reign of Benito Mussolini.

While still at Vanderbilt he joined with a group of poets who termed themselves the Fugitives. He later joined other writers in a group known as the Southern Agrarians. As an Agrarian, he defended the practice of segregation in the South, reflecting the conservative philosophy regarding race relations at the time. He recanted those views in the 1950s in an article written for *Life* magazine and in a book, *Who Speaks for the Negro?* (1965), a collection of interviews he conducted with black civil rights leaders including Dr. Martin Luther King, Jr., and Malcolm X.

He served as a consultant in poetry to the Library of Congress in 1944-45. He was named a MacArthur Fellow in 1981 and became the first U.S. Poet Laureate so designated in 1986. He moved to Fairfield, Connecticut, late in life and died in Stratton, Vermont, 15 September 1989 from complications with bone cancer.

Walker Percy
(1916–1990)

Born 28 May 1916, Birmingham AL
Died 10 May 1990, Covington LA
Buried St. Joseph's Abbey, Covington LA

Works: *The Moviegoer, The Last Gentleman, Love in the Ruins, Lost in the Cosmos, Lancelot, The Thanatos Syndrome, The Message in the Bottle, Novel Writing in an Apocalyptic Time, Bourbon, Signposts in a Strange Land, The Second Coming*

Born 28 May 1916 in Birmingham, Alabama, Walker Percy was the eldest of three boys. After losing both parents in their youth, the three boys moved to Greenville, Mississippi, and were reared by their cousin William Alexander Percy. In his cousin's home Percy became exposed to an unending stream of scholarly guests, which sparked his early interest in literature.

However, Percy chose a non-literary path and in 1937 was graduated from the University of North Carolina with a degree in Chemistry. In 1941 he received his M.D. degree from the College of Physicians and Surgeons at Columbia University. His medical career was interrupted when he contracted tuberculosis.

After spending several years in sanitariums, Percy began to rethink his faith in science and medicine, and instead focused study on philosophy and European literature. In 1943, he resolved to become a writer and returned home to the South. He married Mary Bernice Townsend in 1946, and shortly after, both converted to Catholicism. In 1950 the Percys moved to Covington, Louisiana, where they raised two daughters.

Percy spent years writing essays, but published his first and most popular novel, *The Moviegoer*, in 1961. The book won the National Book Award for fiction in 1962 and is still his best-known piece of work. He went on to write five more works of fiction and two non-fiction books, the last one appearing in 1987. Walker Percy died at his home in Covington on 10 May 1990.

Alex Haley
(1921–1992)

Born 11 August 1921, Ithaca NY
Died 10 February 1992, Seattle WA
Buried at his boyhood home, Henning TN

Works: *Roots, The Autobiography of Malcolm X, Palmer Town, Madam Walker, A Different Kind of Christmas, Queen, Henning, Fred Montgomery*

Alexander Murray Palmer Haley was born 11 August 1921 in Ithaca, New York. When he was a young child, his mother took him to live with his grandparents in Henning, Tennessee, while his father pursued graduate studies at Cornell University. He lived in this house in Henning from 1921 to 1929, and would return to spend summers there as well.

During his time in Tennessee, his grandparents shared with him the stories of his family's history and genealogy, tracing his ancestry all the way back to the African slave Kunta Kinte, who had been brought to America from Gambia.

Haley's writing career started after serving in the United States Coast Guard, which he entered in 1939. Upon leaving the Coast Guard, he wrote a series of well-received interviews for *Playboy* in 1962. His first interview in Playboy was with jazz legend Miles Davis, and his interview with Dr. Martin Luther King, Jr., was the longest interview King had ever given to a magazine.

In 1965, Haley authored *The Autobiography of Malcolm X*, his first notable book.

Haley documented his family's genealogy in his most famous book with the Pulitzer Prize-winning *Roots*, published in 1976. The novel also won the National Book Award. The worldwide popularity of *Roots* was responsible for some to cite Haley as the father of modern genealogy.

In 1978 Haley agreed to settle a lawsuit charging him with plagiarism, paying Harold Courlander $650,000 in damages. Courlander was the author of *The African* (1967).

While on a speaking tour, Haley suffered a fatal heart attack 10 February 1992. He was buried on the grounds of his grandparents' home in Henning.

Caroline Miller
(1903–1992)

Born 26 August 1903, Waycross GA
Died 12 July 1992, Waynesville NC
Buried Greenhill, Waynesville NC

Works: *Lamb in His Bosom, Lebanon*

Caroline Pafford was born 26 August 1903 in Waycross, Georgia. As a young girl, she exhibited a strong talent for writing and after having been graduated from high school, she married her high school English teacher, William D. Miller. As a wife and mother to three small children she began writing short stories as a way of supplementing her family's income. Her first novel, *Lamb in his Bosom*, was published in 1933. With this book, she became the first Georgian to win the Pulitzer Prize for fiction.

Lamb in His Bosom became a best seller and also won France's *Prix Femina*. Miller was able to paint an accurate portrayal of back-country Georgia life, and based some of her characters on members of her large family (she was the youngest of seven children). The novel reflected her interest in local color and in genealogy. She collected folk tales and figures of speech in South Georgia, and critics admired her depiction of the local dialect and culture. The poor white characters revolve around Cean Carver Smith, who marries at 16 and gives birth to 14 children. In the course of the novel Cean endures the Civil War, a snakebite, a panther attack, and a house fire.

The success she garnered from her first novel put a strain on her marital life, and she and her husband divorced in 1936. She later married a florist, Clyde H. Ray, Jr. They moved from Georgia to the mountains of western North Carolina. Her second novel, *Lebanon*, was published in 1944, but failed to live up to the success of her earlier work.

Miller continued to write, but did not publish another book for the rest of her life. Caroline Miller died 12 July 1992 in Waynesville, North Carolina. A year after she died, *Lamb in His Bosom* was reprinted, and popular and critical interest in her work was revived. She was inducted into the Georgia Writers Hall of Fame in 2007.

Lewis Grizzard
(1946–1994)

Born 20 October 1946, Fort Benning GA
Died 20 March 1994, Atlanta GA
Buried Moreland Cemetery, Moreland GA

Works: *It Wasn't Always Easy But I Sure Had Fun, If I Ever Get Back to Georgia, I'm Gonna Nail My Feet to the Ground, Chili Dawgs Always Bark at Night, I Took a Lickin' and Kept on Tickin', Don't Bend Over in the Garden, Granny, You Know Them Taters Got Eyes, When My Love Returns from the Ladies' Room, Will I Be Too Old to Care?, The Last Bus to Albuquerque: A Commemorative Edition Celebrating Lewis Grizzard, If Love Were Oil, I'd Be about a Quart Low, They Tore Out My Heart and Stomped That Sucker Flat, My Daddy Was a Pistol and I'm a Son of a Gun, You Can't Put No Boogie Woogie on the King of Rock and Roll, Kathy Sue Loudermilk I Love You, Does a Wild Bear Chip in the Woods?, Life Is Like a Dogsled Team.... If You're Not the Lead Dog, the Scenery Never Changes—The Wit and Wisdom of Lewis Grizzard, Elvis Is Dead and I Don't Feel So Good Myself, I Haven't Decided Anything Since 1962 and Other Nekkid Truths, Getting It On: A Down-Home Treasury, Shoot Low, Boys—They're Ridin' Shetland Ponies: In Search of True Grit, Don't Forget to Call, Won't You Come Home Billy Bob Bailey?, Don't Sit Under the Grits Tree with Anyone Else But Me, Southern By the Grace of God, The Most of Lewis Grizzard, Grizzardisms: The Wit and Wisdom of Lewis Grizzard, I Haven't Understood Anything Since 1962, Heapin' Helping of True Grizzard: Down Home Again with Lewis Grizzard, Lewis Grizzard's Advice to the Newly Wed; Lewis Grizzard's Advice to the Newly Divorced, True Grits: Tall Tales and Recipes from the New South, Lewis Grizzard on Fear, The Grizzard Sampler: A Q Collection of the Early Writings of Lewis Grizzard, Glory! Glory! Georgia's 1980 Championship Season: The Inside Story*

Lewis McDonald Grizzard, Jr. was a paste-pot newspaperman wrestling with the computer age. He was haunted by the fact that his father, an Army captain, had left his mother when Grizzard was a young boy. His mother had to begin a career at age 40 after she took her son to her home town of Moreland, Georgia.

He was graduated from the University of Georgia with a degree in journalism, but he had begun his writing career long before, working as a reporter at the Newnan (Georgia) *Times-Herald*. At the University of Georgia, Grizzard chose to avoid the campus newspaper and worked instead at the *Athens Daily News*.

After graduation, he joined the Atlanta *Journal* as a sportswriter. At age 23, he was named the executive sports editor of the newspaper—at that time, the youngest newspaperman ever to hold that title at a major metropolitan daily.

He left Atlanta to become executive sports editor of the Chicago *Sun-Times*, but returned in 1977. For the first eight months he was a sports columnist, but then he began writing human-interest columns. Many of his human interests were funny, but others could be heart-wrenching. He remained devoted to his mother, but he was married four times and struggled with alcoholism. Grizzard's columns were syndicated in 450 newspapers, and he became a "personality," appearing on a number of television shows. He died 20 March 1994 from complications from his fourth heart-valve-replacement surgery.

Andrew Lytle
(1902–1995)

Born 26 December 1902, Murfreesboro TN
Died 13 December 1995, Sewanee TN
Buried University Cemetery, Sewanee TN

Works: *The Long Night, At the Moon's Inn, A Name for Evil, The Velvet Horn, A Novel, A Novella, and Four Stories, I'll Take My Stand, Bedford Forrest and His Critter Company, The Hero with the Private Parts, A Wake for the Living, Reflections of a Ghost, The Lytle-Tate Letters, Southerners and Europeans, From Eden to Babylon, Kristin*

Andrew Nelson Lytle was born in Murfreesboro, Tennessee, but attended Sewanee Military Academy near the University of the South at Sewanee, and received his bachelor's degree at Vanderbilt University in Nashville.

He studied acting at Yale and actually performed on Broadway in his early 20s, but he returned to the South because of the death of a relative, and he remained in the South most of the remainder of his life.

After returning to Tennessee from New York, he became associated with those intellectuals, writers, and poets who came to be known as the Southern Agrarians. This coterie included two poets he had known at Vanderbilt—Robert Penn Warren and Allen Tate—and they all took refuge near Lytle's home in the little town of Monteagle, Tennessee. Lytle became one of the group's best known spokesmen and a leader in the Agrarian movement.

His first book, *Bedford Forrest and his Critter Company* (1931), is considered the classic biography of Major General Nathan Bedford Forrest. His other acclaimed works include *The Velvet Horn* (1957), *The Long Night* (1936), and *A Wake for the Living* (1975). He taught for a year at Southwestern at Memphis (now Rhodes College) and lectured at the Iowa Writer's Workshop. He established the Master of Fine Arts program at the University of Florida in 1948. He also taught at Kenyon College and at the University of Kentucky.

In 1961 he returned to Monteagle to edit *The Sewanee Review*, the oldest continuously published literary quarterly in the country, and to teach creative writing and English at the University of the South. Under his guidance, *The Sewanee Review* was elevated to prominence and became a showcase for the South's best writers.

He withdrew from teaching in 1973 but continued to draw friends to his ancestral log cabin at Monteagle, where his skills as a raconteur and his reputation as an "authentic Southerner" made it a shrine of sorts for scholars, writers, and journalists. He died at Monteagle 13 December 1995.

Andrew Lytle

Eugenia Price
(1916–1996)

Born 22 June 1916, Charleston WV
Died 28 May 1996, Brunswick GA
Buried Christ Church, St. Simons Island GA

Works: *The Beloved Invader, New Moon Rising, Lighthouse, Don Juan McQueen, Maria, Margaret's Story, Savannah, To See Your Face Again, Before the Darkness Falls, Stranger in Savannah, Bright Captivity, Where Shadows Go, Beauty from Ashes, Another Day, The Waiting Time, The Eugenia Price Trilogy, Acts in Prayer, Share My Pleasant Stones: Meditations for Every Day of the Year, Woman to Woman, Beloved World: The Story of God and People, as Told from the Bible, Discoveries Made From Living My New Life, Strictly Personal: The Adventure of Discovering What God is Really Like, A Woman's Choice: Living Through Your Problems, Find Out for Yourself: Young People Can Discover Their Own Answers, God Speaks to Woman Today, Women to Women, What is God Like?, Where God Offers Freedom, Make Love Your Aim, Just As I Am, Learning to Live from the Acts, The Unique World of Women: In Bible Times and Now, Learning to Live From the Gospels, St. Simons Memoir: The Personal Story of Finding the Island and Writing the St. Simons Trilogy of Novels, Discoveries, No Pat Answers: Looking Squarely at Life's Most Difficult Questions, Diary of a Novel, At Home on St. Simons, Leave Yourself Alone: Set Yourself Free from the Paralysis of Analysis, Getting Through the Night: Finding Your Way After the Loss of a Loved One, The Burden is Light: The Autobiography of a Transformed Pagan Who Took God at His Word, What Really Matters: What is Truly Essential to the Authentic Christian Life, Early Will I Seek Thee, Learning to Live, The Wider Place: Where God Offers Freedom from Anything That Limits Our Growth, Inside One Author's Heart: A Deeply Personal Sharing with My Readers*

Eugenia "Genie" Price was born 22 June 1916 in Charleston, West Virginia. At the age of ten, she proclaimed that she wanted to be a writer. Her mother encouraged this goal, and so Price submitted a poem to her school's literary magazine. In 1932, Eugenia became the only female student enrolled in Ohio's Northwestern Dentistry School, but within two years she decided to pursue a career in writing again.

By 1961, Price was well known as a Christian author, but a detour through St. Simons Island, Georgia, changed that path. In the Christ Church cemetery she came upon the tombstones of the Reverend Anson Dodge and his two wives. Price was inspired by them and began to research the history of the area. This fascination created a new genre with the "St. Simons Trilogy," which consists of the books *Beloved Invader* (1965), *New Moon Rising* (1969), and *Lighthouse* (1972).

Price spent the rest of her life writing historical novels set in the American South. At age 79, she finished her last book, *The Waiting Time* (1997), a few weeks before her death on 28 May 1996. She was buried not far from her first inspiration in the Christ Church cemetery. Her epitaph reads, "After her conversion to Jesus Christ October 2, 1949, she wrote 'Light ... and eternity and love and all are mine at last.'"

James Dickey
(1923–1997)

Born 2 February 1923, Atlanta GA
Died 19 January 1997, Columbia SC
Buried All Saints', Pawleys Island SC

Works: *Into the Stone, Drowning With Others, The Suspect in Poetry, Helmets, Buckdancer's Choice, Poems 1957-1967, Babel to Byzantium, Deliverance, The Eye-Beaters, Blood, Victory, Madness, Buckhead and Mercy, Self-Interviews, Sorties, The Zodiac, God's Images, Alnilam, Puella, The Strength of Fields, The Early Motion, To the White Sea, Jericho*

James Dickey was born in Atlanta. He attended Clemson University for one term before dropping out to serve in the Army Air Corps during World War II. After the war he completed his education at Vanderbilt University, earning bachelor's and master's degrees in English.

He taught at Rice University, returned to active military service for two years in Korea, and then joined the English faculty at the University of Florida. After a minor scandal there in 1956—he refused to apologize for reading aloud a controversial poem that had offended his audience—he returned to his native Atlanta, where for a number of years he was a well-paid advertising copy writer.

Dickey then turned all his attentions to the writing of poetry. His collection *Buckdancer's Choice* (1965) won the National Book Award for poetry in 1965. An appointment as Consultant in Poetry to the Library of Congress (a position now known as the poet laureateship) soon followed. The recipient of numerous honors, he was also invited to read his poem "The Strength of Fields" at a pre- inauguration gala for President Jimmy Carter in 1977.

His most successful novel, *Deliverance*, appeared in 1970, after which he accepted an endowed professorship at the University of South Carolina in Columbia, a post he held until his death. Among his other works were the novels *Alnilam* (1987) and *To the White Sea* (1993), and more than a dozen poetry volumes.

Dickey died after a long illness and was buried in All Saints' churchyard at Pawleys Island near Georgetown, South Carolina.

Eugene Walter
(1921–1998)

Born 30 November 1921, Mobile AL
Died 29 June 1998, Mobile AL
Buried Old City Cemetery, Mobile AL

Works: *Monkey Poems, The Byzantine Riddle, The Untidy Pilgrim, Delectable Dishes from Termite Hall, American Cooking: Southern Style, Hints and Pinches, The Likes of Which, Milking the Moon: A Southerner's Story of Life on This Planet, The Pokeweed Alphabet, Love You Good, See You Later, The Easiest Way, Jealousy, Just a Woman*

Eugene Walter was born in Mobile, Alabama, 30 November 1921. In his youth, he ran away from home multiple times, taking shelter with locals who recognized his budding artistic genius. Ultimately, he was taken in by his grandmother. He wrote and staged puppet shows for friends, one of whom was a young Truman Capote, three years his junior. He later would describe his childhood home of Mobile as "…a separate kingdom. We are not North America; we are North Haiti." He earned the label over time as "Mobile's Renaissance Man" due to his varied activities in the arts.

During World War II, Walter was assigned as a cartographer in the Aleutian Islands for three years. After the war, Walter spent time as part of the growing artistic scene in Greenwich Village before moving to Paris in the early 1950s. While in Paris he helped launch the *Paris Review*, a publication "for the good writers and good poets," for which Walter wrote short stories, conducted interviews, and created art. He then moved to Rome where, due to his fluency in Italian, he went to work as a translator for Italian film director Federico Fellini. Walter also acted in more than 20 films, including Fellini's *8½* (1963). While making the most of each of his opportunities, he was also writing.

Walter already had more than a few novels to his name when he returned home to Mobile in 1978, yet he was not financially without care. Rather, he had to rely once again on those who gladly took care of him in exchange for his tales of palling around Europe and New York with Capote, T.S. Eliot, William Faulkner, Judy Garland, and Gore Vidal. Later in life he was interviewed at length for an oral biography (*A Southerner's Story of Life on This Planet* [2001]) by Katherine Clark. And in 2008, *Eugene Walter: Last of the Bohemians*, a documentary about his life, was released.

He is rememberred as a true poet, raconteur, talented actor, and storyteller. He pursued art over everything and had "more delights than regrets" in life. He died in Mobile 29 March 1998 at the age of 76. The epitaph on his grave marker in City Cemetery includes the line: WHEN ALL ELSE FAILS, THROW A PARTY.

Margaret Walker Alexander
(1915–1998)

Born 7 July 1915, Birmingham AL
Died 30 November 1998, Chicago IL
Buried Garden Memorial Park, Jackson MS

Works: *Richard Wright: Daemonic Genius, Jubilee, For Farish Street Green, February 27, 1986, This is My Century: New and Collected Poems*

Margaret Walker Alexander (originally Margaret Abigail Walker) was born 7 July 1915 in Birmingham, Alabama. Her music teacher mother and Methodist minister father encouraged her to read philosophy and poetry as a young child. This early exposure to the literary world led her to earn a degree from Northwestern University in 1935.

The following year she befriended fellow writers Katherine Dunham, Frank Yerby, and Richard Wright, when she began working with the Federal Writers' Project, part of the FDR's Works Progress Administration. In 1937 Alexander penned "For My People," a poem that was published in *Poetry* magazine and proved to be one of her most famous works.

Her work with the Writers' Project exposed her to the struggles of inner-city African-Americans whose families had left the South years earlier. Alexander then returned to school at the University of Iowa, earning a master's (1940) and later a doctorate (1960). She spent several years teaching after earning her master's until she met Firnist James Alexander, whom she married in 1943. The couple soon moved back to the South, settling in Jackson, Mississippi.

Alexander then began an impressive teaching career at Jackson State College that lasted the next 30 years. In 1966 she published the most famous of her novels, *Jubilee*, a narrative based on the collected memories of her maternal grandmother. The novel has never gone out of print, has been translated into seven languages, and has won many awards. *Jubilee* also served at the center of a lawsuit in which Alexander sued Alex Haley for plagiarizing *Jubilee* in *Roots* (1976). Her lawsuit failed.

In 1968 she founded The Institute for the Study of History, Life and Culture of Black People, which now bears her name. She retired in 1979, and served as professor emerita until her death at her daughter's home in Chicago on 30 November 1998.

Willie Morris
(1934–1999)

Born 29 January 1934, Jackson MS
Died 2 August 1999, Jackson MS
Buried Glenwood, Yazoo City MS

Works: *North Toward Home, The Courting of Marcus Dupree, The Last of the Southern Girls, New York Days, Faulkner's Mississippi, James Jones: A Friendship, My Dog Skip, My Cat Spit McGee, Yazoo, Good Old Boy, Always Stand In Against the Curve and Other Sports Stories, Prayer for the Opening of Little League Season, My Mississippi, Homecomings, A Southern Album: Recollections of Some People and Times Gone By, The Ghosts of Medgar Evers: A Tale of Race, Murder, Mississippi and Hollywood, The South Today: 100 Years After Appomattox, Terrains of the Heart and Other Essays on Home, My Two Oxfords, After All, It's Only a Game, Shifting Interludes: Selected Essays, Good Old Boy: A Delta Boyhood, Good Old Boy and Witch of Yazoo, Taps*

William Weaks Morris was born 29 November 1934 in Jackson, Mississippi, into a family of storytellers who had called Mississippi home for six generations. He grew up in Yazoo City "on the edge of the Delta, straddling the memorable divide where the hills end and the flat land begins." He was graduated from high school in 1952 as valedictorian and left for the University of Texas at Austin. Upon graduation in 1956, he continued his education as a Rhodes Scholar at Oxford University.

Morris returned to the United States to become editor of the *Texas Observer* and then *Harper's* before publishing his first autobiographical book in 1967, *North Toward Home*. As editor of *Harper's*, Morris enjoyed friendships with a great number of writers. As James Jones, the author of *From Here to Eternity* (1951), was dying from congestive heart failure, he gave Morris all of his notes for the completion of *Whistle*, the third volume of Jones' trilogy on World War II. Morris completed the novel after Jones died in 1977.

In 1980 Morris returned to Mississippi as the writer-in-residence at Ole Miss, encouraging young writers in whom he saw promise. In 1990, the once-divorced Morris married long-time friend JoAnne Pritchard, editor at University Press of Mississippi. The couple moved back to Jackson where Morris wrote a second autobiography, *New York Days* (1993). In his later years he would continue penning powerful pieces, two of which, *The Ghosts of Medgar Evers: A Tale of Race, Murder, Mississippi and Hollywood* (1998), and *My Dog Skip* (1995), would be adapted into films.

Morris never saw his final novel, *Taps* (2001) published, as he suffered a fatal heart attack on 2 August 1999, shortly before its completion.

His gravestone, a divided granite slab, stands less than 20 yards from the broken chains around the tombstone of The Witch of Yazoo, a marker made famous by Morris in his novel *Good Old Boy and The Witch of Yazoo* (1988).

Richard Marius (1933–1999)

Born 23 July 1933, Lenoir City TN
Died 5 November 1999, Belmont MA
Buried The Knoll at Sleepy Hollow, Concord MA

Works: *The Coming of Rain, Bound for the Promised Land, After the War, An Affair of Honor, Luther, Thomas More, A Writer's Companion, The Columbia Book of Civil War Poetry, Reading Faulkner*

Richard Curry Marius first came to public notice as a fiery youth evangelist at the Dixie Lee Baptist Church. He grew up in the shadow of the church, about a mile from Dixie-Lee Junction, the union of two of the South's great highways.

Marius obtained a degree in journalism from the University of Tennessee while working as a reporter and columnist for the *Lenoir City News*. His column, "Rambling with Richard," drew heavily on the history of Loudon County and some of the stories in those columns were reprised in *The Coming of Rain* (1969), his first novel. He continued in his pursuit of a divinity degree aimed at the ministry, but struggled with his faith. Instead, he became a college professor, first teaching history at Gettysburg College and later at the University of Tennessee.

At Tennessee, Marius was highly critical of the school's annual religious convocations and drew death threats for his part in a lawsuit to force the university to allow black comedian Dick Gregory to appear. He led a protest demonstration against an appearance by evangelist Billy Graham that became unruly. He became professor of expository writing at Harvard in 1978, a position he held for 20 years. As a novelist, Marius was strongly linked to his birthplace—Bourbonville is the central location for his four novels, and three of the novels depict actual histories and some conjecture about his home town of Lenoir City, Tennessee.

As a Reformation historian, the challenges Marius experienced in terms of his personal faith are reflected in his biographies of Sir Thomas More and Martin Luther. He showed that both men had struggles with their daily lives, and he castigated Luther for his anti-Semitic views.

Ironically, Marius was accused of harboring anti-Semitic views because of an article he wrote in the *Harvard Alumni* magazine, in which he likened actions of the Shin Bet, the Israeli secret police, to the actions of the Gestapo under Nazi Germany. The article led Vice President Albert Gore to withdraw an offer for Marius to become a speechwriter at the White House.

In addition to the four novels and the two histories, Marius also wrote *A Writer's Companion* (1985) and *A Short Guide for Writing About History* (1989), both key reference works.

Marius was diagnosed with pancreatic cancer in 1998 and died 5 November 1999. He was buried at The Knolls at Sleepy Hollow Cemetery near his adoptive home town of Belmont, Massachusetts.

Eudora Welty
(1909–2001)

Born 13 April 1909, Jackson MS
Died 23 July 2001, Jackson MS
Buried Greenwood, Jackson MS

Works: *A Curtain of Green, The Robber Bridegroom, The Wide Net, Delta Wedding, The Golden Apples, The Ponder Heart, The Bride of the Innisfallen, The Shoe Bird, Losing Battles, One Time, One Place, The Optimist's Daughter, The Eye of the Story, One Writer's Beginnings, Photographs, The Writer's Eye, Country Churchyards, Welty Complete Novels, Welty Stories, Essays and Memoir, On William Hollingsworth, Some Notes on River Country, On William Faulkner, Early Escapades, Occasions*

Eudora Welty spent nearly all of her life in Jackson, Mississippi, "underfoot," she once said, from 1909 to 2001. She drew acclaim for her writings and her photography and garnered every major literary award except the Nobel Prize. As a young girl she had played in Jackson's Greenwood Cemetery, located less than a block from the house where she was born. "I grew up near it. It was the view from the sleeping porch at our house on North Congress Street. We could look right down on it. I used to go over there and play," she said. The cemetery is prominent in Welty's writing and photography, joining themes of place and family. In her early story, "Magic," Myrtle Cross, who was seduced in a graveyard, mentions "a big stone angel standing up with its arm pointed straight into the sky." The angel is in *Country Churchyards* (2000), used on the cover of the brochure for Greenwood Cemetery.

She writes about her baby brother, who died before she was born, in her memoir, *One Writer's Beginnings* (1984). She was playing and found a box with two nickels in it, and she asked her mother if she could spend them. Her mother told her they had lain on the eyes of the baby before they buried him. In several of her writings, Welty used the placement of graves within a cemetery or the selection of one cemetery over another, to reflect class and social standing among the departed. Neither of her parents qualified as "Old Jackson" elites when she was a young girl—her father was a Yankee from Ohio and her mother was from West Virginia—and both were buried in Jackson's "other" cemetery, Cedar Lawn. Welty had become an institution by the time of her death in 2001. Her fame as an author had convinced Jacksonians that she was "Old Jackson." No one questioned her burial in Greenwood Cemetery.

She won the 1973 Pulitzer Prize for her novel *The Optimist's Daughter* (1972), but is best known as a short story writer. The best-known of her stories are "Why I Live at the P. O." and "A Worn Path."

Welty died from pneumonia in Jackson, and was buried beside her brother at Greenwood Cemetery.

Larry Brown
(1951–2004)

Born 9 July 1951, Oxford MS
Died 24 November 2004, Yocona MS
Buried Brown Family Farm, Tula MS

Works: *Dirty Work, On Fire, Facing the Music, Billy Ray's Farm, Joe, Father and Son, The Rabbit Factory, Fay, Big Bad Love, A Miracle of Catfish: A Novel in Progress*

Larry Brown was born in Oxford, Mississippi, on 9 July 1951, the son of a sharecropper. His family moved to Memphis when he was three. His father held various jobs as a laborer, but his drinking problem kept him from succeeding. The family returned to north Mississippi when he was in the eighth grade.

Brown was graduated from Lafayette High School in Oxford in 1969 and joined the Marines the following year. After two years he was discharged, and married Mary Ann Coleman in 1974, when she was 19 and he was 23.

He worked in a myriad of jobs before becoming a firefighter in 1973. He served as a fireman for 17 years before retiring to become a writer full-time. His first book was a collection of short stories, *Facing The Music* (1988). Brown's first novel, *Dirty Work* (1989), was published one year later. Brown wrote in earnest about the people who inhabit the underbelly of the American South.

He became known as one of the foremost authors who wrote in a style that was tagged as "Grit Lit." He penned a collection of stories, *Big Bad Love* (1990), and another novel, *Joe* (1991).

Brown received numerous awards, including the Mississippi Institute of Arts and Letters Award, the Southern Book Critics Award, the Lila Wallace-Reader's Digest Fund Writers' Award, and the Thomas Wolfe Prize. He also wrote nonfiction, including *On Fire* (1993), a book that acknowledged his tenure as a firefighter.

Brown died from a heart attack 24 November 2004, at his home near Oxford.

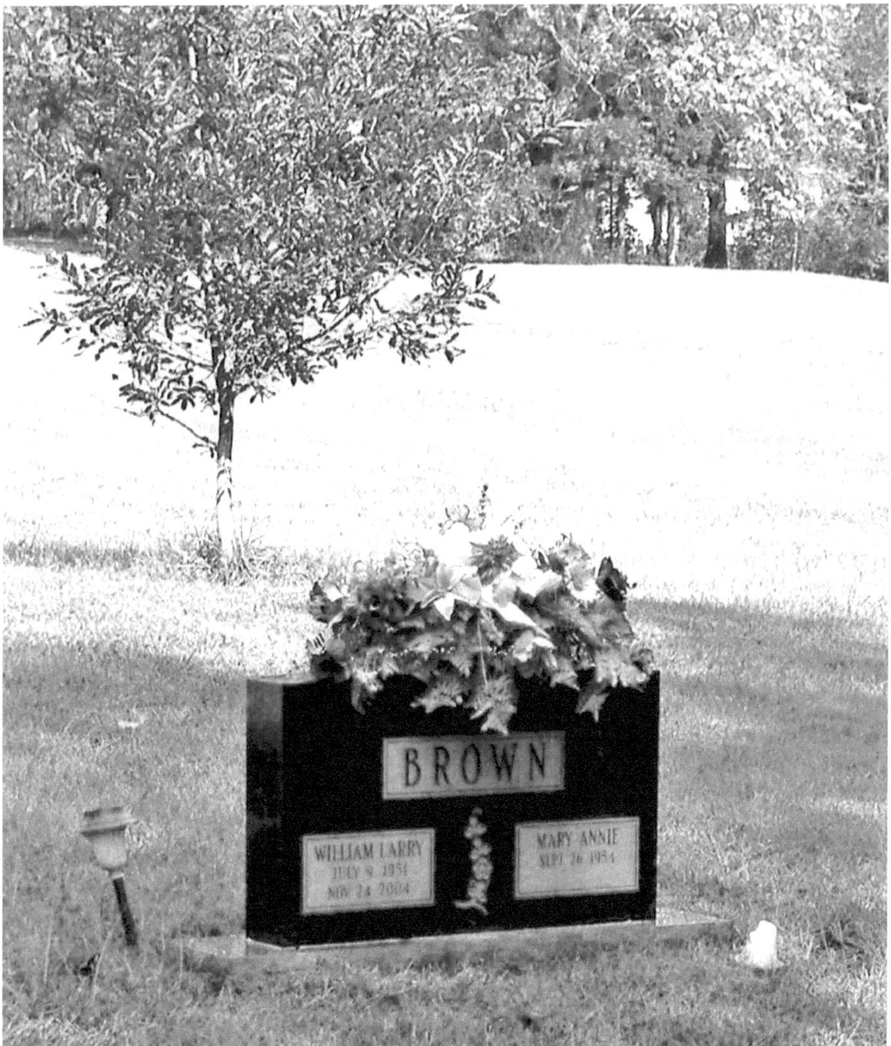
BROWN
WILLIAM LARRY
MARY ANNIE

Shelby Foote
(1916–2005)

Born 17 November 1916, Greenville MS
Died 27 June 2005, Memphis TN
Buried Elmwood, Memphis TN

Works: *The Civil War, Shiloh, Tournament, Follow Me Down, Love in a Dry Season, Jordan County, September, September*

Shelby Foote, who wrote six novels and *The Civil War*, a narrative three-volume history, toiled mainly in obscurity until 1990 when he was selected as a historical narrator for Ken Burns's epic documentary, *The Civil War*, which appeared on the Public Broadcasting System.

Foote made 82 appearances in the 11-hour documentary series, drawing rave reviews from an adoring public. "If we're not too careful," he quipped in a reflection on his sudden popularity, "we Southerners can wind up charming the pants off the rest of the country. We sort of have to keep it in check."

He received the first Tennessee Governor's Award for the Humanities in 1991 and the Frankel Prize from Columbia University in 1992. He wrote everything in longhand, using pen and ink, and was noted for the thoroughness of his research.

For *Shiloh*, a novel in which he relates the course of the horrific Civil War battle through the experiences of different soldiers in the two armies, Foote walked through every battle location. "The ground hasn't changed that much," he explained to a reporter. "I wanted to see what those soldiers saw."

While most Civil War historians focused on the battles in the East, Foote's focus was in the West—particularly battles that raged for control of the Mississippi River. His favorite character was Major General Nathan Bedford Forrest, perhaps the greatest cavalry tactician, though one with no formal military training.

Foote also was interested in the history of Memphis, his adopted home. He was a periodic visitor to Memphis' Elmwood Cemetery, which dates from 1852. He admired the cemetery for "its peaceful isolation in the middle of all the hurrah going on around us."

Elmwood, 80 acres near downtown Memphis, contains the graves of 18 Confederate generals and two Union generals. It also contains the graves of the city's martyrs, including those who sacrificed their lives caring for others during the yellow fever epidemic in 1873.

Foote was buried under a large magnolia in the family plot of Nathan Bedford Forrest.

Burke Davis
(1913–2006)

Born 24 July 1913, Durham NC
Died 18 August 2006, Greensboro NC
Buried Forest Lawn, Greensboro NC

Works: *Amelia Earhart, America's First Army, Appomattox: Closing Struggle of the Civil War* (1958, 1963, 1974), *Bassett Hall: The Williamsburg Home of Mr. and Mrs. John D. Rockefeller, Jr., The Billy Mitchell Affair, The Billy Mitchell Story, Biography of a Fish Hawk, Biography of a King Snake, Biography of a Leaf, Black Heroes of the American Revolution, The Campaign that Won America: The Story of Yorktown, The Cowpens-Guilford Courthouse Campaign, A Fierce Personal Pride: The Story of Mount Hope Finishing Company and Its Founding Family, George Washington and the American Revolution, Get Yamomoto, Getting to Know Jamestown, Getting to Know Thomas Jefferson's Virginia, Gray Fox: Robert E. Lee and the Civil War, Heroes of the American Revolution, Jeb Stuart, the Last Cavalier, The Long Surrender, Marine! The Life of Lt. Gen. Lewis B. (Chesty) Puller, USMC (ret.), Mr. Lincoln's Whiskers, Old Hickory: A Life of Andrew Jackson, Our Incredible Civil War, The Ragged Ones, Rebel Raider: A Biography of Admiral Semmes, Roberta E. Lee: The Sad But Almost True Story of the Rabbit Who Longed to Be Prettier Than Scarlett O'Hara or Anybody Else, Runaway Balloon: The Last Flight of Confederate Air Force One, Sherman's March, The Southern Railway: Road of Innovators, The Summer Land, They Call Him Stonewall: A Life of Lt. General T. J. Jackson, C. S. A., Three for Revolution, To Appomattox, Nine April Days, War Bird: The Life and Times of Elliott White Springs, Whisper My Name, A Novel, A Williamsburg Galaxy, The World of Currier and Ives, Yorktown, Yorktown: The Winning of American Independence*

Burke Davis was born in Durham, North Carolina on 24 July 1913, but was reared in Greensboro, North Carolina. He studied at Guilford and Duke before ultimately earning a degree from the University of North Carolina at Chapel Hill. Shortly thereafter he began his first career as a journalist, writing for the *Charlotte News*. He later joined the *Baltimore Evening Sun* and the *Greensboro Daily News*. In 1949 he penned *Whisper My Name*, a novel about a Charlotte businessman with characters so thinly disguised that it caused a sensation among locals who found the alleged fiction all too familiar.

Davis spent some twenty years writing so-called "special projects" for Colonial Williamsburg, Inc., beginning in 1960. Throughout the rest of his career as an author he wrote more than a dozen fiction and nonfiction books for young readers, historical tales, novels, and biographies. He is perhaps best known for his books involving the Civil War. He amassed large, detailed files on Civil War topics like uniforms, personalities, firearms, geography, and even historical accounts of weather in order to depict events in the most accurate form possible. Later in life he received many awards for his volumes of work and served as a juror for the Pulitzer Prize in biography.

He died 8 August 2006 at the age of 93 in Greensboro.

William Styron (1925–2006)

Born 11 June 1925, Newport News VA
Died 1 November 2006, Martha's Vineyard MA
Buried West Chop, Tisbury MA

Works: *Lie Down in Darkness, Sophie's Choice, Confessions of Nat Turner, The Long March, Set This House on Fire, In the Clap Shack, This Quiet Dust, Darkness Visible, A Tidewater Morning, Havanas in Camelot*

William Clark Styron, Jr., is considered among the best American writers of the second half of the twentieth century. A rebellious youth was channeled into academic pursuit when he attended Christchurch School, an Episcopal college preparatory school in the Tidewater area of Virginia. After graduation, he enrolled at Davidson College, but as a member of the Marine Reserves, he was transferred to Duke University in 1943. He was called to active duty and commissioned as a lieutenant in 1945, but the war ended before his deployment.

He accepted a job with McGraw-Hill in New York, editing books. *Lie Down in Darkness*, Styron's first novel, was published in 1951. He was awarded the *Prix de Rome* by the American Academy in Rome and the American Academy of Arts and Letters. He was to go to Rome to accept the prize and to undertake a year of study there, but was recalled to active duty with the Marines for the Korean War.

Styron was released from military service in 1952 because of a vision problem, and went to Europe to pick up his prize. During an extended stay on the continent he became friends with Romain Gary, George Plimpton, Irwin Shaw, James Baldwin, James Jones, Peter Matthiessen, and others. The group founded the *Paris Review* in 1953. Styron married poet Rose Burgunder in Paris in the spring of 1953.

He wrote *The Long March* (1952) as a serial about his military experiences, but later expanded the serial into a book by the same title (1956). His European experiences were reflected in *Set This House on Fire* (1960).

Styron spent the next five years researching and writing *The Confessions of Nat Turner* (1967), a novel depicting the leader of a slave uprising in Virginia in 1831. The novel won the Pulitzer Prize for Fiction in 1968 and the William Dean Howells Medal from the American Academy of Arts and Letters. *Sophie's Choice* (1979), told of a Polish Catholic Holocaust survivor and her love life. The novel was a national best seller. It won the National Book Award in 1980 and was made into a movie in 1982, starring Meryl Streep and Kevin Klein. Streep won the Academy Award for Best Actress as Sophie.

Styron received the *Prix Mondial Cino Del Luca* in 1985, but suffered a serious bout of depression. His memoir on depression: *Darkness Visible: A Memoir of Madness* (1990), became another national best seller. He died of pneumonia at Martha's Vineyard 1 November 2006.

Wilma Dykeman
(1920–2006)

Born 20 May 1920, Asheville NC
Died 22 December 2006, Asheville NC
Buried Beaverdam Baptist Church, Asheville NC

Works: *The French Broad, The Tall Woman, The Far Family, Return the Innocent Earth, Neither Black nor White*

Wilma Dykeman was born 20 May 1920 in Asheville, North Carolina. She was an only child whose family had called the North Carolina mountains home for generations. Later in life she would state that her interest in stories came from the early memories she had of her parents reading stories to her. As a student in elementary school she was creating stories, plays, and poems of her own.

She attended high school in Asheville before seeking and earning a bachelor's degree in Speech from Northwestern University. Not long after graduation, she married poet and nonfiction writer James R. Stokely, Jr., a member of the prominent Stokely vegetable canning family. The couple maintained homes in both Asheville and Newport, Tennessee, Stokely's home town. They collaborated on several books that dealt with issues in the South such as race relations and integration.

Early in her career Dykeman wrote radio scripts, short stories, and articles for *Harper's, New York Times Magazine, Reader's Digest*, and others. In all, Dykeman published more than 16 books, including critically acclaimed novels that leaned heavily on her understanding of the people, the places, and the way of life of the mountain people. She was a lecturer and adjunct professor at the University of Tennessee from 1975 until 1995.

Dykeman received a Guggenheim Fellowship in 1956 and a senior fellowship from the National Endowment for the Humanities

She earned other awards throughout her career and was Tennessee State Historian from 1981 until her death. She never wandered too far from the area she wrote about and called home, living all of her days near the French Broad River in the mountains of North Carolina and Tennessee. She died in Asheville 22 December 2006 at the age of 86.

A quotation: "The talent comes from developing the aptitude. The writer comes from developing the attitude."

"Scattered, Smothered, and Covered"

Here are collected the authors whose grave markers couldn't be photographed, for assorted reasons. A few of these honored dead are outside the country, but most of them were cremated, with their ashes scattered or retained by family members.

Harry Scott Ashmore (28 July 1916 Greenville SC – 20 January 1998 Santa Barbara CA) was a Clemson graduate and journalist who won two Pulitzer Prizes in 1958, one for editorial writing and the other for public service. His ashes were scattered in the Pacific Ocean at Santa Barbara, California.

◊

Joseph Glover Baldwin (21 January 1815 Winchester VA – 30 September 1864) wrote *Flush Times of Alabama and Mississippi* (1853), said to be Abraham Lincoln's favorite book, then moved to California. A lawyer, he became a judge and eventually served on the California Supreme Court. His grave at Mountain View Cemetery in Oakland, California, is unmarked.

◊

Roark Bradford (21 August 1896 Lauderdale Co. TN – 13 November 1948 New Orleans LA) wrote dialect works including *Ol' Man Adam and His Chillun* (1928), which was translated to the stage and screen by Marc Connelly as *Green Pastures* (1936), a popular play and movie. Bradford's ashes were scattered in the Mississippi River at New Orleans.

◊

Laura Bragg (8 October 1881 Northridge MA – 16 May 1978 Charleston SC) was curator of the Charleston Museum, the first such institution in the United States. She was a founder of the Poetry Society of South Carolina. Her ashes were scattered in the Santee River in South Carolina.

◊

Herschel Brickell (13 September 1889 Senatobia MS – 29 May 1952 Ridgefield CT) was an editor and critic, notably the editor of the O. Henry short story collections. A suicide, he was cremated, and his ashes were given to his wife, Norma.

◊

Olive Ann Burns (17 July 1924 Banks Co. GA – 4 July 1990 Atlanta GA) began writing late in life, and authored the novel *Cold Sassy Tree* (1984), adapted as a successful opera (2000) by Carlisle Floyd. She was cremated, and her ashes were kept by her family.

ॐ

Erskine Caldwell (17 December 1903 Moreland GA – 11 April 1987 Paradise Valley AZ) was a prolific bestselling novelist, most famously for *Tobacco Road* (1932) and *God's Little Acre* (1933), about lower-class Georgians. He was cremated in Arizona, and his ashes were kept by his wife.

ॐ

Mary Boykin Miller Chesnut (31 March 1823 Stateburg SC – 22 November 1886 Camden SC) was the daughter of a governor and wife to a Confederate general. She kept an exemplary diary during the Civil War. Her grave is on private property in Camden on the former Knights Hill plantation. The location of the grave is kept secret to discourage vandals and plunderers.

ॐ

Octavus Roy Cohen (26 June 1891 Charleston SC – 6 January 1959 Los Angeles CA) attended Clemson, practiced law, wrote for newspapers, then became a novelist, with more than 50 books, many in African-American dialect, to his credit. He created the character Florian Slappey. He moved to Los Angeles and was a successful screenwriter. His grave in Forest Lawn Memorial Park, Glendale, California, is unmarked.

ॐ

Wyatt Emory Cooper (1 September 1927 Quitman MS – 5 January 1978 New York NY) was a magazine writer, editor, and actor. He wrote screenplays and the autobiography *Families: A Memoir and a Celebration* (1975). He was the fourth husband of heiress Gloria Vanderbilt and the father of CNN journalist Anderson Cooper. Only people with the surname Vanderbilt are permitted to be buried in the Vanderbilt mausoleum, the largest private mausoleum in the country; therefore, Cooper is buried *near* the mausoleum, on private property adjacent to the Moravian Cemetery, New Dorp, Staten Island, New York.

ॐ

Guy Davenport (23 November 1927 Anderson SC – 4 January 2005 Lexington KY) wrote stories, novels, poems, and essays. He donated his body to Duke Medical Center.

☙

W. E. B. DuBois (23 February 1868 Great Barrington MA – 27 August 1963 Accra, Ghana) studied at Fisk University, Harvard, and the University of Berlin, and was the first African-American to earn a Ph. D. from Harvard. He taught at Atlanta University (now Clark Atlanta University) from 1897 to 1910. His best-known work is *The Souls of Black Folk* (1903). His tomb is in Accra, Ghana.

☙

Willie Snow Ethridge (10 December 1899 Savannah GA – 1 December 1982 Key West FL) wrote many travel- and history-related novels, including *Let's Talk Turkey* (1952) and *It's Greek to Me* (1948). *Strange Fires* (1971) is a novel about John Wesley in Georgia. Her ashes were spread in the garden at the home of her youngest son in the Florida Keys.

☙

Caroline Gordon (6 October 1895 Todd Co. KY – 11 April 1981 San Cristobel Mexico) was a novelist, story writer, and critic. A convert to Catholicism, she was married twice and divorced twice from Allen Tate. She was buried (with Native American funeral rites) in San Cristobel, Mexico, where she had moved to be with her daughter.

☙

Joseph Holt Ingraham (26 January 1809 Portland ME – 18 December 1860 Holly Springs MS) was an Episcopal priest who wrote many novels. He died after shooting himself accidentally inside Christ Church in Holly Springs, Mississippi, where he was rector. His grave marker in Hillcrest Cemetery in Holly Springs has been overtaken by an English yew tree.

☙

Gerald White Johnson (6 August 1890 Riverton NC – 22 March 1980 Baltimore MD) was a prolific newspaperman and writer. He was cremated, with his ashes placed in the columbarium at Green Mount Cemetery in Baltimore, now closed to the public.

☙

Grace Lumpkin (3 March 1891 Milledgeville GA – 23 March 1980 Columbia SC) wrote many novels and had Communist associations. Her grave in the Lumpkin family plot in Elmwood Cemetery in Columbia, South Carolina, is unmarked.

☙

Merrill Moore (11 September 1903 Columbia TN – 20 September 1957 Boston MA) was a poet, particularly a sonneteer, and psychologist, and the son of John Trotwood Moore. He donated his body to Harvard.

☙

Henry Junius Nott (4 November 1797 Union District SC – 13 October 1837 off the North Carolina coast) was a lawyer and professor at South Carolina College. His one book, *Novellette of a Traveller; or, Odds and Ends from the Knapsack of Thomas Singularity* (1834), was "a sprightly tale, well written, yet there was much in it which was displeasing to the religious community," according to his biographer. He died in the shipwreck of the steamer *Home*.

☙

Alexandra Ripley (8 January 1934 Charleston SC – 10 January 2004 Richmond VA) was the author of *Scarlett* (1991), a sequel to Mitchell's *Gone With the Wind* (1936). Her cremated remains are in the possession of a friend.

☙

Irwin Russell (23 July 1853 Port Gibson MS – 23 December 1879 New Orleans LA) wrote "Christmas Night in the Quarters" and other African-American dialect stories. His grave in Bellafontaine Cemetery in St. Louis is unmarked.

☙

Emma Speed Sampson (1 December 1868 Louisville KY – 7 May 1947 Richmond VA) wrote many children's books, including 11 sequels to France Boyd Calhoun's *Miss Minerva and William Green Hill*. Her grave in Hollywood Cemetery, Richmond, Virginia, is unmarked.

☙

Celestine Sibley (23 May 1914 Holley FL – 15 August 1999 Atlanta GA) was a longtime columnist for the *Atlanta Journal-Constitution*. She was cremated, and her ashes are held by the family.

☙

Mickey Spillane (3 September 1918 Brooklyn NY – 17 August 2006 Murrells Inlet SC) wrote many detective novels, notably beginning with *I, the Jury* in 1947. Not a Southern writer, he did live for many years at Murrells Inlet on the South Carolina coast. His ashes were scattered in a creek near his home.

☙

Peter Taylor (8 January 1917 Trenton TN – 2 November 1994 Charlottesville VA) was a story writer and novelist, winner of the 1987 Pulitzer Prize for *A Summons to Memphis* (1986) late in his career. He was cremated and his ashes were buried at University Cemetery in Sewanee, Tennessee, but later taken to Charlottesville, Virginia.

☙

Richard Wright (4 September 1908 Natchez MS – 28 November 1960 Paris France) is remembered as the author of *Native Son* (1940). He was cremated, and his ashes, together with those of the manuscript of *Native Son*, are in the columbarium at Père Lachaise Cemetery in Paris.

BIBLIOGRAPHY

Print Sources

Aiken, David. *Fire in the Cradle: Charleston's Literary Heritage*. Charleston: Charleston Press, 1999.
Alderman, Edwin Anderson. Joel Chandler Harris, and Charles William Kent. *Library of Southern Literature*. Atlanta: Martin and Hoyt, 1910.
Anderson, Mary Crow, ed. *Two Scholarly Friends: Yates Snowden—John Bennett Correspondence, 1902-1932*. Columbia: UP of South Carolina, 1993.
Ayers, Edward L., and Bradley C. Mittendorf. *The Oxford Book of the American South*. New York: Oxford UP, 1997.
Bailey, Beatrice Naff. "Broadcasting and Preserving Upcountry Music Near and Far." *The South Carolina Review* 39.2: 61-73 (Spring 2007).
Bain, Robert and Joseph M. Flora, eds. *Fifty Southern Writers Before 1900*. New York: Greenwood, 1987.
—. Robert, Joseph M. Flora, and Louis D. Rubin, Jr., eds. *Southern Writers: A Bibliographical Dictionary*. Baton Rouge: Louisiana State UP, 1979.
Barley, Nigel. *Grave Matters*. New York: Henry Holt, 1997.
Baskervill, William Malone. *Southern Writers: Biographical and Critical Studies, Volume 2*. Nashville: Publishing House of the Methodist Episcopal Church South, 1922.
Bayne, John. "Eudora Welty's Use of Tombstones and Cemeteries." *Eudora Welty Newsletter* 27.2 (Summer 2003).
Beidler, Philip D. "Caroline Lee Hentz's Long Journey." *Alabama Heritage* (Winter 2005).
Bellows, Barbara L. *A Talent for Living: Josephine Pinckney and the Charleston Literary Tradition*. Baton Rouge: Louisiana State UP, 2006.
Benoit, Tod. *Where Are They Buried? How Did They Die?* New York: Black Dog and Leventhal, 2003.
Bergreen, Laurence. *James Agee: A Life*. New York: Dutton, 1984.
Bergman, Edward F. *Woodlawn Remembers: Cemetery of American History*. Utica: North Country Books, 1988.
Black, Patti Carr and Marion Barnwell. *Touring Literary Mississippi*. Jackson: UP of Mississippi, 2002.
Calhoun, Frances Boyd. *Miss Minerva and William Green Hill*. Chicago: Reilley and Britton, 1909.
Capote, Truman. *In Cold Blood*. New York: Vintage, 1994.
Caron, James C., and M. Thomas Inge, eds. *Sut Lovingood's Nat'ral Born Yarnspinner*. Tuscaloosa: UP of Alabama, 1996.
Carr, Virginia Spencer. *The Lonely Hunter: A Biography of Carson McCullers*. New York: Doubleday, 1975.
Carter, Hodding III. "The Difficult Isolation Courage Can Bring." *Nieman Reports*, n. d.
Cash, Jean W. *Flannery O'Connor: A Life*. Knoxville: UP of Tennessee, 2002.
—, and Keith Perry, eds. *Larry Brown and the Blue-Collar South*. Jackson: UP of Mississippi, 2008.
Chapman, C. Stuart. *Shelby Foote: A Writer's Life*. Jackson: UP of Mississippi, 2003.
Childs, Henry Clay. *Gardens and Graveyards of the Southeastern Seaboard*. Washington: Painter Ridge, 1994.
Cohen, Hennig, and William B. Dillingham, eds. *Humor of the Old Southwest*. Athens: UP of Georgia, 1994.
Coogler, J. Gordon. *Purely Original Verse*. Columbia: Vogue Press, 1974.
Crampton, Nancy. *Writers*. New York: Quantuck Lane, 2005.
Cullen, Lisa Takeuchi. *Remember Me*. New York: Collins, 2006.
Curl, James Stevens. *Death and Architecture*. Thrupp Stroud: Sutton, 2002.
—. *The Egyptian Revival*. Abingdon: Routledge, 2005.
—. *The Victorian Celebration of Death*. Thrupp Stroud: Sutton, 2000.
Dameron, J. Lasley, and James W. Mathews, eds. *No Fairer Land: Studies in Southern Literature before 1900*. Troy, New York: Whitson, 1986.
Davidson, Donald. *Southern Writers in the Modern World*. Athens: UP of Georgia, 1958.
Dollarhide, Louis. *Of Art and Artists*. Jackson: UP of Mississippi, 1981.
Dunaway, John M., ed. *Exiles and Fugitives: The Letters of Jacques and Raissa Maritain, Allen Tate, and Caroline Gordon*. Baton Rouge: Louisiana State UP, 1992.
DuPriest, James E. Jr. *Hollywood Cemetery: A Tour*. Richmond: Richmond Discoveries, 1989.
Elie, Paul. *The Life You Save May Be Your Own: An American Pilgrimage*. New York: Farrar, Straus and Giroux, 2003.
Epps, Edwin C. *Literary South Carolina*. Spartanburg: Hub City Writers Project, 2004.

Faulkner, William. *Novels 1926-1929*. New York: Library of America, 2006.
Ferris, Marcie Cohen, and Mark I. Greenberg, eds. *Jewish Roots in Southern Soil*. Waltham: Brandeis, 2006.

Fisher, Benjamin F., ed. *Masques, Mysteries, and Mastodons: A Poe Miscellany*. Baltimore: Edgar Allan Poe Society, 2006.
Fletcher, Joel L. *Ken & Thelma: The Story of* A Confederacy of Dunces. Gretna: Pelican, 2005.
Flora, Joseph M., and Amber Vogel, eds. *Southern Writers: A New Biographical Dictionary*. Baton Rouge: LSU Press, 2006.
—. and Robert Bain, eds. *Fifty Southern Writers After 1900*. New York: Greenwood, 1987.
Gandolfo, Henri A. *Metairie Cemetery: An Historical Memoir*. New Orleans: Stewart Enterprises, 1998.
George-Graves, Nadine. *The Royalty of Negro Vaudeville*. New York: Macmillan, 2000.
Gerarty, Virginia Mixson. *Porgy: A Gullah Version*. Charleston: Wyrick, 1990.
Givner, Joan. *The Life of Katherine Anne Porter*. London: Jonathan Cape, 1983.
Gonzales, Ambrose E. *The Black Border: Gullah Stories of the Carolina Coast*. Columbia: The State Company, 1922.
Gooch, Brad. *Flannery: A Life of Flannery O'Connor*. New York: Little, Brown, 2009.
Goodman, Fred. *The Secret City: Woodlawn Cemetery and the Buried History of New York*. New York: Broadway, 2004.
Goodman, Susan E. *Ellen Glasgow: A Biography*. Baltimore: Johns Hopkins UP, 1998.
Greene, Harlan. *Mr. Skylark: John Bennett and the Charleston Renaissance*. Athens: UP of Georgia, 2001.
Guss, John Walker. *Savannah's Laurel Grove Cemetery*. Charleston: Arcadia, 2004.
Hacker, Debi. *Iconography of Death*. Columbia: Chicora Foundation, 2001.
Harris, George Washington. *High Times and Hard Times*. Ed. M. Thomas Inge. Nashville: Vanderbilt, 1967.
—. *Sut Lovingood Travels with Old Abe Lincoln*. Ed. Edd Winfield Parks. Chicago: Black Cat Press, 1937.
—. *Sut Lovingood's Yarns*, ed. M. Thomas Inge. New Haven: College UP, 1966.
Hart, Bertha Sheppard. *Introduction to Georgia Writers*. Macon: Burke, 1929.
Hayne, Paul Hamilton. *Poems of Paul Hamilton Hayne*. Boston: Lothrop, 1882.
Hertzberg, Max J., ed. *The Reader's Encyclopedia of American Literature*. New York: Thomas Crowell, 1962.
Hibbard, Addison, ed. *Stories of the South*. Chapel Hill: UP of North Carolina, 1931.
Higgs, Robert J., and Ambrose N. Manning, eds. *Voices from the Hills: Selected Readings of Southern Appalachia*. New York: Frederick Ungar, 1975.
Hill, Samuel S., ed. *The New Encyclopedia of Southern Culture, Volume 1: Religion*. Chapel Hill: UP of North Carolina, 2006.
Historic Oakland Foundation. *Your Gateway to Historic Oakland Cemetery*. Atlanta: Historic Oakland Foundation, 1999.
Hobbs, June Hadden, ed. *Literature of the Graveyard, Studies in the Literary Imagination*. Atlanta: Georgia State UP, 2006.
Howell, Elmo. *Mississippi Home-Places*. Memphis: Elmo Howell, 1988.
—. *Notes on Southern Lit*. Memphis: Langford & Associates, 2005.
Hutchisson, James M. and *DuBose Heyward: A Charleston Gentleman and the World of Porgy and Bess*. Jackson: UP of Mississippi, 2000.
—. *Poe*. Jackson: UP of Mississippi, 2005.
—. and Harlan Greene, eds. *Renaissance in Charleston: Art and Life in the Carolina Low Country, 1900-1940*. Athens: UP of Georgia, 2003.
Inge, M. Thomas, ed. *Conversations with William Faulkner*. Jackson: UP of Mississippi, 1999.
—. ed. *The New Encyclopedia of Southern Culture Volume 9: Literature*. Chapel Hill: UP of North Carolina, 2008.
—. "Searching for Sut: Solving the Mystery of George Washington Harris's Gravesite." *Now and Then* 24.2: 65-67 (Winter 2008).
Inge, M. Thomas and Edgar E. McDonald, eds. *James Branch Cabell: Centennial Essays*. Baton Rouge: Louisiana State UP, 1983.
—, and Edward J. Piacentino, eds. *The Humor of the Old South*. Lexington: UP of Kentucky, 2001.
Johnson, David E. *Douglas Southall Freeman*. Gretna: Pelican, 2002.
Jarrell, Mary von Schrader. *Remembering Randall: a Memoir of Poet, Critic and Teacher Randall Jarrell*. New York: Harper Collins, 1999.
Johnson, Rossiter, and John Howard Brown, *The Twentieth Century Biographical Dictionary of Notable Americans*. Baltimore: The Biographical Society, 1904.
Johnson, Thomas L. *A Day in May*. Hartsville: Coker College Press, 1996.
Jones, Anne Goodwyn. *Tomorrow is Another Day: The Woman Writer in the South, 1859-1936*. Baton Rouge: Louisiana State UP, 1981.

Jones, Charles Colcock Jr. *The Life, Literary Labors And Neglected Grave of Richard Henry Wilde.* NP: Kessinger Rare Reprints, ND.
—. *The Siege of Savannah in December, 1864, and the Confederate Operations in Georgia and the Third Military District of South Carolina during General Sherman' March from Atlanta to the Sea.* New York: Munsel, 1874.
Junior League of Charleston, *Charleston Receipts.* Charleston: Walker, Evans and Cogswell, 1950.
Kaemmerlen, Cathy J. *The Historic Oakland Cemetery of Atlanta: Speaking Stones.* Charleston: The History Press, 2007.
Keister, Douglas. *Forever Dixie: A Field Guide to Southern Cemeteries and Their Residents.* Salt Lake City: Gibbs Smith, 2008.
—. *Going Out in Style: The Architecture of Eternity.* New York: Facts on File, 1997.
—. *Stories in Stone: A Field Guide to Cemetery Symbolism and Iconography.* Salt Lake City: Gibbs Smith, 2004.
King, Grace. *Memories of a Southern Woman of Letters.* Gretna: Pelican, 2007.
King, Larry L. *In Search of Willie Morris.* New York: Public Affairs, 2006.
Klosterman, Chuck. *Killing Yourself to Live: 85% of a True Story.* New York: Scribner, 2005.
Kreyling, Michael. *Inventing Southern Literature.* Jackson: UP of Mississippi, 1998.
Lamb, Brian. *Who's Buried in Grant's Tomb?* Washington: National Cable Satellite Corp., 2000.
Largo, Michael. *Genius and Heroin.* New York: Harper, 2008.
Leonard, Stephanie. *Imortelles of Catholic Columbian Literature.* New York: D. H. McBride, 1897.
Levy, Buddy. *American Legend: The Real-Life Adventures of David Crockett.* New York: Putnam, 2005.
Linden, Blanche M. G. *Silent City on a Hill.* Boston: UP of Massachusetts, 2007.
Manly, Louise. *Southern Literature from 1579-1895.* Richmond: R. F. Johnson, 1895.
Marius, Richard. *An Affair of Honor.* New York: Knopf, 2001.
Marston, John C. H. *A Tour of Historic Magnolia Cemetery, Mobile, Alabama.*
Masek, Mark J. *Hollywood Remains to Be Seen.* Nashville: Cumberland House, 2001.
Mason, Mary. *The Young Housewife's Counsellor and Friend.* New York: Hale, 1875.
McAlexander, Hubert Horton. *Peter Taylor: A Writer's Life.* Baton Rouge: Louisiana State UP, 2001.
—. *The Prodigal Daughter: A Biography of Sherwood Bonner.* Baton Rouge: Louisiana State UP, 1981.
McClatchy, J. D. *American Writers at Home.* New York: Library of America, 2004.
—. ed. *Truman Capote Conversations.* Jackson: UP of Mississippi, 1987.
—. *William Faulkner.* New York: Overlook, 2006.
McHaney, Pearl ed. *Eudora Welty: The Contemporary Reviews.* Cambridge: Cambridge UP, 2005.
Menachemson, Nolan. *A Practical Guide to Jewish Cemeteries.* Bergenfield: Avotaynu, 2007.
Meyer, Richard E., ed. *Cemeteries and Gravemarkers: Voices of American Culture.* Logan: Utah State UP, 1989.
Miller, Dan B. *Erskine Caldwell: The Journey from Tobacco Road.* New York: Knopf, 1995.
Mitford, Jessica. *The American Way of Death.* New York: Simon and Schuster, 1963.
Morris, Willie and William Eggleston. *Faulkner's Mississippi.* Birmingham: Oxmoor, 1990.
Neely, Jack, and Aaron Jay. *The Marble City.* Knoxville: UP of Tennessee, 1999.
Norrell, Robert J. *Up from History: The Life of Booker T. Washington.* Cambridge: Belknap, 2009.
O'Connell, David. *Furl That Banner: The Life of Abram J. Ryan, Poet-Priest of the South.* Macon: Mercer UP, 2006.
O'Neall, John Belton. *Biographical Sketches of the Bench and Bar of South Carolina.* Charleston: S. G. Courtenay, 1859.
Parks, Edd Winfield. *Segments of Southern Thought.* Athens: UP of Georgia, 1938.
Phillips, Ted Ashton Jr. *City of the Silent: The Charlestonians of Magnolia Cemetery.* Columbia: UP of South Carolina, 2010.
Plimpton, George. *Truman Capote.* New York: Doubleday, 1997.
Polk, Noel. *Faulkner and Welty and the Southern Literary Tradition.* Jackson: UP of Mississippi, 2008.
Pomerantz, Gary M. *Where Peachtree Meets Sweet Auburn.* New York: Scribner, 1996.
Proprietors of Green Mount Cemetery. *Green Mount Cemetery One Hundredth Anniversary 1838–1938.* Baltimore: 1938.
Ravenel, Beatrice Witte. *Arrow of Lightning.* Ed. Louis D. Rubin, Jr. Chapel Hill: UNC Press, 1969.
Reed, J. D., and Maddy Miller. *Stairway to Heaven: The Final Resting Places of Rock's Legends.* New York: Wenner Books, 2005.
Richter, Curt. *A Portrait of Southern Writers.* Athens: Hill Street Press, 2000.
Rickles, Milton. *George Washington Harris.* New York: Twayne, 1965.
Ridgely, J. V. *Nineteenth-Century Southern Literature.* Lexington: UP of Kentucky, 1980.
Roberts, Jimm. *Southernmost Art and Literary Portraits.* Macon: Mercer UP, 2005.

Rosengarten, Theodore, and Dale Rosengarten, eds. *A Portion of the People: Three Hundred Years of Southern Jewish Life*. Columbia: UP of South Carolina, 2002.
Rubin, Louis D. Jr., ed. *A Bibliographical Guide to the Study of Southern Literature*. Baton Rouge: Louisiana State UP, 1969.
Ryan, Abram Joseph. *Selected Poems of Father Ryan*. Ed. Gordon Weaver. Jackson: UP of Mississippi, 1973.
Samway, Patrick S. J. *Walker Percy: A Life*. New York: Farar, Straus, and Giroux, 1997.
Savigneau, Josayne. *Carson McCullers: A Life*. New York: Houghton Mifflin, 1995.
Serafin, Steven, ed. *The Continuum Encyclopedia of American Literature*. New York: Continuum, 2001.
Simpson, Lewis P. *The Fable of the Southern Writer*. Baton Rouge: Louisiana State UP, 1994.
Skaggs, Merrill Maguire. *The Folk of Southern Fiction*. Athens: UP of Georgia, 1972.
Solomon, Jack, and Olivia. *Gone Home: Southern Folk Gravestone Art*. Montgomery: NewSouth Books, 2004.
Spears, Ross, Jude Cassidy, and Robert Coles. *Agee: His Life Remembered*. New York: Holt Rinehart Winston, 1985.
Spencer, Elizabeth. "Remembering Eudora," *Raleigh-Durham-Chapel Hill Indy*, 15 August 2001.
Spielman, David G., and William W. Starr. *Southern Writers*. Columbia: UP of South Carolina, 1997.
Stanton, Scott. *The Tombstone Tourist: Musicians*. Portland: 3T Publishing, 1998.
Stone, David Charles. *The Last Great Necessity*. Baltimore: Johns Hopkins, 1991.
Stribling, T.S. *Laughing Stock*. Ed. R.K. Cross and J.T. McMillan. Memphis: St. Luke's, 1982.
Styron, William. *This Quiet Dust And Other Writings*. New York: Random House, 1982.
Taliaferro, Tevi. *Historic Oakland Cemetery*. Charleston: Arcadia, 2001.
Taylor, Jerome. *In Search of Self: Life, Death & Walker Percy*. Cambridge, MA: Cowley, 1986.
Tetzlaff, Monica Maria. *Cultivating a New South: Abbie Holmes Christensen*. Columbia: UP of South Carolina, 2003.
Thomas, James W. *Lyle Saxon: A Critical Biography*. Birmingham: Summa Publications, 1991.
Tippins, Sherill. *February House: The story of W. H. Auden, Carson McCullers, Jane and Paul Bowles, Benjamin Britten, and Gypsy Rose Lee Under One Roof in Brooklyn*. New York: Mariner, 2005.
Tobias, Thomas J. *Tombstones That Tell Stories: The Historic Coming Street Cemetery of Congregation Beth Elohim, Charleston, S. C.*, revised by Solomon Breibart. Charleston: Kahal Kadosh Beth Elohim, 2000.
Unrue, Darlene Harbour. *Katherine Anne Porter: The Life of an Artist*. Jackson: UP of Mississippi, 2005.
Walker, Margaret. *Richard Wright: Daemonic Genius*. New York: Warner Books, 1988.
Welch, William C. and Greg Grant. *The Southern Heirloom Garden*. New York: Taylor, 1995.
Welty, Eudora. *Country Churchyards*. Jackson: UP of Mississippi, 2000.
—. "Magic," *Eudora Welty Newsletter*. 28.2 (Summer 2003).
—. *Occasions*. Ed. Pearl Amelia McHaney. Jackson: UP of Mississippi, 2009.
—. *The Optimist's Daughter*. New York: Random House, 1972.
Williams, Benjamin Buford. *A Literary History of Alabama: The Nineteenth Century*. Rutherford: Fairleigh Dickinson, 1979.
Wilson, Amie Marie, and Mandi Dale Johnson, *Historic Bonaventure Cemetery*. Charleston: Arcadia, 1998.
Wilson, Charles Reagan, and William Ferrris, eds. *Encyclopedia of Southern Culture*. Chapel Hill: UP of North Carolina, 1989.
Wolfe, Theodore F. *Literary Haunts and Homes*. Philadelphia: Lippincott, 1898.
—. *A Literary Pilgrimage*. Philadelphia: Lippincott, 1895.
—. *Literary Rambles*. Philadelphia: Lippincott, 1900.
—. *Literary Shrines*. Philadelphia: Lippincott, 1895.
Wright, Roberta Hughes, and Wilbur B. Hughes III, *Lay Down Body: Living History in African-American Cemeteries*. Detroit: Visible Ink, 1996.
Yates, Norris Wilson. *William T. Porter and the Spirit of the Times*. New Hampshire: Ayer Publishing, 1977.
Young, Thomas Daniel. *Tennessee Writers*. Knoxville: UP of Tennessee, 1981.
—. *Selected Essays 1965-1985*. Baton Rouge: Louisiana State UP, 1990.
Young, Timothy White. "Hamilton Basso Papers," *Yale University Beinecke Rare Book and Manuscript Library*, (September 1992).

Web Sources

"Allen, Hervey." <http://pabook.libraries.psu.edu/palitmap/bios/Allen__Hervey.html>.
Beavers, Herman. "James Weldon Johnson's Life and Career." *Modern American Poetry*. <http://www.english.illinois.edu/Maps/poets/g_l/johnson/life.htm>.

"Biography." <http://www.sc.edu/library/spcoll/amlit/johnson/johnson1.html>.
"Biography." *Internet Poetry Archive.* <http://www.ibiblio.org/ipa/poems/walker/biography.php>.
"Biography of John Kennedy Toole (1937–1969)." *Grade Saver.* <http://www.gradesaver.com/author/john-toole/>.
"Booker T. Washington." *National Park Service.* <http://www.nps.gov/bowa/index.htm>.
Butterfield, Herbie. "John Peale Bishop." *The Literary Encyclopedia.* <http://www.litencyc.com/php/speople.php?rec=true&UID=420>.
"Caroline Lee Whiting Hentz." <http://momo348.tripod.com/carolineleewhitinghentz/>.
"Caroline Miller." *Georgia Writers Hall of Fame.* <http://www.libs.uga.edu/gawriters/miller.html>.
"Christensen Family Papers, 1806-1987." *University of South Carolina.* <http://www.sc.edu/library/socar/uscs/1999/christn.html>.
"Christian Reid." <http://toto.lib.unca.edu/WNC_women/reid_christian.htm>.
Eidelman, Jay M. "Penina Moïse." *Jewish Women's Archive.* <http://jwa.org/encyclopedia/article/Moïse-penina>.
English, Lisa. "Walter Tevis." *KYLIT.* <http://www.english.eku.edu/SERVICES/KYLIT/tevis.htm>.
"Eugene Walter Biography." Book Rags. <http://www.bookrags.com/wiki/Eugene_Walter>.
"Eugene Walter: Last of the Bohemians." *Waterfront Pictures.* <http://www.waterfrontpix.com/eugenewalter2.htm>.
"Eugenia Price." *Wikipedia.* <http://en.wikipedia.org/wiki/Eugenia_Price>.
Fox, Margalit. "Wilma Dykeman, 86, a Writer on the Environment and Race, Dies." *The New York Times.* <http://www.nytimes.com/2006/12/29/books/28dykeman.html?_r=1>.
"Genesis & Apocalypse of the 'Old South' Myth: Two Virginia Writers at the Turn of the Century." *Publishers' Bindings Online.* University of Alabama. <http://bindings.lib.ua.edu/gallery/glasgow.html>.
"Gonzales Family: Charleston, SC & Beyond - Odds and Ends." <http://www.vergie.com/gonzales_odds_and_ends.html>.
"Harry Golden." <http://www.answers.com/topic/harry-golden>.
"Harry Stillwell Edwards." *Strangers to Us All.* <http://myweb.wvnet.edu/~jelkins/lp-2001/edwards.html>.
Havird, David. "Allen Tate's Life and Career." *Modern American Poetry.* <http://www.english.illinois.edu/maps/poets/s_z/tate/life.htm>.
"Howard, Robert Ervin." *The Handbook of Texas Online.* <http://www.tshaonline.org/handbook/online/articles/HH/fho92.html>.
"John Charles McNeill House and Memorial Gardens." *Learn NC.* <http://www.learnnc.org/lp/pages/2083>.
"John Crowe Ransom." *The Academy of American Poets.* <http://www.poets.org/poet.php/prmPID/12>.
"John Crowe Ransom Biography." *Famous Poets and Poems.* <http://famouspoetsandpoems.com/poets/john_crowe_ransom/biography>.
"John Kennedy Toole." *Wikipedia.* <http://en.wikipedia.org/wiki/John_Kennedy_Toole>.
"John Peale Bishop." Encyclopedia Britannica. <http://www.britannica.com/EBchecked/topic/66925>.
"John Peale Bishop Biography." *Book Rags.* <http://www.bookrags.com/biography/john-peale-bishop-dlb/>.
Jones, Sandy. "Eugenia Price Dies at Age 79." <http://www.gacoast.com/navigator/ep2.html>.
"Kate Chopin: Her Novels and Stories." *The Kate Chopin International Society.* <http://www.katechopin.org/>.
"Katherine Anne Porter." *American Masters.* <http://www.pbs.org/wnet/americanmasters/episodes/katherine-anne-porter/about-katherine-anne-porter/686/>.
"Lillian Eugenia Smith." *Georgia Women of Achievement.* <http://www.georgiawomen.org/_honorees/smithl/smith.pdf>.
"Lillian Smith." *Wikipedia.* <http://en.wikipedia.org/wiki/Lillian_Smith_(author)>.
"Mobile: William March, Albert Murray & Eugene Walter." *Southern Literary Trail.* <http://www.southernliterarytrail.org/mobile.html>.
Odom, Maida. "Margaret Walker, poet and novelist." *UPENN.* <http://writing.upenn.edu/~afilreis/50s/walker-margaret.html>.
"O. Henry Bio." *Random House.* <http://www.randomhouse.com/anchor/ohenry/bio.html>.
Powell, William S. ed. "Mary Ann Bryan Mason, 1802-1881." *Documenting the American South.* <http://docsouth.unc.edu/nc/mason/bio.html>.
Rainwater, Catherine. "Ellen Glasgow." *The Literary Encyclopedia.* <http://www.litencyc.com/php/speople.php?rec=true&UID=1766>.
Reuben, Paul P. "PAL: Perspectives in American Literature - A Research and Reference Guide - An Ongoing Project." <http://www.csustan.edu/english/reuben/pal/chap7/porter.html>.
Sansing, David G. "Alexander G. McNutt, Twelfth Governor of Mississippi: 1838-1842." *Mississippi History Now.* <http://mshistory.k12.ms.us/articles/265/index.php?s=extra&id=117>.

"Sons of Confederate Veterans: A Heritage of Honor." *Tennessee Division, SCV*. <http://tennessee-scv.org>.
"Thomas Holley Chivers (1809–1858)." *Georgia Encyclopedia*. <http://www.georgiaencyclopedia.org/nge/Article.jsp?id=h-513>.
"Tiernan, Frances (Christine) Fisher." <http://www.novelguide.com/a/discover/aww_04/aww_04_0119.html>.
"Walker Percy." <http://www.lib.unc.edu/rbc/percy/percy.html>.
"Walter Tevis." <http://www.waltertevis.com/>.
Watkins Family History Society. <http://www.watkinsfhs.net/>.
"William Clark Falkner." *The Mississippi Writers Page*. <http://www.olemiss.edu/mwp/dir/falkner_william_clark/index.html>.
"William Elliott, III Biography." *Book Rags*. <http://www.bookrags.com/biography/william-elliott-iii-dlb/>.
"William Hervey Allen, Jr.: First Lieutenant, United States Army." *Arlington National Cemetery*. <http://www.arlingtoncemetery.net/whallenjr.htm>.
Wilson, Charles Reagan and William Ferris, eds. "Ellen Anderson Gholson Glasgow, 1873-1945." *Documenting the American South*. <http://docsouth.unc.edu/southlit/glasgowbattle/bio.html>.

Index

Abel's Hill Cem., Chilmark, MA, 220, **221**
Abernathy, Ralph David, 56
abolitionist, 10, 50, 52, 114
Absalom, Absalom!, 170
Academy Award, 140, 154, 260
Accra, Ghana, 266
actor, 134, 238, 244, 265
Adams Run, SC, 92
Adams, Alexander St Clair, 46
Adams, E. C. L., 114
adultery, 160
advertising, 242
Advocate, 202
Africa, 232, 266
African Methodist Episcopal, 56
African Queen, The, 154
African, The, 232
African-American, 50, 54, 56, 82, 90, 100, 102, 110, 114, 118, 124, 126, 134, 138, 150, 158, 168, 190, 200, 216, 232, 246, 265, 266, 267
Agee Farm, Hillsdale, NY, 154, **155**
Agee, James, 154, **155**
Agrarian, 96, 124, 144, 172, 176, 190, 206, 208, 228, 238
Aiken, Conrad, 202, **203**
Aiken, SC, 14, **15**
Ainslie's, 156
Alabama, 10, 20, 40, **41,** 72, **73,** 80, **81,** 82, **83,** 98, 130, 152, 166, 180, 200, 226, **227,** 230, 244, **245,** 246
Alamo, 2
Alaska, 244
alcohol, 8, 12, 56, 78, 104, 136, 170, 188, 194, 218, 236, 254
Aleutian Islands, 244
Alexander, Firnist James, 246
Alexander, Margaret Walker, 246, **247**
Alexandria, LA, 200
Allen, Annette Andrews, 142
All Saints' Waccamaw, Pawleys Island, SC, 242, **243**
All The Way Home, 154
Allan, John, 8
Allegheny, PA, 20
Allen Temple, Atlanta, 56
Allen, Hervey, 120, 142, **143,** 156, 158
Alnilam, 242
Alston, Robert, 46
Altamont, NC, 112
American Academy in Rome, 260
American Academy of Arts and Letters, 132, 260
American Expeditionary Forces, 128
American Mercury, The, 122, 226
Americanization of Emily, The, 226

Amherst College, 172
Amherst, MA, 172
Andalusia, 178
Anderson Independent, 126
Anderson, Elizabeth, 136
Anderson, SC, 18, 126, 266
Anderson, Sherwood, 100, 136, 176
Andrews Allen, Annette, 142
Angel of the Tenement, The, 138
Angel, 120
Annals of Tennessee, 38
Anthony Adverse, 142
anthropologist, 166
anti-Semitism, 250
Antioch Cem., Island Grove, FL, 150, **151**
Arbuthnot, Fletcher Florence Emily (Daisy), 144
Arizona, 265
Arkansas, 144, **145**
Arlington National Cem., Arlington, VA, 142, **143**
Arp, Bill, 62, **63**
Arrow of Lightning, The, 156
arthritis, 144
As I Lay Dying, 170
Asheville, NC, 78, **79,** 112, **113,** 262, **263**
Ashmore, Henry Scott, 264
Ashwood, TN, 58
Ashworth, Mary Wells, 146
Associated Press, 152
Association of Southern Women for the Prevention of Lynching, 138
Aswell, Edward, 112
Athens Daily News, 236
Athens, GA, 46
Atlanta Constitution, 46, 60, 62, 70, 96, 164, 268
Atlanta Daily Herald, 46
Atlanta Journal, 96, 140, 236, 268
Atlanta Ring, 46
Atlanta University, 110, 266
Atlanta, Battle of, 58, 140
Atlanta, GA, 46, **47,** 56, **57,** 58, 70, **71,** 96, **97,** 104, 140, **141,** 186, 236, 242, **265,** 268, 216
Atlantic Monthly, 42, 86, 102, 106, 122, 138, 156
Auden, W. H., 188
Audubon, John James, 14
Augusta Chronicle, 68
Augusta Mirror, 34
Augusta, GA, 4, **5,** 24, 34, 40, 42, **43,** 48, **49,** 50, 68, 68, **69**
Austin, TX, 172
Author's Club, 138
Authors Guild, 222
Autobiography of an Ex-Coloured Man, The, 110
Autobiography of Malcolm X, The, 232
autograph, **153**
Awakening, The, 64

Bailey, Frederick Augustus Washington, 50
Bailey, Pearl, 200
Balch, Edwin, 148
Balch, Emily Clark, 148, **149**
Baldwin Co. (GA) High School, 178
Baldwin, James, 260
Baldwin, Joseph Glover, 264
Ball, William Watts, 156
Ballad of the Bones and Other Poems, 164
"Balloon Hoax, The," 8
Baltimore College, 26
Baltimore Evening Sun, 122, 258
Baltimore, MD, 8, **9,** 26, **27,** 30, **31,** 34, 68, 80, 112, 134, 258, 266
Bank of Tennessee, 38
Banks Co., GA, 265
Banner of the South, 40
Baptist Church, Beaufort, SC, 114, **115**
Baptist, 134, 152
Barbados, 16
Bardstown, KY, 214
Bartlett Cable, Louise Stewart, 90
Bartow Co., GA, 104, **105**
Baskervill, William Malone, 54, **55**
Baskin, Norton, 150
Basso, Hamilton, 176, **177**
Baton Rouge, LA, 136, **137**
Battle of Angels, 218
Bayles, AL, 152
Bayou Folk Museum, 64
Beaufort, SC, 16, 114, **115**
Beaverdam Baptist Churchyard, Asheville, NC, 262, **263**
Bedford Forrest and His Critter Company, 238
Beersheba Springs, TN, 86
Bell, Sam, 20
Bellamann, Henry, 130, **131,** 168
Bellamann, Katherine McKee Jones, 130, **131**
Bellefontaine Cem., St Louis, MO, 267
Belles, Beaux and Brains of the 60's, 80
Bellingham, WA, 136
"Bells for John Whiteside's Daughter," 206
Belmont, MA, 250
Beloved Invader, 240
bench, **85, 203, 235**
Bénet, Stephen Vincent, 142
Bennett, John, 120, 158, **159**
Bennington College, 168
Berendt, John, 202
Berkeley, CA, 228
Berry, Martha, 104
Beth Elohim, Charleston, SC, 28
Better a Dinner of Herbs, 164
Beulah, 72
Bienville, 100

Big Bad Love, 254
Big Bear of Arkansas, The, 6
Bigsby Grays, 58
Bilbo, Theodore, 198
Billy and the Major, 74
biographer, 142, 146
birdbath, **235, 261**
Birmingham, AL, 152, 230, 246
Birth of a Nation, The, 102, 134
Birthright, 180
Biscuit Eater, The, 152
Bishop, John Peale, 128, **129**
Black April, 168
blacklist, 220
blind, 28, 80
Blood Mountain, GA, 164
Bollingen Prize, 202, 208, 206
Bonaventure Cem., Savannah, GA, 202, **203**
Bonner McDowell, Sherwood, 36, **37**
Bontemps, Arna, 200, **201**
Book of the Month Club, 160
Boston, MA, 8, 30, 36, 46, 52, 96, 267
boulder, **19, 31, 71, 83, 155, 181**
Bourbonville, TN, 250
Bow Down In Jericho, 164
Bowles, Jane and Paul, 188
Boyle, Virginia Fraser, 118, **119**
Bradford, Roark Whitney Wickliffe, 264
Bragg, Laura, 142, 264
Bread Loaf, 188
Breakfast at Tiffany's, 224
Brennan, Walter, 152
Brickell, Henry Herschel, 264
Bridge St. Cem., Northampton, MA, 90, **91**
Bright Skin, 168
Bright's disease, 48
Britten, Benjamin, 188
Broadway, 188, 218, 220, 238
Brock Cem., Trenton, GA, 20, **21**
Brooklyn, NY, 110, 111, 188, 268
Brown Family Farm, Tula, MS, 254, **255**
Brown, Larry, 254, **255**
Brownwood, TX, 108, **109**
Brunswick, GA, 240
Bryan Mason, Mary Ann, 32, **33**
Bryant, William Cullen, 42
Bryson City, NC, 112
Buchanan, VA, 106
Buckdancer's Choice, 242
Buckley, William F., 226
Burgunder, Rose, Styron, 260
Burnett, Frances Hodgson, 88, **89**
Burnett, Lionel, Swann, and Vivian, 88
Burns, Ken, 58
Burns, Olive Ann, 265
Burns, Robert, 70

Burroughs Adding Machine Co., 210
By Valor and Arms, 152
Byhalia, MS, 170

"C. S. A.," 40
Cabell, James Branch, 96, 162, **163**
Cabin Road, 174
Cable, Eva C. Stephenson, Hannah Cowing, and Louise Stewart Bartlett, 90
Cable, George Washington, 54, 90, **91**
Caldwell, Erskine, 265
Calhoun, Frances Boyd, 74, **75,** 267
Calhoun, John C., 24
Calhoun, SC, 126
California Supreme Court, 264
California, 170, 200, 220, 222, 224, **225,** 228, 264, 265
Calvary Cem., Nashville, TN, 190, **191**
Calvary Cem., St Louis, MO, 64, **65,** 218, **219**
Cambridge, MA, 52, **53**
Camden, SC, 265
Campbellsville, TN, 190
Canada, 216
cancer, 32, 36, 160, 186, 220, 222, 228, 230, 250
Candler, Warren, 104
Canyon, TX, 214
Capote, Truman, 224, **225,** 244
car accident, 110,150
Caribbean, 156
Carmer, Carl, 142
Carolina Chansons, 120, 142
Carolina Israelite, The, 216
Carolina Sports, 16
"Carolina," 18
Caroline Sinkler Award for Poetry, 160
Carrie, Caroline Amour, Thompson, 34
Carroll, John Alexander, 146
Carson, Joanne and Johnny, 224
Carter, Hodding, 198, **199**
Carter, Jimmy, 202, 242
Cartersville, GA, 62, **63**
Carthage, MS, 130
Cary, Jennie, 68
Cash, Wilbur Joseph, 122, **123**
Cason, Zelma, 150
Cassique of Kiawah, A, 22
Cat on a Hot Tin Roof, 218
Catholic, 40, 84, 152, 178, 208, 230, 260, 266
Catholic Cem., Mobile, AL, 40, **41**
Cave Hill Cem., Louisville, KY, 138, **139**
Cedar Lawn Cem., Jackson, MS, 252
"Celebrated Jumping Frog of Calaveras County, The," 76
Cembry, R. Emmett, 86, **87**
cenotaph, 2, 70
Centenary College, 24

Century, 66
Church of the Heavenly Rest, New York, NY, 130, **131**
Chegary Institute, 86
Chalotte News, 258
Chancellorsville, VA, 114
Chaney, James, 226
Chapel Hill, NC, 10, 152, **153,** 182, 214, **215,** 230
Charles S. Johnson Award, 186
Charles Town, WV, 128
Charleston Museum, 264
Charleston News and Courier, 14, 92, 126, 192
"Charleston," 18
Charleston (dance), 176
Charleston, SC, 8, 14, 16, **17,** 18, 22, **23,** 28, **29,** 42, 120, **121,** 142, 156, **157,** 158, **159,** 160, **161,** 192, **193,** 204, 264, 265, 267
Charleston, WV, 240
Charlotte News, 122
Charlotte Observer, 66, 122
Charlotte, NC, 38, 216, **217,** 258
Charlottesville, VA, 268
Chattanooga, TN, 20
Chesnut, Mary Boykin Miller, 265
Chesnutt, Charles Waddell, 102, **103**
Chestnut Hill, Salisbury, NC, 84, **85**
Chicago Lyric Opera, 210
Chicago Post, 122
Chicago Sun-Times, 236
Chicago World's Fair, 56
Chicago, IL, 200, 210, 236, 246, 262, 200
Chickamauga, GA, 58
Chicora College, 130, 168
Children in the Mist, 138
Children of Pride, The, 48
Children's Hour, The, 220
Chillicothe, OH, 158
Chilmark, MA, 220, **221**
Chivers, Thomas Holley, 12, **13**
Chopin, Kate, 64, **65**
Chopin, Oscar, 64
Christ Church Cem., St Simons Island, GA, 240, **241**
Christ Episcopal Church, Holly Springs, MS, 36, 266
Christ Episcopal Church, New Bern, NC, 32
Christchurch School, 260
Christensen, Abbie Mandana Holmes, 114, **115**
Christensen, Niels, 114
Christian Brothers, 40
"Christmas Night in the Quarters," 267
Chronicles of Pineville, John's Alive, 34
Chunkey and Jem, 6
Church of the Heavenly Rest, New York, NY, 130, **131**
Cincinnati Conservatory of Music, 208, 210

Cincinnati, OH, 10, 76, 208, 210
Circuit Rider's Wife, A, 104
cirrhosis, 78
City College of New York, 216
City Cem., Hartselle, AL, 226, **227**
Civil War, 16, 18, 20, 22, 28, 38, 40, 46, 48, 52, 58, 76, 80, 86, 90, 98, 100, 106, 116, 118, 140, 172, 234, 256, 258, 265
Civil War, The (Burns), 58, 256
Civil War, The (Foote), 256
Clansman, The, 134
Clark Balch, Emily, 148, **149**
Clark Co., KY, 210
Clark University, 196
Clark, Katherine, 244
Clayton, GA, 186, **187**
Clemens, Orion, 76
Clemens, Samuel, 20, 70, 76, **77**, 90, 102
Clemm Poe, Virginia, 8
Clemson University, 126, 242, 264
Cleveland Co., NC, 134
Cleveland Press, 122
Cleveland, OH, 102, **103**
Clifton Masonic Academy, 180
Clifton, TN, 180, **181**
Cloutierville, LA, 64
Cohen, Octavus Roy, 265
Coker College, 196
Cold Sassy Tree, 265
Coleman, Mary Ann, 254
Coleman, Sarah Lindsey, 78
Collected Stories of Katherine Anne Porter, The, 212
Collected Stories, The (O'Connor), 178
College of Charleston, 42, 160
College of Physicians and Surgeons, 230
College of William and Mary, 162
College Park, MD, 212
Colonial Williamsburg, Inc., 258
Colorado, 212
columbarium, 130, **131**, 266, 268
Columbia University, 110, 142, 146, 160, 172, 184, 188, 194, 196, 230, 256
Columbia, SC, 18, **19**, 60, **61**, 80, 92, **93**, 168, 242, **267**
Columbia, TN, 58, **59**, 267
Columbus, GA, 10, 72, 188
Columbus, MS, 218
Coming of Rain, The, 250
Coming St. Cem., Charleston, SC, 28, **29**
Committee for Interracial Cooperation, 138
Communist, 267
Como, MS, 172, **173**
Co. Aytch: A Side Show of the Big Show, 58
Company H, 58
Conan the Barbarian, 108
Concord, MA, 250, **251**

Confederacy of Dunces, A, 194
Confederate Army, 16, 18, 20, 24, 30, 40, 44, 58, 76, 80, 90, 106, 118, 146, 265
Confessions of Nat Turner, The, 260
Conjure Woman, The, 102
Connecticut, 76, 176, **177**, 228
Connelly, Marc, 264
"Conquered Banner, The," 40
Conroy, Jack, 200
Converse College, 168, 192
Coogler, John Brown Gordon, 60, **61**
cook book, 32
Cooper, Anderson, 265
Cooper, James Fenimore, 22
Cooper, Wyatt Emory, 265
"Corn," 30
Cornell University, 232
Cornwall, England, 16
Cosmopolitan, 152
Cosmopolite, 80
"Cotton Boll, The,"' 18
Country Churchyards, 252
Courlander, Harold, 232
Covington, LA, 230, **231**
Covington, TN, 74, **75**
Cowing Cable, Hannah, 90
Cowper, William, 12
Craddock, Charles Egbert, 86, **87**
Crag-Nest, 80
Creekmore, Hubert, 184, **185**
cremated, 2, 122, 130, 212, 224, 250, 264, 265, 266, 267, 268
Creole, 90, 100
Crescent Beach, FL, 150
Crisis, The, 102
critic, 8, 212
Crockett, David, 2, **3**
Croix de Guerre, 124
Crooked Pond, 224
Cross Creek, FL, 150
Cross Creek and *Cross Creek Cookery,* 150
Cross Plains, TX, 108
cross, **33**, **41**, **49**, **63**, **85**, **87**, **97**, **149**, **157**, **161**
Cross, Myrtle, 252
Crozier, Margaret, Ramsey, 38
Cruise of the Dry Dock, 180
Cuba, 92
Cullen, Countee, 200
Cumberland Mountains, 86
Cumberland Plateau, 94
Curtis Institute, 130

Dabbs, James McBride, 196, **197**
Dabney family, 152
Daffodils Are Dangerous, 184
Daily American, The, 110

Daily Courier, 198
Dallas Morning News, 122
"Dancin' Party at Harrison's Cove, The," 86
Daniel Baker College, 108
Dante, 4
Daughters of the American Revolution, 148
Daughters of the Confederacy, 84
Davenport, Guy, 266
David Copperfield, 98
Davidson College, 260
Davidson, Donald, 124, 144, 190, **191**
Davis, Burke, 258, **259**
Davis, Jefferson, 70, 80, 84, 106, 118, 208
Davis, Miles, 232
Davy Crockett: His Own Story, 2
Day, Mary, Lanier, 30
Days to Come, 220
de Havilland, Olivia, 142
De Lara, or The Moorish Bride, 10
De Leon, Edwin, 80
De Leon, Thomas Cooper, 80, **81**
de Soto, Hernando, 118
De Wilde, Brandon, 152
"De Wolf, de Rabbit an' de Tar Baby," 114
Dead Lovers are Faithful Lovers, 96
Death in the Family, A, 154
Decatur, AL, 20
Decatur, GA, 12, **13**
Declaration of Independence, 120, 204
DeKalb County, GA, 12, 186
Delaware, 32
Deliverance, 242
Delta, The, 68
Delta Democrat-Times, 198
Democrat, 20, 34
Denmark, 114
Denver, CO, 212
DePauw University, 54
depression, 88, 144, 182, 260
Descendant, The, 132
De Soto Co., MS, 6
diabetes, 78
dialect, 16, 34, 36, 48, 62, 92, 94, 102, 114, 118, 168, 234, 264, 265, 267
Diary of a Slave Girl, 52
Dick Cavett Show, The, 220
Dickens, Charles, 26, 98
Dickey, James, 242, **243**
Dickinson, Emily, 202
D'Invilliers, Tom, 128
Dirty Work, 254
divorce, 36, 88, 144, 150, 160, 208, 212, 234, 248
Dix, Dorothy, 136
Dixie Lee Baptist Church, 250
Dixon, Thomas, 134, **135**
Dobbs, John Wesley, 56

Doctor to the Dead, The, 158
Dodge, Anson, 240
Doko (Blythewood), SC, 60
Dolittle, Eliza, 74
Dollar Cotton, 174
Dominican College, 194
dos Passos, John, 136
Double-Dealer, The, 176
Douglas, Margery Stoneman, 142
Douglass, Frederick, 50, **51**, 102
Dr. J. G. M. Ramsey: Autobiography and Letters, 38
Drama Critics Circle Award, 218, 220
Dreiser, Theodore 162
drowning, 144, 267
drugs, 96, 104, 188, 218
Dublin, Ireland, 4
DuBois, W. E. B., 82, 266
Duke University, 132, 258, 260, 266
Dunham, Katherine, 246
Durham, NC, 258
Dutton, E. P., 164
Dykeman, Wilma, 262, **263**
Dylan, Bob, 18

East Tennessee Historical Society, 38
Eatonton, GA, 70
Ebenezer Academy, 38
Edenton, NC, 52
editor, 8, 34, 46, 110, 122, 124, 265
Edwards, Harry Stillwell, 116, **117**
Egyptian, 157
$8^{1/2}$, 244
Elbert Co., GA, 104
elder, 20
Eliot, T. S., 170, 202, 244
Elliott, Sarah Bull Barnwell, 94, **95**
Elliott, Stephen, 94
Elliott, William, 16, **17**
Elmira, NY, 76, **77**
Elmwood Cem., Columbia, SC, 60, **61**, 92, **93**
Elmwood Cem., Memphis, TN, 118, **119**, 256, **257**
Emmy Lou: Her Book and Heart, 138
Emory College and University, 24, 104, 164, 186
Eneas Africanus, 116
England, 8, 50, 60, 88, 144, 202, 248
Engle, Paul, 178
Episcopal, 32, 168, 176, 210, 218, 260, 266
epitaph, 36, 126, **127**, 180, 186, 196, 202, 240, 244
Equal Suffrage League of Virginia, 106
Essays on the Ten Plagues and Other Miscellaneous Poems, 56
"Ethnogenesis," 18
Ethridge, Willie Snow, 266
Eugene Walter: Last of the Bohemians, 244
Europe, 34, 76, 84, 124, 144, 156, 170, 176, 260

Evans Wilson, August Jane, 72, **73**
Evans, Walker, 154
Everglades, 142
Everglades: River of Grass, The, 142
Evergreen Cem., Harwich, MA, 128, **129**
Evergreen Cem., Murfreesboro, TN, 86, **87**
Everything That Rises Must Converge, 178
Execution of Private Slovik, The, 226

Fable, A, 170
Fabulous New Orleans, 136
Facing the Music, 254
Fairfax Co., VA, 208
Fairfield, CT, 228
Falkner, John, 174, **175**
Falkner, William Clark, 44, **45**
Families: A Memoir and a Celebration, 265
Family Companion and Ladies' Mirror, The, 34
Fancy's Sketch Book, 28
Faneuil Hall, Boston, MA, 46
Father Mississippi, 136
Father of the Blues, 200
Fathers, The, 208
Faulkner, Estelle Oldham Franklin, 170
Faulkner, John, 174, **175**
Faulkner, William, 20, 76, 124, 136, 156, 170, **171**, 174, 176, 198, 244
Fayette Co., TN, 54
Fayetteville, NC, 102
Federal Writers Project, 184, 136, 246
Fellini, Federico, 244
Felton, Rebecca, 104
feminism, 10 64, 96, 132, 138
Ferncliff Cem., Hartsdale, NY, 264
Fifty Years and Other Poems, 110
Fillmore, Millard, 14, 26
Fingers of the Night, 184
Finn, Huckleberry, 76
firefighter, 254
fireplace, 186, **187**
First Families of Virginia, 148
First Presbyterian Church, Knoxville, TN, 20
Fisher, Col. Charles F, 84
Fisher Tiernan, Frances Christine, 84, **85**
Fisk University, 186, 200, 266
Fitzgerald, F. Scott, 128, 150
Fitzgerald, Robert, 154
Flags in the Dust, 44
flat maker, **5,** 37, 57, 65, 81, 101, 103, 111, 119, 153, 159, 185, 191, 199, 207, 211, 221, 231, 235, 237, 239, 247, 251, 255, 257, 259, 221, 247, 251, 257
Fletcher, John Gould, 144, **145**
Florence Normal School, 180
Florence, AL, 180
Florence, SC, 18

Florida, 10, **11,** 90, 110, 142, 150, **151,** 152, 166, **167,** 186, 266
Florida, MO, 76
Flower in Drama, The, 172
"Flowering Judas," 212
Floyd, Carlisle, 265
Flush Times of Alabama and Mississippi, 264
Flye, Harold, 154
Foote, Henry S., 6
Foote, Shelby, 198, 256, **257**
"For My People," 246
Forest Lawn Memorial Park Cem., Glendale, CA, 265
Forest Lawn Cem., Greensboro, NC, 258, **259**
Forrest, Nathan Bedford, 238, 256
Forsyth, GA, 70
Ft Benning, GA, 236
Fort Motte, SC, 168, **169**
Fort Moultrie, 8
Ft Pierce, FL, 166, **167**
Fort Worth, TX, 212
Fortune, 154
Four Years in Rebel Capitals, 80
France, 124, 128, 156, 178, 206, 210, 234, 260, 268
Frankel Prize, 256
Franklin (State of), 38
Franklin Co., VA, 82
Franklin Faulkner, Estelle Oldham, 170
Frederick Douglass Paper, 50
Freedom Summer, 226
Freeman, Douglas Southall, 146, **147**
French Broad River, 262
Freud, Sigmund, 170
Friendship Cem., Como, MS, 172, **173**
Frobisher School, 134
From Here to Eternity, 248
Froman, Jane, 126
Frost, Robert, 150
Fugitive, 98, 124, 190, 206, 208, 228
Fugitive, The, 206, 208
Fulton, MO, 130
Future of the American Negro, The, 82

Gaffney, SC, 122
Gambia, 232
Gambier, OH, 182, 206, **207**
Garden of Heavenly Rest, Ft Pierce, FL, 166, **167**
Garden Memorial Park Cem., Jackson, MS, 246, **247**
Gardner, Isabella, Tate, 208, 216
Garland, Judy, 244
Garrison, William Lloyd, 50
Gary, Romain, 260
Gauntlet, The, 152
genealogy, 14, 20, 162, 192, 232, 234
George Washington: A Biography, 146

Georgetown College and University, 80, 68
Georgetown, SC, 242
Georgia College and State University, 178
Georgia Institute of Technology, 96
Georgia Scenes, 24
Georgia State College for Women, 178
Georgia Writer's Association, 164
Georgia Writers Hall of Fame, 234
Georgia, 4, **5,** 10, 12, **13,** 20, **21,** 24, 30, 34, 34, **35,** 42, **43,** 46, **47,** 48, **49,** 50, 56, **57,** 58, 62, **63,** 68, **69,** 70, **71,** 72, 94, 96, 96, **97,** 104, **105,** 114, 116, **117,** 140, **141,** 164, **165,** 178, **179,** 186, **187,** 188, 192, 202, **203,** 234, 236, **237,** 240, **241,** 242, **265,** 268
German, 18, 156
Germany, 54, 122
Gershwin, George, 120
Gestapo, 250
Gettysburg College, 250
Gettysburg, PA, 114, 250
Ghana, 266
Ghosts of Medgar Evers, The, 248
Ghosts of Mississippi, The, 248
"Gift of the Magi, The," 78
Giles County, TN, 190
Glasgow, Anne Jane Gholson and Francis Thomas, 132
Glasgow, Ellen, 132, **133,** 148
Glass Menagerie, The, 218
Glendale, CA, 265
Glenwood Cem., Yazoo City, MS, 248, **249**
Go Down, Moses, 170
Goblins and Pagodas, 144
God Sends Sunday, 200
Goddess of Reason, The, 106
Godey's Lady's Book, 88
God's Little Acre, 265
Godwin Timrod, Katie, 18
Gold Fish Bowl, The, 96
Gold Medal for Poetry, 202
"Gold-Bug, The," 8
Golden Apples, 150
Golden, Harry, 216, **217**
Gone With the Wind, 140, 172, 267
Gonzales, Ambrose Elliott, 92, **93,** 114
Gonzales, Ambrosio Jose and Nicoso, 92
Good Bye, My Lady, 152
Good Man is Hard to Find, A, 178
Good Old Boy and The Witch of Yazoo, 248
Goodman, Andrew, 226
"Goophered Grapevine, The," 102
Gordon, Caroline, 208, 266
Gordon, John Brown, 60
Gore, Al, 250
Gossip, The, 80

governor, 6, 265
Gowdy, Anne, 36
Grady, Henry, 46, **47,** 60, 70
Graham, Billy, 216, 250
Graham's Magazine, 12
Grand Isle, LA, 64
Grandissimes, The, 90
Grant, Cesar, 158
Grant, U. S., 36
Gravelly Springs, AL, 180
Gray Court, SC, 168
Great Barrington, MA, 266
Great Depression, 108, 136, 154, 184
Great Flood of 1927, 124
Great Mischief, 160
Greek, 4, 266
Greeley, Horace, 52
Green Fruit, 128
Green Mount Cem., Baltimore, MD, 26, **27,** 30, **31,** 266
Green Pastures, 264
Green Thursday, 168
Green, Paul, 214, **215**
Greenfield, 174
Greenhill Cem., Waynesville, NC, 234, **235**
Greenleaf Cem., Brownwood, TX, 108, **109**
Greensboro Law School, 134
Greensboro, NC, 78, 182, **183,** 258, **259**
Greenville News, 126
Greenville, MS, 124, **125,** 174, 198, **199,** 230, 256
Greenville, SC, 114, 264
Greenwich Village, 244
Green-Wood Cem., Brooklyn, NY, 110, **111**
Greenwood Cem., Jackson, MS, 6, **7,** 252, **253**
Greenwood Cem., Nashville, TN, 200, **201**
Greenwood Cem., New Orleans, LA, 194, **195**
Greenwood, MS, 174
Gregory, Dick, 250
Griffith, D. W., 134
Grizzard, Lewis, 236, **237**
Grovetown, GA, 42
Guggenheim Fellowship, 122, 214, 228, 262
Guildford College, 258
Gullah, 16, 48, 92, 114, 158, 168
Gumbo Ya-Ya, 136
Guthrie, KY, 228

Habit of Being, The, 178
Hagerstown, MD, 40
Haley, Alex, 232, **233,** 246
Hamilton, Charles, 140
Hamlet, The, 170
Hammett, Dashiell, 220
Hammond, Lilian Kirk, 36
Hampton Institute, 82
Hampton Plantation, 204, **205**

Handy, W. C., 200
Hannibal Journal, 76
Hannibal, MO, 76
Hapgood, Norman, 156
Hard-Boiled Virgin, The, 96
Harlem Renaissance, 166, 200
Harlem, 110
Harper Brothers, 36
Harper's Bazaar, 88
Harper's Weekly, 36, 118, 138
Harper's, 42, 156, 248, 262
Harris, Corra Mae White, 104, **105**
Harris, George Washington, 20, **21**
Harris, Joel Chandler, 34, 54, 70, **71**, 92, 114
Harris, Julia Collier and Julian LaRose, 70
Harris, Lundy, 104
Hart Co., KY, 56
Hartsdale, NY, 264
Hartselle, AL, 226, **227**
Hartsville, SC, 196
Harvard Alumni, 250
Harvard University, 16, 48, 124, 144, 154, 156, 202, 250, 266
Harwich, MA, 128, **129**
Hattiesburg American, 152
Havre de Grace, MD, 50
Hawaii, 76
Hawk and the Sun, The, 164
Hawthorne, FL, 150
Hawthorne, Nathaniel, 22, 160
Haxton, Kenneth, 198
Hayne, Paul Hamilton, 18, 42, **43**
Hayward, Susan, 104
He Slew the Dreamer, 226
headstone, **15**, **17**, **29**, **33**, **43**, **53**, **59**, **61**, **89**, **91**, **95**, **99**, **107**, **109**, **115**, **127**, **133**, **135**, **137**, **143**, **147**, **161**, **165**, **167**, **169**, **174**, **177**, **181**, **197**, **201**, **209**, **213**, **215**, **217**, **219**, **223**, **229**, **233**, **243**, **249**, **253**, **255**, **263**
heart attack, 72, 76, 120, 170, 198, 232, 248, 254
heart disease, 78, 220, 222, 236, 240, 248
Heart is a Lonely Hunter, The, 188
Hearts of Hickory: A Story of Andrew Jackson and the War of 1812, 98
Heaven's Trees, 172
Hebrew, Charlotte, NC, 216, **217**
Heinz, Helen, Tate, 208
Helen, GA, 104
Hellman, Lillian, 220, **221**
Hemingway, Ernest, 76, 150
hemorrhage, 64, 162, 96, 150
Hendersonville, NC, 112
Henning, TN, 232, **233**
Henry, O., 78, **79**
Hentz, Caroline Lee, 10, **11**
Hentz, Nicholas Marcellus, 10

Herndon, A. C., 56
Heyward, DuBose, 92, 114, 120, **121**, 142, 148, 156, 158
Hickock, Richard Eugene, 224
Higgins, Henry, 74
High Calling, The, 152
High Times and Hard Times, 20
Hill, Jamie, 104
Hill, William Green, 74
Hillcrest Cem., Holly Springs, MS, 36, **37**, 266
Hillsdale, NY, 154, **155**
Hindman, Robert, 44
His Majesty's Servant, 94
historian, 38, 262, 264
Hitler, Adolf, 122
Holiday, 176
Holley, FL, 268
Holly Springs, MS, 36, **37**
Hollywood, CA, 170, 220, 154
Hollywood Cem., Richmond, VA, 106, **107**, 132, **133**, 146, **147**, 148, **149**, 162, **163**, 267
Holocaust, 260
Home, 267
Hood, John Bell, 140
Hoover, Herbert, 124
Horn in the West, 214
Horse-Shoe Robinson, 26
Horton, George Moses, 10
"Hours, The," 128
House of Fulfillment, The, 138
"House of Haunted Shadows, The," 180
Houston Daily Post, 78
Houston, Sam, 94
Howard Payne University, 108
Howard University, 152
Howard, Hester Jane and Mordecai, 108
Howard, Robert Erwin, 108, **109**
Hughes, Langston, 200
Huguenot, 14, 156, 192
Huie, William Bradford, 226, **227**
humorist, 20, 24, 34, 62, 76, 78, 216, 236
Hunt, Chivers, Harriet, 12
Hunter College, 194
Hunter, Kermit, 214
Huntingdon Southern Normal University, 180
Huntingdon, TN, 180
Hurston, Zora Neale, 150, 166, **167**
Hustler, The, 222
Hutchins, Bishop, Margaret, 128
Hyannis, MA, 128

"I Wonder as I Wander," 210
I, The Jury, 268
I'd Climb the Highest Mountain, 104
I'll Take My Stand, 144, 172, 190, 206, 208, 238
Illinois, 200, 210, 236, 246, 262

In Abraham's Bosom, 214
In Cold Blood, 224
"In Search of Zora Neale Hurston," 166
In the Tennessee Mountains, 86
In This Our Life, 132
Incident and Other Happenings, An, 94
Incidents in the Life of a Slave Girl, 52
Indian Creek, TX, 212, **213**
Indiana Asbury University, 54
Indiana, 54
Inez: A Tale of the Alamo, 72
influenza, 88
Inge, M. Thomas, 20
Ingraham, Joseph Holt, 266
Innocence Abroad, 148
Innocents Abroad, The, 44, 76
Institute for the Study of History, Life, and Culture of Black People, The, 246
inventor, 14, 20, 24
Iowa Writer's Workshop, 238
Ireland, 4, 50
Irradiations: Sand and Spray, 144
Island Grove, FL, 150, **151**
Israel, 250
Israfel, 142
Italy, 4, 122, 156, 228, 244
Ithaca, NY, 232
It's Greek to Me, 266
Ives, Charles, 130

Jackson College, 58
Jackson State College, 246
Jackson, Andrew, 2, 6, 98
Jackson, MS, 6, **7**, 184, **185**, 246, **247**, 248, 252, **253**
Jackson, Stonewall, 208
Jacksonville, FL, 110
Jacobs, Harriet Ann, 52, **53**
Jacobs, John S., 52
Japanese-American, 198
Jarrell, Randall, 182, **183**
Jasper, FL, 186
Jefferson Davis: His Rise and Fall, 208
Jem and Chunkey, 6
Jeremy, 132
Jerry, 94
Jewish, 28, 80, 216, 220, 265
Joe, 254
John Doyle Writing Group, 192
John Holden, Unionist, 80
Johns Hopkins University, 30, 94, 134, 146
Johnson, Gerald White, 266
Johnson, James Weldon, 110, **111**, 200
Johnston, Annie Fellows, 138
Johnston, Mary, 106, 107
Jones, Charles Colcock Jr., 4, 48, **49,** 92

Jones, James, 248
Jones Bellamann, Katherine McKee, 130, **131**
Jones, Major Joseph, 34
journalist, 8, 18, 46, 50, 76, 80, 96, 148, 154, 176, 198, 212, 216, 226
Joyce, James, 170
Jubilee, 246
judge, 24, 264
Juilliard, 130, 188
Jurgen, a Comedy of Justice, 162

Kahal Kadosh Beth Elohim, Charleston, SC, 28
Kansas, 56
Kennedy, John F., 186, 226
Kennedy, John Pendleton, 26, **27**
Kennedy, Robert, 186
Kentucky, 12, 40, 56, 138, **139,** 208, 210, **211,** 214, 222, **223,** 228, 238
Kenyon College, Gambier, OH, 182, 206, **207,** 238
Kenyon Review, The, 206
Kerby, Marion, 210
Key West, FL, 266
Killers of the Dream, 186
King, Dr. Martin Luther Jr., 56, 186, 226, 228, 232
King, Grace, 100, **101**
King, Julia, 46
King, Martin Luther Sr., 56
Kingfisher Cabin, 116
Kings Row, 130
Kinte, Kunta, 232
Klein, Kevin, 260
Knights Hill Cem., Camden, SC, 265
Knoll at Sleepy Hollow, Concord, MA, 250, **251**
Knopf, Alfred, 122
Knopf, Blanche, 122
Knox Co., TN, 44
Knoxville, TN, 20, 38, **39,** 154, 250
Kober, Arthur, 220
Koontz, John Henry, 212
Korea, 242, 260
Korean War, 260
Ku Klux Klan, 70, 102, 134, 226

Laetare Medal, 84
LaFarge, Oliver, 176
Lafayette High School, Oxford, MS, 254
Lafayette, LA, 100
Lafitte the Pirate, 136
LaForgue, James, 96
Lake Maggiore, Italy, 156
Lake View Cem., Cleveland, OH, 102, **103**
Lakewood Cem., Jackson, MS, 184, **185**
Lamar, L. Q. C. II, 24
Lamb in His Bosom, 234
"Lament of the Summer Rose," 4
Lancaster, MA, 10

Lang Syne Plantation, 168
Lanier, Sidney, 30, **31,** 42, 218
Lanterns on the Levee, 124
Lauderdale Co., TN, 264
laureate, 18, 56, 60, 66, 68, 80, 118, 202, 204, 228, 242
Laurel Daily Leader, 152
Laurel Falls Camp, 186
Laurel Grove Cem., Savannah, GA, 34, **35**
"Lauriger Horatius," 68
law, 4, 6, 14, 18, 24, 26, 30, 42, 44, 46, 62, 66, 102, 110, 116, 118, 122, 124, 134, 176, 180, 264, 267
Lawrence, Jerome, 216
Lawrenceville, GA, 62
Lebanon, 234
Lebanon in the Forks Presbyterian Churchyard, Knoxville, TN, 38, **39**
ledger stone, **41, 51,** 73, 89, **99,** 117, **125, 129, 137, 154, 149, 151, 167, 171, 173,** 174, **175, 179,** 182, **183,** 204, **205,** 232, **233, 241, 245**
Lee, Gypsy Rose, 188
Lee, Robert E. (Gen.), 40, 146
Lee, Robert E. (playwright), 216
Legaré, Hugh Swinton, John D. and Mary D. M, 14
Legaré, James Mathewes, 14, 15
legislature, 16, 26, 44, 62, 66, 134, 198
Leipzig, Germany, 54
Lenoir City News, 250
Lenoir City, TN, 250
Leopard's Spots, The, 134
Let Us Now Praise Famous Men, 154
Letitia: Nursery Corps, U. S. Army, 138
Let's Talk Turkey, 266
"Letter to the Editor, A," 152
Levee Press, 198
Lexington, KY, 210, 266
Liberator, The, 50
Liberty, SC, 126, **127**
Library of Congress, 116, 208, 228, 242
Lie Down in Darkness, 260
Life, 176, 228
"Lift Ev'ry Voice and Sing," 110
Light in August, 170
Light Infantry Ball, The, 176
Lighthouse, 240
Lightning, 116
Like unto Like, 36
Lila Wallace-Reader's Digest Fund Writers' Award, 254
Lillian E. Smith Center, Clayton, GA, 186, **187**
Lillington, NC, 214
Lincoln, Abraham, 50, 62, 264
Lipetz, Niles, Rena, 210

Lisbon, Portugal, 126
Little Brick Church, The, 44
Little Foxes, The, 220
Little Lord Fauntleroy, 88
Little Princess, A, 88
Little Rock, AR, 144, **145**
Liveright, Horace, 220
lobotomy, 218
local color, 36, 54, 64, 90, 98, 100, 102, 116, 174, 234
Lomax, John and Ruby, 126
Lombard, Carole, 152
London, 52, 88, 94, 126, 144
Long Island, NY, 88
Long March, The, 260
"Long Reprieve, The," 184
Long, Crawford, 70
Long, Huey P., 198
Longfellow, Henry Wadsworth, 36, 42, 70
Longines Chronoscope, 226
Longstreet, Augustus Baldwin, 24, **25,** 34
Longstreet, James, 24
Look Homeward, Angel, 61, 112
Look, 198
Los Angeles, CA, 224, **225,** 265
Lost Colony, The, 214
Lost Diamond, The, 44
Lost Pleiad, The, 12
Louisiana State University, 136
Louisiana, 4, 68, 90, 100, **101,** 136, **137,** 176, 194, **195,** 200, 220, 224, 230, **231,** 264
Louisville Courier-Journal, 94
Louisville, KY, 40, 138, **139,** 210, **267**
Lourdes, France, 178
Love Songs and Bugle Calls, 118
Lovingood, Sut, 20
Lowell, Amy, 144, 156
Lowell, Robert, 182
Luce, Henry, 154
Lucedale, MS, 152
Lumberton, MS, 152
Lumberton, NC, 66
Lumpkin, Grace, 267
lupus, 178
Luther, Martin, 250
Lynchburg, VA, 146
lynching, 62, 138, 164
Lynn, NC, 30
Lyon, France, 210
Lyons Plain Cem. (Emmanuel Epis.), Weston, CT, 176, **177**
Lytle, Andrew, 178, 208, 238, **239**

Macaria, 72
MacArthur Fellow, 228
MacDowell Colony, 96

Index 285

MacLeish, Archibald, 154
Macon Evening News, 116
Macon Telegraph, 116
Macon, GA, 30, 34, 70, 116, **117**
Madison Co., KY, 222
"Magic," 252
Magnolia Cem., Augusta, GA, 4, **5**, 42, **43**, 68, **69**
Magnolia Cem., Baton Rouge, LA, 136, **137**
Magnolia Cem., Charleston, SC, 16, **17**, 22, **23**, 156, **157**, 158, **159**, 160, **161**, 192, **193**
Magnolia Cem., Mobile, AL, 72, **73**, 80, **81**
Maine, 110
Major Jones's Courtship, 34
Major Jones's Sketches of Travel, 34
Malden, Eva, 138
Mamba's Daughters, 120
Man Who Fell to Earth, The, 222
Manassas, First Battle of, 44, 84
Manchester, England, 88
Mansion, The, 170
Manteo, NC, 214
Many Thousands Gone, 128
Marbeau Cousins, The, 116
March On, 138
March, Frederic, 142
Mardi Gras, 80
"Mariá Concepción," 212
Marianna, FL, 10, **11**
Marion, AL, 98
Marion, Francis, 160
Marius, Richard, 250, **251**
Markham, Edwin, 156
Marsh, Margaret Mitchell (Peggy), 140, **141**
"Marshes of Glynn, The," 30
Martha's Vineyard, MA, 220, 260
Martin, Attwood Reading, 138
Martin, George Madden, 138, 139
Maryland, 8, **9**, 26, **27**, 30, **31**, 34, 40, 48, 50, 68, 112, 134, 212, 258, 266
"Maryland, My Maryland," 68
Mason, Mary Ann Bryan, 32, 33
Massachusetts Anti-Slavery Convention, 50
Massachusetts, 8, 10, 30, 36, 46, 50, 52, **53**, 90, 91, 114, 128, **129**, 138, 172, 202, 220, **221**, 250, **251**, 260, **261**, 267
Master of Fine Arts, 178, 238
Master Skylark, 158

Matthiessen, Peter, 260
Maury Co., TN, 58
mausoleum, **47**, **105**, **195**, 224, **225**, 265
Maybank, Burnet R., 126
Maybe, 220
Mayesville, SC, 196
mayor, 48, 62
Mayrant, Drayton, 192, **193**

Mayrant, Walter, 158
Maysi, Kadra, 192, **193**
McAlexander, Hubert Horton, 36
McCarthy, Joseph, 226
McCarthy, Mary, 220
McClellanville, SC, 204
McClure's Magazine, 138
McCullers, Carson, 188, **189**
McCullers, Reeves, 188
McDowell, David, 154
McDowell, Edward, 36
McDowell, Sherwood Bonner, 36, **37**
McGill, Ralph, 140, 164
McGraw-Hill, 260
McMillan, Bruce, 36
McNeil, John Charles, 66, **67**
McNeill, Duncan and Euphemia, 66
McNutt, Alexander, 6, **7**
Mecklenburg Co., VA, 74
medicine, 12, 36, 38, 54, 230
Melville, Herman, 22
Member of the Wedding, The, 188
Memories of a Southern Woman of Letters, 100
Memory Hill Cem., Milledgeville, GA, 178, **179**
Memory of a Large Christmas, 186
Memphis, TN, 118, **119**, 174, 238, 256, **257**
Men Working, 174
Mencken, H. L., 60, 96, 122, 148, 162, 168
Mercer University, 116
Mercersburg Academy, 204
Metairie Cem., New Orleans, LA, 100, **101**, 106
Methodist, 24, 54, 104, 206, 246
Mexican War, 44
Mexico City, Mexico, 122
Mexico, 84, 122, 212, 266
MGM, 160, 220
Middagh Street, 188
Middle East, 156
Midnight in the Garden of Good and Evil, 202
Mikulintsky, Ukraine, 216
Milledgeville, GA, 30, 178, **179**
Miller Ray, Caroline Pafford, 234, **235**
Miller, William D., 234
Mind of the South, The, 122
Minnesota, 208
Miss Kelly's Female Seminary, 156
Miss Minerva and William Green Hill, 74, 267
Mississippi Institute of Arts and Letters Award, 254
Mississippi Partisan Rangers, 44
Mississippi River, 76, 256, 264
Mississippi State Highway Department, 174
Mississippi, 6, **7**, 24, **25**, 36, **37**, 40, 44, **45**, 124, 125, 130, 152, 170, **171**, 172, **173**, 174, **175**, 184, **185**, 198, **199**, 218, 230, 246, **247**, 248, **249**, 252, **253**, 254, **255**, 256, 266

286 *Gravely Concerned*

Missouri, 44, 64, **65,** 76, 130, 152, 218, 219, **267**
Mitchell Marsh, Margaret, 104, 140, **141,** 150, 267
Mitchell-Hollingsworth Annex, Florence, AL, 180
mixed race, 52, 100, 102
Mobile Register, 80
Mobile, AL, 40, **41,** 72, **73,** 80, 81, 244, **245**
Mockingbird, 222
Modern Times, 18
Moïse, Penina, 28, **29**
Monroe, James, 106
Monteagle, TN, 238
Moore, Erasmus, 44
Moore, John Trotwood, 98, **99**
Moore, [Austin] Merrill, 98
Moravian Cem., New Dorp, Staten Island, NY, 265
More, Thomas, 250
Moreland, GA, 236, 237
Morning Watch, The, 154
Morris, Willie, 248, **249**
Mosel, Tad, 154
Mount Auburn Cem., Cambridge, MA, 26, 52, **53**
Mount Holly Cem., Little Rock, AR, 144, 145
Mount Holyoke, 114
Mount Hope Cem., Rochester, NY, 50, **51**
Mount Olivet Cem., Nashville, TN, 54, **55**
Mountain View Cem., Oakland, CA, 264
Moviegoer, The, 230
Mozart, Wolfgang Amadeus, 164
Mrs. Mason's New Cookery, 32
Ms., 166
Mud on the Stars, 226
Munford Cem., Covington, TN, 74, **75**
"Municipal Report, A," 78
Munsey's Magazine, 60
murder, 6, 20, 44, 162, 202, 224, 226, 248
Murfree, Mary Noailles, 86, **87**
Murfreesboro, TN, 86, **87**
Murphy, NC, 210
Murrells Inlet, SC, 268
Museum of Arts and Science, Macon GA, 116
musician, 30, 32, 110, 130, 168, 186, 188, 208, 210
Mussolini, Benito, 122, 228
My Brother Bill, 174
My Dog Skip, 248
My Son and Foe, 160
Myers, Robert Manson, 48

NAACP, 82, 102, 110, 114, 122
Names in South Carolina, 192
Narrative of the Life of Frederick Douglass, An American Slave, 50
Nashville Banner, 94
Nashville Female Academy, 86
Nashville, TN, 20, 54, **55,** 86, 98, **99,** 180, 182, 190, **191,** 200, **201,** 206
Nassau, Jamaica, 110

Natchez, MS, 268
Nation, The, 128, 154
National Book Award, 176, 48, 176, 178, 202, 206, 212, 220, 230, 232, 242, 260
National Endowment for the Humanities, 262
National Institute of Arts and Letters, 176, 202
National Medal for Literature, 202
National Theater Conference Award, 214
Native American, 12, 266
Native Son, 268
Nazism, 122, 250
NBC, 202
Nebula Award, 222
Negro Question, The, 90
Nelson, Randy, 12
Neon Bible, The, 194
New Albany, MS, 170
New Bedford, MA, 50
New Bern, NC, 32
New Criticism, The, 206
New Dorp, NY, 265
New England Society, 46
New Garden Friends Cem., Greensboro, NC, 182, **183**
New Hampshire, 96
New Jersey, 24
New Market, TN, 88
New Moon Rising, 240
New Orleans Delta, 68
New Orleans, LA, 4, 64, 70, 90, 100, 101, 136, 176, 194, 195, 220, 224, 264, 267
New Republic, The, 172
"New South, The," 46
New York, 8, 30, 32, 48, 50, **51,** 52, 76, **77, 78,** 88, **89,** 96, 110, **111,** 130, **131,** 134, 152, 154, **155,** 160, 172, 178, 184, 188, **189,** 194, 200, 204, 210, 212, 216, 218, 222, 224, 232, 238, 244, 260, 264, 265
New York Age, 110
New York Days, 248
New York Herald, 126, 162
New York Society for the Supression of Vice, 162
New York Times, 18, 122, 172, 184, 224, 262
New York Tribune, 52
New York University, 208, 220
New York World-Telegram, 152
New York, NY, 8, 30, 48, 50, 52, 76, 78, 80, 96, 102, 110, 128, 130, 131, 134, 152, 154, 160, 172, 178, 184, 188, 194, 200, 204, 208, 210, 212, 216, 218, 220, 222, 224, 238, 244, 260, 265
New Yorker, The, 176
Newbery Honor, 150
Newman, Frances, 96, **97**
Newnan Times-Herald, 236
Newport News, VA, 260

Newport, RI, 26
Newport, TN, 262
News Leader, 146
newspaper, 8, 18, 34, 46, 60, 66. 68, 70, 76, 80, 90, 92, 122, 146, 152, 176, 198, 212, 216, 236, 258, 264
Newsweek, 164
Niagara Movement, 82
Nicaragua, 110
Night Gallery, 202
Night of the Iguana, 218
Niles, John Jacob, 210, **211**
Nisei, 198
Nixon, Richard, 216
Nobel Prize, 170, 212, 252
North Carolina, 10, 30, 32, **33**, 38, 52, 66, **67,** 78, **79,** 84, **85,** 102, 112, **113,** 120, 122, **123,** 134, **135,** 152, **153,** 176, 182, **183,** 210, 214, **215,** 216, **217,** 230, 234, **235,** 258, **259,** 262, 262, 266, 267
North Star, The (Douglass), 50
North Star, The (Hellman), 220
North Toward Home, 248
Northampton, MA, 10, 90, **91**
Northridge, MA, 264
Northrop, Cash, Mary Ross, 122
Northwestern University, 240, 246, 262
Norway, 156
Not a Man, and Yet a Man, 56
"Not in Memoriam, but in Defense," 172
Notasulga, AL, 166
Nothing Sacred, 152
Notre Dame University, 84
Nott, Henry Junius, 267
Novellette of a Traveller, or, Odds and Ends from the Knapsack of Thomas Singularity, 267
Now is the Time, 186
Now with His Love, 128
Nyack, NY, 188, 189

O. Henry Award, 78, 264
Oak Hill Cem., Cartersville, GA, 62, **63**
Oak Hill Cem., Nyack, NY, 188, **189**
Oakdale Cem., Hendersonville, NC, 112
Oakland Cem., Atlanta, GA, 140, **141**
Oakland, CA, 264
Oakwood Cem., Raleigh, NC, 32, **33**
obelisk, **7, 9, 11, 21, 25, 39, 67**
O'Briant, Lucy Nash, Street, 152
Ocala, FL, 150
Ochs, Adolph, 172
O'Connor, Flannery, 178, **179,** 194
"Ode to Tennessee," 118
"Ode to the Confederate Dead," 18, 118, 208
Oglethorpe University, 30
O, Promised Land, 152

"O, Tannenbaum," 68
O'Hara, Scarlett, 140
Ohio University, 222
Ohio, 10, 34, 56, 102, **103,** 122, 158, 182, 206, 207, 208, 210, 214, 222, 238, 240, 252
Ol' Man Adam and His Chillun, 264
Old Chapel Hill Cem., Chapel Hill, NC, 152, **153**
Old City Cem., Mobile, AL, 244, **245**
Old Creole Days, 90
Old Louisiana, 136
Old Union Cem., Young Harris, GA, 164, **165**
Old Westminster Churchyard, Baltimore, MD, 8, **9**
Oldham Franklin Faulkner, Estelle, 170
On Fire, 254
One Writer's Beginnings, 252
Only in America, 216
Open Letter Club, 54
Optimist's Daughter, The, 252
Orangeburg, SC, 168
Other Side, The, 118
Oxford University, 206, 228, 248
Oxford, GA, 104
Oxford, MS, 24, **25,** 170, **171,** 174, **175,** 184, 248, 254

P. M., 126
Pacific Ocean, 264
Pafford Miller Ray, Caroline, 234, **141**
painter, 14, 32, 172, 174
Paradise Valley, AZ, 265
Paramount Pictures, 128
Paris Review, 244, 260
Paris, 96, 128, 156, 210, 244, 260, 268, 268
Parker, Dorothy, 220
Path of Sorrow, The, 12
Paulo Parish, Colleton Co., SC, 92
Pavilion, The, 172
Pawleys Island, SC, 242, **243**
Payne, Daniel Alexander, 56, 58
PBS, 58, 256
Peabody Conservatory, 30
Peachtree Street, 140
Peaster, TX, 108
pen name, 62, 76, 78, 84, 86, 138, 192, 218
Penland, 112
Pennsylvania, 8, 20, 30, 34, 50, 52, 142, 148, 204, 250
Pensacola Journal, 152
Pentimento, 220
Pentland, 112
Percy, LeRoy and Phinizy, 124
Percy, Mary Bernice Townsend, 230
Percy, Walker, 124, 194, 230, **231**
Percy, William Alexander, 124, **125,** 198, 230
Père Lachaise Cem., Paris, France, 268
Perkins, Max, 112

Permit Me Voyage, 154
Personal Sun, the Early Poems of Hubert Creekmore, 184
Persons, Truman Streckfus, 224
Peter Ashley, 120
Peterborough, NH, 96
Peterkin Cem., Fort Motte, SC, 168, **169**
Peterkin, Julia, 92, 114, 130, 148, 168, **169**, 210
Peterkin, William George, 168
Petersburg, VA, 46
Peterson's Ladies' Magazine, 88
Petigru, James L., 14
Philadelphia, PA, 8, 30, 34, 50, 52, 76, 86, 130, 148
Philips Exeter Academy, 154
photography, 154, 168, 210, 252
Pinckney, Eliza Lucas, 160
Pinckney, Josephine, 142, 156, 160, **161**
Pine Log, Bartow Co., GA, 104, **105**
Pioneers of the Old South, 106
Pittsburgh, PA, 142
plagiarism, 12, 232, 246
Plandome, NY, 88, **89**
Plantation Christmas, A, 168
Playboy, 224
Pleasant Ways of St. Medford, The, 100
Plimpton, George, 260
Pluck, 80
pneumonia, 56, 252, 260
Poe, Edgar Allan, 8, **9**, 12, 24, 26, 40
Poems about God, 206
Poems of Henry Timrod, The, 18
Poetry Society of South Carolina, 120, 130, 142, 156, 158, 160, 192, 264
Poetry, 246
Point Coupee, LA, 68
Poitier, Sidney, 152
polio, 120
Ponder Heart, The, 72, 252
Ponder, Edna Earle, 72
Pontellier, Edna, 64
Pontotoc, MS, 44
Porgy and Bess, 120
Porgy, 120
Port Gibson, MS, 267
Port Royal Experiment, 114
Porter Military Academy, 142, 204
Porter, Katherine Anne, 188, 192, 212, **213**
Porter, William Sidney, 78, **79**
Porter, William Trotter, 6
Portland, ME, 266
portrait, **9**, 45, 71, 77, **89**, 233
Portugal, 126
Pound, Ezra, 144, 170
Poydras College, 68
Prairie Schooner, 164

Presbyterian, 20, 38, 48, 58, 196
Price, Eugenia, 240, **241**
Princeton University, 48, 128
prison, 78, 216
Prisoner of Hope, 106
Pritchard Morris, JoAnne, 248
Prix de Rome, 260
Prix Femina, 234
Prix Mondial Cino Del Luca, 260
Prophet of the Great Smoky Mountains, The, 86
Proust, Marcel, 170
Pseudophilia, 186
Pulaski, TN, 206
Pulitzer Prize, 70, 122, 132, 140, 144, 146, 148, 150, 154, 164, 168, 170, 180, 194, 198, 202, 212, 214, 218, 228, 232, 234, 252, 258, 260, 264, 268, 122
pulp, 108
Puritan's Daughter, The, 80

Quarter Race in Kentucky, A, 6
Quitman, MS, 265

racism, 90, 152, 186, 190, 216, 262
Radcliffe College, 156, 160
railroad, 20, 44
Raleigh, NC, 32, **33**
"Rambling with Richard," 250
Ramsey, J. G. M., 38, **39**
Randall, William Ryder, 68, **69**
Randolph-Macon College, 54
Ransom Hall, 206
"Ransom of Red Chief, The," 78
Ransom, John Crowe, 124, 144, 182, 206, **207**
Rapid Ramblings in Europe, 44
"Raven, The," 12
Ravenel, Beatrice Witte, 156, **157**
Ravenel, Beatrice St. Julian (Kitty), Francis and Samuel Prioleau, 156
Ravenna, OH, 34
Rawlings, Charles, 150
Rawlings, Marjorie Kinnan, 150, **151**
Ray, Caroline Pafford Miller, 234, **141**
Ray, Clyde H. Jr., 234
Ray, James Earl, 226
Reader's Digest, 262
Reavill, Ransom, Robb, 206
reburied, 4, 8, 250, 268
Reconstruction, 36, 48, 62, 90, 100, 134, 180, 198
Red Cross, 118
Red Hills and Cotton, 126
Redding, CT, 76
Reece, Byron Herbert, 164, **165**
Reformation, 250
Reid, Christian, 84, **85**
Reidsville, GA, 186

Reivers, The, 170
Remus, Uncle, 54, 70, 114
reporter, 136
Reviewer, The, 148, 168
Rhode Island, 26
Rhodes College, 238
Rhodes Scholar, 206, 228, 248
Rice University, 242
Rice, Alice Hegan, 138
Richmond Co., GA, 24
Richmond College, 146
Richmond Evening Journal, 148
Richmond Temperence and Literary Society, 66
Richmond, KY, 222, **223**
Richmond, VA, 8, 106, **107**, 132, **133**, 146, **147**, 148, **149**, 162, **163**, 267
Rich's department store, 186
Ridgefield, CT, 264
Rip Raps Plantation, 196
Ripley Advertiser, 44
Ripley, Alexandra Braid, 267
Ripley, MS, 44, **45**, 174
River House, 172
riverboat, 20, 76
Rivers of America, 142, 190
Riverside Cem., Asheville, NC, 78, **79**
Riverton, NC, 66, **67**
Robertson, Ben, 126, **127**
Rochester, NY, 50, **51**
Rockbridge Co., VA, 6
Rocky Mountain News, 212
Rogersville, TN, 2
Roll, Jordan, Roll, 168, 210
Rolling Stone, The, 78
Rome Courier, 46
Rome, GA, 62
Rome, Italy, 244, 260
Roosevelt, Theodore, 82
Roots, 232, 246
Rose Hill Cem., Macon, GA, 116, **117**
Rose Tatoo, The, 218
"Rose, The," 12
Rosicrucians, 114
Roslyn Cem., Plandome, NY, 88, **89**
ROTC, 218
Round Hill Academy, 10
Rowan Oak, 170
Royal Air Force of Canada, 170
rural cemetery, 26
Russell, Irwin, 267
Rutledge, Archibald, 204, **205**
Ryan, Abram Joseph, 40, **41**

Sacred Heart Church, Milledgeville GA, 178
Sagapanack, NY, 224
"Sahara of the Bozart, The," 60

St Andrews School, 154
St Augustine, FL, 150
St Charles, MO, 152
St Elmo, 72
St Hubert Cem., Winchester, Clark Co., KY, 210, **211**
St Joseph Abbey Cem., Covington, LA, 230, **231**
St Louis Woman, 200
St Louis, MO, 64, **65**, 76, 218, **219**, 267
St Luke's Episcopal Cem., Marianna, FL, 10, **11**
St Martin Parish, LA, 100
St Mary's College, Baltimore, 14
St Nicholas, 36
St Paul's Episcopal Church, Charleston, SC, 22
St Peter's Cem., Oxford, MS, 24, **25**, 170, **171**, 174, **175**
St Petersburg, FL, 90
St Philip's Cem., Charleston, SC, 120, **121**
St Simons Island, GA, 240, **241**
St Simons Trilogy, 240
St Thaddeus's Cem., Aiken, SC, 14, **15**
Salem Black River Presbyterian Church Sumter, SC, 196, **197**
Salisbury, NC, 84, **85**
Sampson, Emma Speed, 267
San Antonio, TX, 2, **3**
San Cristobal, Mexico, 266
San Fernando Cathedral, San Antonio, TX, 2, **3**
San Francisco, CA, 222, 264
Sanctuary, 170
Sandburg, Carl, 168, 216
Santa Ana, Antonio Lopez de, 2
Santa Barbara, CA, 264
Santee River Delta, SC, 264
Santee River, 264
"Sara Crewe," 88
sarcophagus, **13, 63, 163**
Sartoris, 44
Saturday Evening Post, 152, 156
Saturday Review, 122, 176
Savannah Morning News, 34
Savannah, GA, 34, **35**, 48, 50, 70, 94, 178, 202, **203**, 266
Saxon, Lyle, 100, 136, **137**
Scarlet Sister Mary, 148, 168
Scarlett, 267
schizophrenia, 218
Schoenbrunn, OH, 214
Schwerner, Michael, 226
Science Fiction and Fantasy Writers of America, 222
Scola Cantorum, 210
Scoundrel Time, 220
Scribner's, 88, 94
Sea-Drinking Cities, 160
Searching Wind, The, 220
Season of Flesh, The, 164

Seattle, WA, 232
Second Seminole War, 34
Secret Garden, A, 88
Secret River, The, 150
Secretary of the Navy, 26
segregation, 100, 134, 186, 190, 216, 228, 262
Selected Poems (Aiken), 202
Selected Poems (Fletcher), 144
Selected Poems (Ransom), 206
Selina, 138
Selznick, David O., 142, 152
Senatobia, MS, 264
Serena, 118
Set This House on Fire, 260
Sewanee Miltary Academy, 238
Sewanee Review, The, 208, 238
Sewanee, TN, 94, **95,** 154, 208, **209,** 218, 238, **239**
Shakespeare, Lain, 70
Shakespeare, William, 138, 158
Shaw, Irwin, 260
Shearit Israel, Charleston, SC, 28
Shelby Academy, 134
Shelby, NC, 122, **123,** 134, **135**
Sherman, William Tecumseh, 18, 48, 58, 62, 140
Sherwood Anderson and Other Famous Creoles, 176
Shiloh, 256
Shiloh, Battle of, 58, 256
Shin Bet, 250
Ship Island, Ripley and Kentucky Railroad, 44
Ship of Fools, 212
Short Guide for Writing About History, A, 250
Short Story's Mutations, The, 96
Sibley, Celestine, 268
Siege of Monterrey, The, 44
Sigma Kappa Delta, 20
"Silent Snow, Secret Snow," 202
Simms, William Gilmore, 14, 22, **23,** 42
Simon and Schuster, 194
Simon, Charlie May, Fletcher, 144
Simons, Katherine Drayon Mayrant, 192, **193**
Simons, Sedgewick Lewis, 192
Singularity, Thomas, 267
Sir Mortimer, 106
Slappey, Florian, 265
slavery, 20, 50, 52, 134, 260
Sleepy Hollow Cem., Concord MA, 250
Smart Set, 168
Smith, Cean Carver, 234
Smith, Charles Henry, 62, **63**
Smith, Lillian, 186, **187**
Smith, Perry Edward, 224
Smythe, Bennett, Susan, 158
So Red the Rose, 172
Socialist Party, 114
Song of Joy, A, 164

"Song of the Chattahoochee, The," 30
Sons and Fathers, 116
Sophie's Choice, 260
Sorbonne, 96
Souls of Black Folk, The, 266
Sound and the Fury, The, 170
South Carolina College, 24, 267
South Carolina, 8, 14, **15,** 16, **17,** 18, **19,** 22, **23,** 24, 28, **29,** 42, 54, 60, **61,** 80, 92, **93,** 114, **115,** 120, 121, 122, 126, **127,** 130, 142, 156, **157,** 158, **159,** 160, **161,** 168, **169,** 176, 192, **193,** 196, **197,** 204, **205,** 242, **243,** 264, 265, 267, 268
South Carolinian, The, 18
South Moon Under, 150
Southern Agriculturalist, The, 16
Southern Book Critics Award, 254
Southern Literary Messenger, The, 8, 18, 24, 24, 130, 160
Southern Literary Renaissance, 130, 160
Southern Miscellany, The, 34
Southern Writers Conference, 132
Southern Writers: Biographical and Critical Studies, 54
Southerner's Story of Life on this Planet, A, 244
South-View Cem., Atlanta, GA, 56, **57**
Southwest humor, 2, 6, 20, 24, 34
Southwestern Theological Seminary, 152
Southwestern, 238
Spain, 92, 184, 220
Spanish Civil War, 220
Spanish Heroine, The, 44
Spartanburg, SC, 168, 192
Spaulding, James Reed, 72
Spillane, Frank Morrison, 268
Spirit of the Times, The, 6, 20
Splendid in Ashes, 160
Spratling, William, 176
Spring Hill, Scotland Co., Riverton, NC, 66, **67**
Stanford Children's Convalescent Home, 222
Star-Spangled Virgin, The, 120
state legislature, 2, 4
State Rights Sentinel, 34
State, The, 16, 92, 156
Stateburg, SC, 265
statue, **45,** 88, **89,** 124, **125, 235, 239**
Stein, Gertrude, 148, 170
Steinbeck, John, 136
Stephen Foster Story, The, 214
Stephens, Alexander, 70
Stevenson Cable, Eva C., 90
Stokely, James, 262
Stone, Phil, 170
Stones River, Battle of, 238
Stonewall Jackson: The Good Soldier, 208
Store, The, 180

Stowe, Harriet Beecher, 10, 14
Strange Fires, 266
Strange Fruit, 186
"Strange Moonlight," 202
Stratton, VT, 228, **229**
Streep, Meryl, 260
Street, James, 152, **153**
Streetcar Named Desire, A, 218
Stribling, T. S., 180, **181**
Strickland, Lily, 18
stroke, 92, 172, 174, 188
Stuart, Jesse, 164
Stuffed Peacocks, 148
Styron, William, 260, **261**
suffrage, 50, 64, 94, 100, 106, 114
suicide, 104, 108, 122, 144, 164, 168, 182, 188, 194, 202, 264
Summer Place, 204
"Summer Tragedy, A," 200
Summerville Cem., Augusta, GA, 48, **49**
Summons to Memphis, A, 268
Sumter, SC, 196, **197**
"Sunburnt Boys, The," 66
Sunset, Shelby, NC, 122, **123**, 134, **135**
Sut Lovingood: Yarns Spun, 20
Swallow Barn, 26
Swan Pond, TN, 38
Sweet Bird of Youth, 218
"Sword of Robert Lee, The," 40
"Symphony, The," 30

Tagus River, 126
Talbot Co., MD, 48
Tap Roots, 152
Taps, 248
"Tar Baby, The," 114
Tasso, Torquato, 4
Tate, Allen, 124, 144, 148, 208, **209**, 238, 266
taxi, 140, 154, 184
Taylor, Peter, 182, 268
Taylor, Robert Love (Bob), 98
Taylor-Trotwood Magazine, 98
Teckla's Lilies, 138
Teeftallow, 180
temperence, 114
Tennessee Equal Suffrage Association, 94
Tennessee Federation for Constitutional Government, 190
Tennessee Governor's Award for the Humanities, 256
Tennessee History Committee, 98
Tennessee River, 38, 190
Tennessee State Library and Archives, 98
Tennessee Valley Authority, 190
Tennessee, 2, 20, 38, **39**, 40, 44, 54, **55**, 58, **59**, 74, 75, 86, **87**, 94, **95**, 98, **99**, 118, **119**, 130, 154, 174, 180, **181**, 182, 190, **191**, 200, **201**, 206, 208, **209**, 218, 232, **233**, 238, **239**, 250, 256, **257**, 262
Tennessee, The, 190
Tennesseean, The, 190
Tennyson, Alfred, Lord, 42
Territorial Enterprise, 76
Tevis, Walter, 222, **223**
Texas Observer, 248
Texas Review, 172
Texas, 2, **3**, 36, 56, 78, 108, **109**, 130, 172, 212, **213**, 214
Texas, 214
The Glades, FL, 142
Theater Arts Magazine, 172
Theater Practice, 172
Theater, The, 172
Their Eyes Were Watching God, 166
"Their Story Runneth Thus," 40
These Three, 220
This Side of Paradise, 128
Thomas Wolfe Prize, 254
Thomas, G. H., 72
Thomas, Norman, 114
Thompson, William Tappan, 34, **35**
Three Lives for Mississippi, 226
Three O'Clock Dinner, 160
Thurmond, Richard Simon, 44
Tiernan, Frances Christine Fisher, 84, **85**
Tiernan, James, 84
Till, Emmett, 226
Tillman, Benjamin Ryan, 92
Time, 122, 154, 176
Times-Picayune, 136
Timrod, Henry, 18, **19**, 42
Timrod, Willie, 18
Tisbury, Marthas Vinyard, MA, 260, 261
To Have and to Hold, 106
To the White Sea, 242
Tobacco Road, 265
Todd Co., KY, 266
Tommey, Eneas, 116
Tomorrow We Reap, 152
Toole, John Kennedy, 194, **195**
Torches Flare, The, 172
Town, The, 170
Townsend Percy, Mary Bernice, 230
Townsend, Stephen, 88
Toys in the Attic, 220
Traitor, The, 134
Transylvania University, 12
Travelers Rest, 126
Travis, William Barrett, 2
Trenton, GA, 20, **21**
Trenton, TN, 268
Trinity Cathedral, Columbia, SC, 18, **19**

Trotwood, Aunt Betsy, 98
Trotwood's Monthly, 98
True Tale of Slavery, A, 52
Trumpet in the Land, 214
Tryon, NC, 120
tubercular meningitis, 112
tuberculosis, 14, 18, 30, 78, 164, 212, 230
Tula, MS, 254, **255**
Tulane University, 4, 100, 176, 194
Turnbull plantation, 70
Tuscaloosa, AL, 10, 180
Tuskegee, AL, 10, 82, **83**
Twain, Mark, 20, 44, 70, 76, **77,** 90, 102
Tyler, John, 14, 106

U. S. Military Academy, 8
Ukraine, 216
"Ulalume," 12
Ulmann, Doris, 168, 210
Uncle Tom's Cabin, 14
Under the Southern Cross, 84
Unfinished Woman, An, 220
Union Army, 114
Union College, 204
Union District, SC, 267
Union Pacific College, 200
United Confederate Veterans, 118
University Cem., Sewanee, TN, 94, **95,** 208, **209,** 238, **239,** 268
University of Alabama, 180, 226
University of Berlin, 266
University of California at Los Angeles, 164
University of California, 228
University of Chicago, 200
University of Colorado, 184
University of Denver, 130
University of Florida, 238, 242
University of Georgia, 46, 236
University of Illinois, 200
University of Iowa, 178, 218, 246
University of Kentucky, 222, 238
University of Louisiana (now Tulane), 4
University of Lyon, 210
University of Michigan, 212
University of Minnesota, 208
University of Mississippi, 24, 170, 172, 174, 184, 248
University of Missouri, 126, 218
University of North Carolina at Greensboro, 182
University of North Carolina, 112, 156, 180, 182, 214, 230, 258
University of Northern Alabama, 180
University of Pittsburgh, 142
University of Richmond, 132
University of South Carolina, 24, 267, 196, 242
University of Southwestern Louisiana, 194

University of Tennessee, 250, 262
University of Texas, 172, 212, 248
University of the South, 124, 218, 238
University of Virginia, 8, 46, 132, 132, 148, 170
University of Wisconsin, 150
University Press of Mississippi, 248
University System of Georgia, 104
Unto These Hills, 214
Unvanquished, The, 170
Up From Slavery, 82
urn, **55, 73**
US Army Air Corps, 242
US Army, 8, 124, 142, 194, 210, 236
US Coast Guard, 232
US Colored Infantry, 114
US House of Representatives, 2, 4, 26
US Marines, 254, 260
US Military Academy, 8
US Navy, 184, 222
US Senate, 6, 124
US Treasury Department, 116

Valparaiso College, 122
Vanderbilt University, 54, 182, 190, 206, 208, 228, 238, 242
Vanderbilt, Gloria, 265
Vanity Fair, 128
Vassar College, 130, 142
Venezuela, 110
Vermont, 228, **229**
"Vertical Negro Plan," 216
Vicksburg, MS, 6, 36, 124
Vidal, Gore, 244
View from Pompey's Head, The, 176
Vincentians, 40
Violent Bear It Away, The, 178
Virginia City, NV, 76
Virginia Quarterly Review, 148
Virginia, 6, 8, 46, 54, 74, 82, 106, 107, 132, **133,** 142, **143,** 146, **147,** 148, **149,** 162, **163,** 170, 260, 267, 268
voodoo, 156

Wagram, NC, 66
Waiting Time, The, 240
Wake Forest College, 66, 122, 134
Walker, Alice, 166
Walker Alexander, Margaret, 246, **247**
Walter, Eugene, 244, **245**
War of 1812, 26
Warm Springs, VA, 106
Warner Brothers, 142
Warner, Charles Dudley, 100
Warren, Robert Penn, 124, 228, **229,** 238
Warwickshire Lad, A, 138
Washington (state), 136, 232

Washington College, 6, 38
Washington, Booker T., 82, **83**
Washington, DC, 48, 52, 80, 88, 96, 150
Washington, GA, 12
Washington, George, 146
Wasson, Ben, 198
Watch on the Rhine, 220
Water Valley, MS, 184
Watkins, Sam, 58, **59**
Watling, Belle, 140
Waycross, GA, 234
Waynesville, NC, 234, **235**
wedge stone, **37, 93, 113, 121, 139, 189, 193, 215**
Weird Tales, 108
Welcome, The, 184
Wellesley School, 138
Wellesley, MA, 138
Welty, Eudora, 72, 184, 188, 198, 252, **253**
Wesley, John, 266
West Chop Cem., Tisbury, Martha's Vineyard, MA, 260, **261**
West Indies, 84
West Point, NY, 8
West View Cem., Liberty, SC, 126, **127**
West Virginia, 128, 240, 252
West Wardsboro, VT, 228
Westborough, MA, 114
Western Continent, 34
Westminster College, 130
Weston, CT, 176, **177**
Westview Cem., Atlanta, GA, 46, **47**, 70, **71**, 96, **97**
Westwood Cem., Los Angeles, CA, 224, **225**
"What Comes Down My Cheek," 116
Where the Battle Was Fought, 86
Whisper My Name, 258
"White Baby Plan," 216
White Citizens Council, 190, 198
White House, 250
White Rose of Memphis, The, 44
Whiteville Academy, 66
Whitman Sisters, 56
Whitman, Albery Alson, 56, **57**
Whitman, Caddie (Katie), 56
Who Speaks for the Negro?, 228
Whole Wide World, The, 108
"Why I Live at the P. O.," 252
Wilberforce University, 56
Wild Palms, The, 170
Wilde, Richard Henry, 4, **5**
Wilkes, Melanie, 140
William Dean Howells Medal, 260
Williams, Dakin and Rose, 218
Williams, Thomas Lanier (Tennessee), 188, 218, **219**
Williamsburg, VA, 162, 258
Willis Cem., Stratton, VT, 228, **229**
Wilson, Augusta Jane Evans, 72, **73**

Wilson, Col. Lorenzo Madison, 72
Wilson, Edmund, 128, 136
Wilson, Woodrow, 134
Winchester, Clark Co., KY, 208, 210, **211**
Winchester, VA, 264
Wirey, Phil, 20
Wiscasset, ME, 110
Wise Blood, 178
Witch of Yazoo, 248
With a Song in My Heart, 126
Witte Ravenel, Beatrice, 156, **157**
Wofford College, 54, 122
Wolf Whistle and Other Stories, 226
Wolfe, Thomas, 112, **113**
Women's Committee on National Defense, 118
Woodhull, Victoria Clifford, 64
Woodlawn Cem., Bronx, NY, 92
Woodlawn Cem., Elmira, NY, 76, **77**
Works Progress Administration, 136, 184, 246
World War I, 98, 120, 124, 138, 142, 170, 190, 206, 210
World War II, 184, 198, 220, 226, 244, 248
"Worn Path, A," 252
wounded, 114, 120, 142
Wreath from the Woods of Carolina, 32
Wren's Nest, 70
Wright, Richard, 188, 246, 268
Wright's Sanitarium, 170
Writer's Bureau on Public Information, 118
Writer's Companion, A, 250
Writer's Workshop, University of Iowa, 178

X, Malcolm, 228, 232

Yaddo, 188
Yale University, 24, 124, 154, 184, 200, 228, 238
Yale Younger Poets, 124, 154
Yazoo City, MS, 248, **249**
Yearling, The, 150
Yemassee, The, 22
Yerby, Frank, 246
Yocona, MS, 254
Yoknapatawpha, 44
Young Harris College, 164
Young Harris, GA, 164, **165**
Young Housewife's Counsellor and Friend, 32
Young, Stark, 172, **173**
Youth's Companion, 36, 66

Zion Presbyterian Churchyard, Columbia, TN, 58, **59**

About the Author

JOHN BAYNE is a mathematician, book collector, and literary pilgrim in Atlanta, Georgia, where he is a Senior Consultant for AT&T. He was born in Lenoir City, Tennessee, grew up in Anderson, South Carolina, and holds bachelor's and master's degrees from Clemson University. His articles have appeared in the *Eudora Welty Newsletter*, the *Eudora Welty Review*, *The Journal of the Georgia Philological Association*, *Studies in American Culture*, and *Firsts*. He is active in the Cemeteries and Gravemarkers Section of the American Culture Association.

www.ingramcontent.com/pod-product-compliance
Lightning Source LLC
Chambersburg PA
CBHW030524230426
43665CB00010B/758